PAINTING ○ COLOR ○ HISTORY

COLLECTION PLANNED AND DIRECTED BY
ALBERT SKIRA

FLEMISH PAINTING

FROM BOSCH TO RUBENS

TEXT BY JACQUES LASSAIGNE
AND ROBERT L. DELEVOY

Albert Skira Publisher

TRANSLATED BY STUART GILBERT

★

Library of Congress Catalog Card Number: 57-11640

© by Editions d'Art Albert Skira, 1958

Flemish Painting
From Hieronymus Bosch to Rubens

Though the spirit of the Flemish Primitives remained active throughout the 15th century in all the towns where that art of precise and patient craftsmanship had arisen, it is with the age-old city of Bruges that we associate its most brilliant manifestations. But in the next century, when the tranquillity of Flanders was rudely shaken by the influx of Renaissance ideology, by the religious controversies of the Reformation and Counter-Reformation, by the rise of nationalism and the political upheavals of the western world, the center of gravity shifted to Antwerp, which now became the headquarters of the leading artists and humanists of the day. It was at Antwerp that the vital forces of Flemish genius found expression in the 16th century and from there that they spread abroad, making their imprint on many foreign schools.

To begin with, however, the northern painters came under the spell of Italy, enraptured by her revelation of antiquity and an uncharted world of beauty. But though they took over the forms and modalities of Roman, Florentine and Venetian art, the Flemings were no slavish copiers and brought to these such creative zest that the successive forms of Antwerp "mannerist" painting developed an originality and an earthy pungency not to be found in the works from which they stemmed. Indeed this capacity for at once assimilating and transforming foreign influences is one of the characteristics of the Flemish temperament. Similarly, at a later period, Rubens reinterpreted Italian Baroque in terms of his own genius and, explicit as was the content of his pictures, pointed the way to the modern conception of "pure painting."

Readers will find that there is not so great a contrast as might be expected between this volume and its predecessor, devoted to the period of Flemish painting beginning with Van Eyck, when there was as yet no hint of the spiritual and political unrest that prevailed in Flanders during the 16th century and is reflected in the restless, temperamental, in some cases almost incoherent art of the great painters discussed in this volume. In the light of certain "constants," however, the inevitable dichotomies of an age when moral values were in the melting-pot and at the same time art techniques were rapidly changing, can be regarded as the "mutations" conditioning a ceaseless evolutionary process. Thus in the expressive resonances of Quentin Massys, in Jan Gossart's predilection for ornament and in those agitated forms that were an obsession with the Romanists, we have a foretaste of Baroque opulence and dynamism.

There was at once a remarkable continuity and a wealth of brilliant innovation in the developments of Flemish painting, and these led up not only to the composite classical landscape but also to "impressionistic" renderings of scenes of nature. What had *hitherto been only a setting or background for religious scenes became, in the hands of Bosch and Patinir, a subject in its own right and the dominant theme of the picture. Figures and the ostensible subject ceased to play the leading part and depictions of nature gave the painter opportunities for dramatic—sometimes even homiletic—effects of a quite new order. And so the landscape came to fill the entire canvas with far-flung vistas of plains and mountains and great sea spaces, which the play of light, directed by the artist's imagination, invested with fantastic or poetic intimations.*

To Pieter Bruegel falls the credit of setting order in the disposition of the picture elements and, while sacrificing nothing of his cosmic vision, of assigning its exact, tactile value to each detail—and, last but not least, of restoring to man his due place in the center of things. Bruegel's work is pervaded by the rhythm of the seasons, by those eternal laws of nature which govern all the works and days of men, and, while fully alive to the infirmities of the human situation, he confers an epic grandeur on the humble, hand-to-mouth existence of the Flemish peasant.

One of his admirers was Rubens, who collected Bruegel's pictures and occasionally drew inspiration from his scenes of Flemish country fairs. The universal genius of Rubens dominates the first half of the 17th century. He transfused new life into the ancient myths by interpreting them in a boldly modern spirit. In his vast religious compositions and peerless sketches, in his lyrical, tree-shaded landscapes pointing the way to Watteau's exquisite art, in his intimate, revealing portraits and in his gorgeous nudes, Rubens solved with smiling ease all the problems that had so often baffled earlier painters. No technique has ever been freer, more spontaneous than his. Though the art of Rubens was carried on with elegant variations by Van Dyck and its forms were amplified and consolidated by Jordaens, it has retained its splendid primacy, as the consummation and apotheosis of Flemish art.

There is a wonderful diversity in the trends of Flemish painting during the two centuries covered by this volume; a wealth of new discoveries and high achievements. Behind this art lay flawless technical skill, but the exigencies of perfect craftsmanship never curbed its native vigor, racy of the soil. It found in nature an unfailing source of inspiration, which by a free recourse to fantasy it exploited to the limit of the visible, and, while enlarging the landscape to cosmic dimensions, never lost sight of man's place in it. And, finally, with its plenitude of forms and its feeling for living, vibrant light, it made good the creative efficacy of color as an independent means of expression.

Bosch: Master of the Fantastic

Hieronymus Bosch (c. 1450-1516).

Fragment of a Last Judgment, 1504? (23⅝×45″) Alte Pinakothek, Munich.

Bosch: Master of the Fantastic

FLEMISH painters in the century from Jan van Eyck to Gerard David had gradually built up a world of tranquil dreams, melodious quietude. The disciplines of hieratic thought had been tempered by the *Golden Legend* and the artist could now indulge in gentler moods and finer shades of feeling. Moreover, thanks to his conquest of the visible, he could convert everything he saw into religious images, transfigured by a fervent faith, and all the churches of the West had become peopled with silent figures. Angels and Madonnas, saints and donors filled men's hearts with a peace that seemed inviolable.

Then, out of the blue, there swept down from the heights of the cathedrals a horde of monsters that had, men thought, been put to sleep for ever, and out of the medieval darkness there sounded once again the trumpets of Apocalypse. Gothic quietude was threatened by the teratology of Romanesque imagination, and the dawn of the new age darkened by a recrudescence of the age-old superstitions of the East. A pious Christian artist living on the confines of Flanders took stock of this and, basing his imagery on the signs and wonders premonitory of the Last Judgment, gave expression to the spiritual unrest of the time, its uneasy preoccupations with witchcraft, with the sins of Pride and Lust. Against the grave, unsmiling faces sponsored by the intense religious feeling of the earlier age, Hieronymus Bosch conjured up a world no longer ruled by Divine Order but at the mercy of Nature's craziest whims. The terror cycle begins at midnight. Suddenly the whole horizon reddens with the flames of a Dantesque Inferno, the earth quakes and, bursting open, lays bare the depths of Hell. The waters of the sea are burning, monsters of the deep bellowing with fury, plants steeped in fiery dew. At the bidding of angels the dead rise from their graves, blinking dazed eyes at an unearthly light. One wears a bishop's miter, another a papal tiara, another a royal crown—kings and prelates are among the Damned. Miscegenations of the animal and vegetable kingdoms reflect the chaos of the Fall; a man's body is covered with fish scales, has a bird's head and ostrich plumes; seaweed sprouts wings, an octopus becomes a mammal. Phantasms and hybrid monsters armed with swords, harpoons and knives, emissaries of the great impostor Antichrist, inflict hideous tortures on the race of men. All religions tend to this dualistic concept of the scheme of things, as an eternal conflict between light and darkness, Good and Evil, angels and devils, and starting out from this antinomy, Bosch built up a strange and baffling art, based on the ever-changing flux of forms in matter and in the mental underworld.

Thus a poetry of the imaginary played havoc with the facts of Faith. The remote sources of Bosch's inspiration may have been oral, written or figural traditions, but his demonology is essentially a product of his imagination, an imagination unique of its kind, prodigious, irrepressible. The Munich *Last Judgment* bears the imprint of a style that has achieved complete maturity, and it has a visionary sweep, a dazzling wealth of colors, a virtuosity that takes every executional problem in its stride. Charles de Tolnay believes it to be a fragment of a large-scale picture commissioned by Philip the Fair in 1504—in which case we have here a truly "central" work. Treated like a scene in an aquarium, it has a curiously oriental air; queer creatures and plants are delineated with an exquisite precision reminding us of Persian art. Submarine fireworks, sudden bursts of flame, glittering aigrettes, phosphorescent bodies—all combine to give each organism a weird life of its own, and the whole an enigmatic unreality. The paint is laid on with extreme delicacy, and the essentially decorative treatment of each sign makes it seem without depth. Implicit in this work (which is closely linked up with flamboyant Gothic) are the germs of that mannerist lyricism which was soon to pervade all 16th-century art. We are tempted to describe it as one of those singular creations which best retain their dewy bloom when left unprobed by erudite analysis and whose message can be sensed only when we surrender to their mood, uncritically.

Though from the morphological viewpoint it may appear utterly unlike the Munich fragment, the *Bearing of the Cross* (Ghent) is a continuation of the same art, but infused with a poignancy appropriate to the subject. The presence in this picture of an emotive tension of a like order and a similar color scheme suggests that it was painted at about the same time, that is to say around 1505. Here fantasticality gives place to tragedy, "color gravely enounces all that it embodies," as Valéry's Eupalinos would say. Bosch rigorously omits all that does not serve to convey the tragic implications of the scene. The face of the Man of Sorrows is anguish incarnate; treated in "close-up," it seems to engulf the somber background that projects it towards the observer. The ugliness of evil is bodied forth under all its aspects; bestial, bloated, grinning faces under grotesque headdresses, an assortment of humanity at its lowest level. Features are distorted by hatred, mendacity and malice; even complexions are tainted by fear and vice. They closely frame the serenely noble face of Christ who, lost in mournful meditation, has shut his eyes. In the top righthand corner of the picture the Penitent Thief, his cheeks an ashen grey, his eyes narrowed to two white slits, twists his lips in disgust as he listens to the rantings of a foul-faced Dominican. And in contrapposto, on the left, we have the pale, ethereal form of Veronica holding the veil. Though the entire composition lies flat on the picture surface (Bruegel was to employ the same technique in the *Fall of the Rebel Angels*), it has a tremendous dynamism, due to the conflict of emotions, to skillful, balanced grouping—profiles are alternated round the central face seen in three-quarter view—and to the brilliant color orchestration whose subtly conceived nuances have been restored by a judicious cleaning in the Laboratoire Central des Musées de Belgique (1957). The magical sheen of the colors is heightened by some deft pointillist touches and high lights delicately flicked on in white.

Successive stages of the artist's progress towards the grand style of the Ghent *Bearing of the Cross* (the best replica of which is in the Fine Arts Gallery, San Diego) can be seen in the *Crowning with Thorns* (Prado and London) and *Christ before Pilate* (Princeton). Forming an isolated group in Bosch's œuvre, these pictures were the starting-point of a tradition followed up by Bruegel, Callot, Goya, Chodowiecki, Daumier and Ensor: that of forthright pictorial satire devoid of literary allusion. Here the caricatural expressions have nothing in common with the "grotesques" that Leonardo was producing at about the same time. It has been suggested that Bosch got the idea of them from the leather or papier-mâché masks worn in processions, mystery plays and the festivities of Carnival. This theory is based on the fact that Bosch is often mentioned in records of the period 1480-1512 as being a member of the orchestra and taking part in theatrical performances sponsored by the Confraternity of Our Lady at Bois-le-Duc ('s-Hertogenbosch in Dutch), capital of North Brabant, where he was born about 1450. But it is doubtful if the painter resorted to any such expedient. The mask is a simple, obvious device for creating a comical or quaint effect. It is purely superficial and its set, mechanical grimace never gives the feeling of a real human face, depicted with an eye to expressive values and distorted so as to convey more powerfully the truth within.

Hieronymus Bosch (c. 1450-1516).

The Bearing of the Cross, c. 1505. (29¼×32⅜″) Musée Royal des Beaux-Arts, Ghent.

Hieronymus Bosch (c. 1450-1516).

The Bearing of the Cross, detail: The Penitent Thief and the Dominican, c. 1505.

Musée Royal des Beaux-Arts, Ghent.

Hieronymus Bosch (c. 1450-1516).

The Bearing of the Cross, detail: Veronica, c. 1505.

Musée Royal des Beaux-Arts, Ghent.

And if the leer on the brutal faces of the men escorting Christ is no less terrifying than the flames of Bosch's Hell, this is because it signifies the beast lurking within the human heart, and conveys emotions experienced and observed.

For the age Bosch lived in was an age of excess; behind the colorful façade which sometimes makes it seem like "one long jovial kermess," there was a general breakdown of morals; suicides and crimes were everyday occurrences. The ever-present threat of famine, the horrors of torture, social and economic instability, led to a feeling that the End of Things was near, revived the belief in evil spirits and encouraged superstitious practices. The pseudo-miracles of alchemists, who often performed in public, troubled men's minds still further and tended to undermine Christian faith. The church authorities assimilated witches to heretics, heretics to magicians, and all alike were hounded down remorselessly. Persecution, Huizinga writes, was regarded as a token of religious zeal and a warrant for judicial savagery. The *Vauderie d'Arras* (an outbreak of witchcraft accompanied by mass hysteria that took place in 1461) was followed by trials of an unprecedented ruthlessness and their "revelations" filled the superstitious-minded with apprehensions of impending doom. The immense success of the Netherlandish version of the *Visio Tondali* (printed at Antwerp in 1472 as *Het Boek van Tondalus' Visioen* and republished at Bois-le-Duc in 1484), which describes an Irish knight's vision of the lost souls in Hell, shows how ready was the populace to lend credit to the most extravagant delusions. The papal Bull *Summis desiderantes affectibus* issued by Innocent VIII in 1484 reflects the anxiety caused the Church by the vogue for books and pamphlets challenging its authority and, still more, by "the accursed charms and crafts, enormities and horrid offenses" of the traffickers in black arts. The works of the Dominican monk Alain de la Roche (Alanus de Rupe), who died at Zwolle in 1475, had already shown how deeply religious thought was being influenced by the current Manichaean heresies and a belief in diabolic intervention. In 1487 his disciple Jakob Sprenger, Dominican inquisitor of Cologne, and Heinrich Krämer (Institor) published at Strasbourg the famous *Malleus Maleficarum* (Hammer of Witches) as a manual for the use of inquisitors. It contains a full description of the monstrous regiment of wizards and witches which God, "angered by the world's corruption, has permitted the devil to let loose on earth." An underground movement, bred of the atavistic fears that haunt the subconscious mind, was extending its domain, filling men's minds with nightmare imaginings—and only in the light of Reason could its occult energy be quelled.

But the great currents of modern thought had not yet reached this provincial hinterland. Untouched by the new forces which were soon to shatter the structure of medievaldom, Bosch could appraise with calm detachment the changing values of the world around him, and in all his works we have a fascinating, if sometimes baffling, interpretation of the superstitions of his age. He transposes the well-nigh demoniac eloquence of the popular preachers into the language of art, creates plastic equivalents of written or spoken homilies, gives striking forms to proverbs and a prodigious actuality to abstractions. Thanks to a singularly coherent system of thought—poised midway between faith and skepticism, hope and despair—coupled with an audacious imagination he built up a personal, original language, owing nothing to the forms and colors bequeathed by Flemish national tradition.

The words *insignis pictor* appended to the record (1516) of his death in the archives of the Confraternity of Our Lady at Bois-le-Duc indicate the high esteem in which Bosch was held by his contemporaries. And in 1585 Gian Paolo Lomazzo, in his *Trattato della Pittura, Scultura et Architettura*, speaks of "Girolamo Boschi the Fleming who in his depictions of strange, terrifying creatures and horrific dreams was unique, and truly divine."

If André Malraux is right in saying that "every artist's career begins with the pastiche," and that, however great is a creator, his work always contains, to start with, elements taken over from another artist—that, in short, the life history of forms is determined by a succession of influences—then the art world of Hieronymus Bosch is a remarkable exception to the rule. For it has the compelling power of a wholly new revelation, product of the untrammelled workings of an imagination nourished by the secret well-springs of life. Nothing foreshadowed the emergence, in that remote provincial backwater, of this arch-magician of the fantastic.

Hieronymus Bosch (c. 1450-1516).
The Temptation of St Anthony, c. 1500. Triptych.
National Museum of Antique Art, Lisbon.

True, Bois-le-Duc, "situated two leagues distant from the river Meuse and twelve from Antwerp," was a flourishing commercial center. The Italian traveler Ludovico Guicciardini (in his *Descrittione di tutti i Paesi Bassi*, 1567) comments on the fact that here the "congenital unruliness" of the Belgians was more in evidence than in any of the neighboring regions. But Bois-le-Duc did not lie on any of the highways of the art of the day and had no local art tradition. In any case there is no trace of any contacts Bosch might have had with his contemporaries of the North, chiefly active at Haarlem. Except perhaps for some vague affinities with the Master of the Virgin among Virgins, his works show no attempt to render the effects of plasticity, the phlegmatic attitudes, or the *mise en scène* at once punctilious and naive favored by the Dutch Primitives. Friedländer's theory that he may have studied under some miniature painter seems to be borne out by the elaborate patterning of his pictures, the freedom of his line and the intricate ornamentation of the more specifically Boschian portions of his compositions.

No contemporary records throw any light on his life and, as none of the forty works ascribed to him is dated, there is no knowing which came earliest. Only five are signed: *St John in Patmos* (Berlin), one *Temptation of St Anthony* (Lisbon), one *Adoration of the Magi* (Prado), the *Altarpiece of the Hermits* (Ducal Palace, Venice), the *Altarpiece of St Julia* (Ducal Palace, Venice). Though these works have marked differences in style and quality, it is hard to place them chronologically—all the more so since there is no consensus of opinion regarding the evolution of Bosch's style. It is, however, generally accepted that the Philadelphia *Adoration of the Magi*, the Rotterdam *Marriage at Cana* and the Frankfort *Ecce Homo* are early works. In all three surprising liberties are taken with traditional iconography and religious values are replaced by anecdotal motifs, ironical in tone. These anti-realistic transferences involve some curious anachronisms and anomalies; the persons around Christ in the *Marriage at Cana* are "heretics." His mockers in *Ecce Homo* are the hosts of Satan, while the shepherds of the *Adoration* are ironical observers. There are already signs of Bosch's obsession with Witches' Sabbaths, and also indications of a highly personal manner, technique and way of seeing. Thus we find gaunt, elongated or grotesquely thick-set figures, with aquiline, knife-blade profiles and colors "invented" to suit the figuration instead of the realistic local colors favored by other Flemish artists. The *Cure of Folly* (Prado), the *Conjuror* (Saint-Germain-en-Laye) and the *Seven Deadly Sins* (Prado) mark, it seems, the end of the painter's first period. They inaugurate the picture with a social content, the thesis-picture. Their moral is obvious; by way of popular proverbs they denounce the incorrigible folly of mankind, *vanitas vanitatum*, leading theme of that famous work, affiliated to this group, the *Hay Wagon* (Prado), in which the whole human race is shown in mad pursuit of its illusions, with Hell its destination. Here Bosch is beginning to give free rein to his fantastic imaginings and the promptings of his visionary genius; the *Hay Wagon* is a prelude to one of the most extraordinary pictures that exist: the Lisbon *Temptation of St Anthony*.

This is the crowning point of Bosch's career and the most original, most sensational display of demonic inventions, hybrid monsters, dream-begotten phantasmagoria ever conjured up from the abysses of a human mind. "Henceforth," writes Michel Florisoone, "all forms are conceivable, all are possible, all permissible." Bosch's demonology seems inexhaustible, and he makes his fiends so convincing that he almost seems to have thought himself into their ugly personalities. (Yet it has been suggested, plausibly enough, that "a man who really believes in the devil does not paint him on a wall.") This great work is not made to be taken in at a glance. It is one vast anecdotal discourse, teeming with motifs of every conceivable—and inconceivable—description. Though the composition seems to reflect the incoherence of a nightmare, it is held together by the color orchestration. And such is its suggestive power that, while the hidden meanings of details often escape us, the general effect is overwhelming. For many years erudite researchers have been exploring this mausoleum of dead hieroglyphs which in their own day may well have been clear and comprehensible. Begun by Charles de Tolnay and Jacques Combe, these researches have recently been prosecuted with exemplary success by Charles D. Cuttler.

Hieronymus Bosch (c. 1450-1516).

The Temptation of St Anthony, detail of the left panel: St Anthony succored, c. 1500.

National Museum of Antique Art, Lisbon.

Bosch's predilection for this theme (seven or eight versions of it are attributed to him) was probably due to the fact that there was a special local cult of St Anthony at Bois-le-Duc. The cathedral was dedicated to him and the *pièce de résistance* in the annual procession of the Confraternity of Our Lady was a float on which was represented the Temptation of the Saint. We may well believe that the masks worn by the performers were made after designs supplied by Bosch—which would involve a reversal of the generally accepted view. It would seem that the ordeals undergone by the saintly patron of the Antonite Order were represented with almost startling realism on these occasions. Bosch may also have seen a curious work by a Dominican monk of Louvain entitled *The Mystery [Play] of Saint-Trond* and the *Wonderful True Tale of Marieken of Nimeguen*, the story of a woman who cohabited over seven years with a demon. Other sources of Bosch's iconology were probably a woodcut illustration in an *Almanach auf das Jahr 1498*, printed by Johann Zainer at Ulm, and Jean le Tavernier's miniatures in the French translation of the *Liber de quatuor hominum novissimis* by Dionysius van Rijckel, "Denis the Carthusian" (1455, Bibliothèque Royale, Brussels); also, perhaps, as suggested by Charles D. Cuttler, a miniature in MS 11 209 in the Bibliothèque Royale, Brussels. There can, however, be no doubt that Bosch was the inventor of a new iconography, quite independent of that employed by Martin Schongauer in his *Temptation of St Anthony* (c. 1480), generally regarded as the first appearance of the theme in plastic art.

Hieronymus Bosch (c. 1450-1516).

The Temptation of St Anthony, detail of the central panel: The Gourd, c. 1500. National Museum of Antique Art, Lisbon.

Hieronymus Bosch (c. 1450-1516). The Temptation of St Anthony, detail of the right panel:

The Temptress in the Hollow Oak, c. 1500. National Museum of Antique Art, Lisbon.

Hieronymus Bosch (c. 1450-1516).

The Temptation of St Anthony, back of the left panel: The Seizing of Christ, c. 1500. (51⅝×20⅞″)

National Museum of Antique Art, Lisbon.

Hieronymus Bosch (c. 1450-1516).

The Temptation of St Anthony, back of the right panel: The Bearing of the Cross, c. 1500. (51⅝×20⅞″)

National Museum of Antique Art, Lisbon.

No subject could have lent itself better to an exposition of Bosch's personal philosophy. He was convinced that there was something rotten in the state of Christendom. The laws of nature had collapsed and the devil was playing havoc with the distinctions between Truth and Falsehood. The Temptation takes place on a stage-like platform, midway between the fires of hell ravaging the earth (this is the first fire picture in art) and the waters beginning to engulf it. There the saint had thought to find peace and solitude, but he is promptly beset by a Witches' Sabbath. He is deaf to its uproar, equally unaffected by malefic spells, by fleshly provocations, and by the heretical allurements of the alchemists; indifferent to the sound and fury of a pseudo-Apocalypse. He is morally isolated, midway between the figure of Christ gleaming in the dark recess of his little chapel and the magician, in a red mantle and tall hat, master of the unholy ceremonies, lounging against a parapet a few paces behind him. Standing in the fetid, greenish water, a tonsured demon with a pig's snout is reciting a black mass; his pale blue chasuble is torn and through the rent we glimpse his rotting entrails. Two pseudo-monks stand beside him, one wearing on his head an inverted funnel (symbol of madness), the other a bird's nest on top of which is an egg (a symbol of the art of alchemy). The egg, Jacques Combe reminds us, signifies both the oval vessel wherein, according to alchemical theory, the "great work" (i.e. the philosopher's stone) is concocted and also the egg out of which the universe was hatched. This "world-egg" symbol appears again and again: on the dish upheld by a black servant in the center of the picture; moving, bird-like, on the crumbling vault above the hermit's cell; winging its way across the sky. The big hollow gourd or pumpkin whose green-and-red makes a splendid patch of color in the left foreground is an allusion to that essential part of the alchemist's still, called in old texts "the philosopher's cucurbit" (flask or gourd). Devils are pouring out of it. One, wearing a green cloak, bestrides a turtle and is "profaning the angelic harp." Two clusters of demons, balancing each other, are mustered on either side of the composition. In each group is an outstanding figure, his head encased in a hollow, withered treetrunk rising to a point: another emblem of the alchemist's furnace. Pandemonium is at its height. But there are limits to human endurance. On the left wing of the triptych we see the drooping body of the saint, who has fainted, supported by two monks and a peasant. Forming a graceful arabesque, the group tells out against a hillock, spared by the Witches' Sabbath; the rhythms of this fragment of undesecrated nature answer to those of the fragment of forlorn humanity formed by the four men, whose profound dejection is conveyed by their attitudes alone. This beautifully conceived little scene (Bruegel was to draw inspiration from it) has the poignancy of a Station of the Cross. It is an interesting point that the peasant with the blue head-cloth has exactly the same face as the Prodigal Son in the famous picture in the Boymans Museum, Rotterdam. There are other premonitions of the parable in the *Temptation*. In the left wing an obscenely crouching naked man has transformed St Anthony's hut into a bordello and, as Charles D. Cuttler has pointed out, Bosch has been at pains to make his meaning clear: "grass grows on the kneeling man's back and short branches grow from his legs to indicate that he is rooted in earth, which to Bosch meant being rooted in sin." Also the woman at the window, the barrel and the tall staff leaning against the eaves reappear in front of the tavern from which the Prodigal Son is coming forth.

Like the earth, the air is "mad with magic" and fishes are sailing in the sky—grotesque substitutes for the flying carpet of the Arabian Nights: man's time-old dream of the conquest of the air. His hands clasped in prayer, the saint is lying flat on a winged toad. A ship mounted on a whale's back and manned by a fiendish crew escorts him. In the righthand panel another fish-borne flight is taking place, the "pilot" being a fat man with an egg-shaped body. He denotes the sin of gluttony, also exemplified by the table laid with wine and food at the bottom of the panel. The saint gives it a sidelong glance but is as impervious to its lure as to that of the naked girl in a hollow oak in front of him. The insistence, everywhere apparent, on such elemental themes as fire and water, the earth, heat and cold, moisture and dryness, points to the cosmic nature of the artist's initial conception, deriving from the medieval (Aristotelian) conception of matter. Yet behind the proliferation of chimerical forms and

Hieronymus Bosch (c. 1450-1516).

St Jerome in Prayer, c. 1505. (32×24″) Musée Royal des Beaux-Arts, Ghent.

Hieronymus Bosch (c. 1450-1516).

St Jerome in Prayer (detail), c. 1505. Musée Royal des Beaux-Arts, Ghent.

fancies, débris of a credulous age, we sense the beginnings of that critical spirit which was soon to change the outlook of the western world. Out of those atavistic dreams of magic was to be born the scientific mind; as alchemy, purged of its absurdities, was to give birth to chemistry. Viewed from this angle the Lisbon triptych is seen to be a bridge between imagination and reason, a cabalistic prelude to the Renaissance. And the artist was still alive when (in 1509) Erasmus published his *Moriae encomium* (In Praise of Folly), in which he satirized those foolish people "who never weary of listening to the most extravagant tales of specters, ghosts, evil spirits and hell fire."

His creative genius enabled Hieronymus Bosch to reconcile the real with the imaginary in his evocations of scenes of nature. Between the quiet landscape, done in small, light, conventional touches, that acts as a backdrop to the Brussels *Crucifixion* (c. 1480) and the bright, limpid, fully integrated setting of the Prado *Temptation of St Anthony* (c. 1515) his art underwent an evolution, one of whose intermediary phases can be seen in the Ghent *St Jerome in Prayer*. Here Bosch has succeeded in combining to wonderful effect the poetry of the fantastic and that of nature; nature perverted by the devil and nature that has kept her pristine decorum; nature, enemy of man, and that better nature where all is peace, good

Joachim Patinir (c. 1480-1524).

The Flight into Egypt, 1515-1524. (6¾×8⁵/₁₆″) Musée Royal des Beaux-Arts, Antwerp.

Joachim Patinir (c. 1480-1524).

The Rest on the Flight into Egypt, 1515-1524. (24½×30¾") Kaiser Friedrich Museum, Berlin.

will, amenity. In the foreground of the Ghent *St Jerome*, an atmosphere of corruption has lingered on; the embers of hell fire still are smoldering. The soil is scorched and charred, and the vegetation retains its jagged spikes. The thorns suggest instruments of torture, the hollow oak is a reminiscence of a bygone temptation, a broken gourd lies stranded in a shallow pool. Lizards are crawling on the mound of wreckage over which an owl, the bird of darkness (symbol of wisdom or of heresy?), keeps his nightlong vigil. Colors are warm and forms picked out with the luminous specks of white characteristic of Boschian technique. In the midst of this strange setting, where life seems in suspense, the saint, stretched flat, is praying, his eyes shut, a crucifix resting on his emaciated arms. He has flung aside his cardinal's scarlet robe, which lies across the hollow tree. Here there is a striking innovation in the iconography; until now St Jerome had been represented fully dressed and kneeling. It was left to Jan Sanders van Hemessen to carry this process a stage further: to strip the figure completely and to treat it in the style of the heroic nude.

The setting is a stretch of open country, rendered uniformly in a somber reddish brown, with the foreground slanting upwards to the left along a diagonal that at once emphasizes the asymmetry of the composition, articulates the transition between the two planes nearest

Joachim Patinir (c. 1480-1524) and Quentin Massys (1466-1530).

The Temptation of St Anthony, 1515-1524. (61×68″) Prado, Madrid.

the observer, and enables the artist to fill the background with a panoramic vista of distant hills and a lake. Space is suggested by a bright, sunlit zone, a fragment of the Brabantine countryside rendered in the natural hue of high summer: a wan, sunburnt green warmly tinged with ochre. The horizon is set very high and the blue-green of the distant hills, heightening the illusion of depth, foreshadows the vibrancy of "atmospheric" painting. Here Bosch, ruling out all merely decorative effects, points the way to the modern landscape, unified by the artist's direct response to nature.

In this respect *St Jerome in Prayer* may be likened to the Berlin *St John in Patmos*, in which, as Fierens-Gevaert pointed out, Bosch was first of the Flemish school to use a tree placed well in the foreground as a spatial referent, a key to the schema of proportion governing the design. The background consists of a river scene and brightly lit meadows, bathed in shimmering blue air. On the horizon we glimpse a city. Some have identified this as a view of Nimeguen; it is much the same as that which figures in the midst of a desolate plain in the *Cure of Folly* (Prado)—by general consent an early work—and also in the background of a *Bearing of the Cross* (on the reverse of the right wing of the Lisbon *Temptation of St Anthony*). The *St John in Patmos* has a fine spareness anticipating the great developments of landscape art in the 17th century. On the other hand, I find it hard to agree with those who find close resemblances between the Ghent *St Jerome* and *St John the Baptist in the Wilderness* (Lazaro Museum, Madrid). More archaistic, more scriptural and more Gothic, this latter work belongs rather to the Dutch tradition sponsored by Geertgen tot Sint Jans.

Generally speaking, the compositions in which landscape bulks large combine frontality with a high viewpoint. There is also an harmonious relation, but of a plastic and conceptual order, between the human figure and space. Details taken straight from nature are integrated into a skillfully composed whole and implement the third dimension by an interplay of values, ringing the changes on what was to become the conventional triad of three planes: brown, green and blue. We have here the beginnings of the "cosmic," imaginary, panoramic landscape. Thus Bosch prepared the way for Patinir.

In his *Schilderboek* (Haarlem, 1604) that assiduous and invaluable chronicler of Netherlandish painting, Carel van Mander, speaks of a picture by Bosch that he saw in Amsterdam. "Somewhere I was shown a *Flight into Egypt* by his hand, in which Joseph is asking the way of a peasant and Mary riding on the ass; a queerly shaped rock in the background is laid out to resemble a hostelry and there are some odd episodes, such as a big bear that is made

Joachim Patinir (c. 1480-1524).

St Jerome in a Landscape. (29¼×35⅞″) Prado, Madrid.

Cornelis Massys (c. 1500-c. 1580).

Landscape with St Jerome, 1547. (9⅞×12¼″) Musée Royal des Beaux-Arts, Antwerp.

to dance for money. A very entertaining picture." The description is precise enough for us to surmise a connection between this (so far undiscovered) picture and that gem of Antwerp Museum, Joachim Patinir's small *Flight into Egypt*. Though an attentive eye discerns the Holy Family on its way and the Massacre of the Innocents taking place in a fold of the valley, both the religious theme and the human elements are wholly subordinated to a poetic evocation of the beauties of nature. Patinir has replaced the conventional relationship between man and his surroundings which had obtained since the days of the Primitives, by an organic relationship, tending to unify the picture content. When, later, Pieter Bruegel humanized nature herself, this relationship attained its maximum coherence. Reservations must, however, be made regarding the part played by Patinir, considerable though this was. He was no more the originator of the "pure" landscape (that had already been created by Gerard David in the two famous panels in the Rijksmuseum, Amsterdam) than of the "cosmic" landscape, which was entirely Bosch's creation. Patinir's new contribution to art was the classical structure he imposed on far-flung landscape vistas and the lyrical feeling he instilled into them, combined with a keen interest in topographical details and a deliberate specialization, heralding the autonomy of this branch of art.

Social and economic conditions called for a new approach. A demand had arisen among the middle class for a type of picture at once portable, saleable and negotiable. The age of great sea-ventures had quickened "a desire to be shown *terrae ignotae*" (Fierens-Gevaert). Specialists were therefore needed "who could depict a number of geographical and topographical curiosities in a small compass." Patinir was moved to fill this need and thus became the first professional landscapist. "He had a knack," writes Van Mander, "of handling landscape with much care and delicacy. His works were in great demand, sold well and found their way to foreign countries." Hardly anything is known of his life. The name derives from *patinier*, maker of pattens. Seemingly he was born about 1480. According to Italian chroniclers of the 16th century his birthplace was Bouvignes, on the opposite bank of the Meuse from Dinant. Lomazzo calls him "Joachimo Dionatense" (Joachim of Dinant). There is no question that he hailed from the Walloon country, which so far had given the Netherlands only one major artist, Rogier van der Weyden. Certain elements in his style suggest that he worked at Bruges before moving to Antwerp where, it seems, he soon became friendly with Quentin Massys. He qualified as a free master in the Guild of Painters in 1515, the same year in which Gerard David came to Antwerp and applied for professional status. "At this time," Van Mander observes, "Antwerp had become a prosperous trade center and the most eminent artists flocked thither, since art is ever ready to associate with wealth."

In the course of his journey to the Netherlands in 1520-1521 Dürer came in contact with Patinir. In his diary he noted that "Master Joachim" had kindly placed "his apprentice and his colors" at his disposal. Patinir invited Dürer to his wedding with Joanna Nuyts on May 5, 1521. The German artist expressed pleasure with his reception, adding, "I saw two fine plays there; the first, especially, was very pious and devout." Dürer described his Antwerp friend as a *gut landschaftmaler* (a good landscape painter), and in fact his preoccupation with this branch of art prevented Patinir from being successful with the human figure. Dürer came to the rescue and drew for him "four St Christophers" on grey paper. (It is thought that Patinir used one of these drawings for the large *St Christopher* in the Escorial, believed to be by his hand.) Dürer also mentions that he made a portrait of Master Joachim in silver-point; from this Cornelis Cort engraved the portrait of Patinir in Lampsonius' *Pictorum aliquot celebrium Germaniae inferioris Effigies* (Antwerp, 1572). At the end of his visit Dürer presented his friend with "some things by Hans Baldung Grien." Patinir's small painting of *Lot and his Daughters* presented to Dürer by the City of Antwerp has not been traced.

It is impossible to say if the similarities in the two masters' handling of space is due to an influence of one on the other or to chance. Heinrich Wölfflin contents himself with pointing out that the structure of some of Patinir's landscapes is the same as that in Dürer's engraving *Landscape with a Cannon* (1518). The watercolor sketches (Ashmolean Museum, Oxford) made by Dürer in or about 1495, when traveling in the Tirol, show that a lyrical approach to nature was common to both artists. Patinir died suddenly in 1524; his wife was declared a widow on October 5 and Quentin Massys appointed guardian of his two daughters. "He had led an irregular life," Van Mander informs us, "drinking heavily and spending whole days in the tavern."

Though of unusually small dimensions (our reproduction is exactly the same size as the original), the Antwerp *Flight into Egypt* has none of the characteristic crystallization of miniature technique. On the contrary, Patinir loosens up the compact design, the meticulous stylization of leafage and the analytic precision of Gerard David's woodland scenes. True, the mountain formation in the background and its bluish tint remind us of the distant prospect in the *Baptism of Christ* painted in 1507 by the unknown Bruges master with whom, as Friedländer has demonstrated, Patinir collaborated on at least one occasion. Here, however, the mountains have a wraithlike, vaporous consistency, trees and plants are wet with dew, forms tend to melt into the surrounding air. This evocation of a warm summer evening without a breath of wind is at once wholly convincing and strangely modern. Patinir secures this effect by the use of low-pitched colors and an unusual distribution of values. Some tall cliffs in the foreground overhang the scene. They reinforce the oblique linear structure of

Herri met de Bles (c. 1480-c. 1550).

The Copper Mine. (32¾×45″) Uffizi, Florence.

the composition, set the scale of depth and inaugurate a system of plastic rhythms that traverse the entire landscape. André Lhote points out, in his masterly analysis of this picture, that the clouds floating in the sky at a right angle to the cliffs exactly reproduce their rhythms. The transitions from plane to plane are hardly perceptible, so closely are they interlinked by the continuity of the lines of force and the soft manipulation of the picture elements. And composite though these may be, we have the impression of looking at a really existing scene, almost of the *déjà vu*. The same sense of intimate reality is created by two small signed panels that have recently come to light: the *Rest during the Flight into Egypt* (Private Collection, Dijon) and *Landscape with Shepherds* (Comte de Pret Collection, Castle Vordensteyn, Schoten). The latter is somewhat archaistic, in the tradition of the miniature painters.

In the larger works the imaginative element is more pronounced. The *Baptism of Christ* (Vienna) and the Berlin *Rest on the Flight into Egypt*, both signed, are masterpieces of pictorial architecture, bristling with fantastic, jagged-edged rock formations rendered in a characteristic blue. Viewed in bird's eye perspective, the *Temptation of St Anthony* (Prado) contains a vast panoramic landscape prospect (Massys collaborated on this work). The scene is presented in parallel strips under a stormy sky. Alternating woods and meadows stretch out into illimitable distance and there is lavish use of the color perspective preconized by Leonardo da Vinci. "It is known to you that, seen through air of uniform density, distant objects, for example mountains, acquire a bluish tint, by reason of the mass of atmosphere between your eyes

Jan Mandyn (1502-c. 1560).

The Temptation of St Anthony, 1550? (24⅞×32⅞″) Frans Hals Museum, Haarlem.

and the distant scene. Therefore you shall give its natural color to the nearest element...
but when you want to show another twice as far away, paint it a twice deeper blue, and when
it is five times as distant, paint it a five times stronger blue. This I call aerial perspective."
This poetic approach to nature, which tends to bring out, by purely painterly means, the
mysterious, fantastic, pantheistic qualities of landscape, was adopted to some extent by
Gerard David and Quentin Massys, and very possibly it was through them that Patinir
became acquainted with it. To this discovery he owed not only an enrichment of his vision
but a distinctive element of his style. Lombard *sfumato* also gives a softness to the figures
that Massys painted in, in this *Temptation*: figures so characteristic of his elegant, refined,
Mannerist style. Notable, too, is the disposal of the red and blue cloaks on either side of
St Anthony, stressing the horizontal of the foreground plane. In other works Patinir had
Joos van Cleve execute the figures in his landscapes. And, reciprocally, he is said to have
painted the backgrounds of some colleagues' works. This was the beginning of that collaboration between artists which became a common practice in the 17th century. It seems that
Jan Massys, too, resorted to it; De Tolnay has recently suggested that the view of Antwerp
in the background of a *Venus* (1569, Kunsthalle, Hamburg) was the work of Pieter Bruegel.

Patinir's successors—Herri met de Bles, Jan de Cock, Hieronymus and Matthys Cock—
helped to establish landscape as a subject in its own right and in so doing developed a number
of studio formulas. The effect of these was to make the diagonal structure of the picture

more flexible, to render atmosphere more fully and to emancipate the artist's sensitivity to light. By combining fragments of real scenes into an ideal, carefully planned ensemble, they created the style of the composite landscape. Mannerism retarded the full expression of a direct feeling for nature. The outside world was "thought" before it was experienced, and this was in accordance with the philosophy then in vogue. Neo-Platonism, too, subordinated experienced sensations to the primacy of ideas. Theosophy, which "shares with theology a belief in the supernatural and with philosophy its faith in nature" (A. Weber), had already given an undertone of mystery to the world of Hieronymus Bosch, and it pointed the way to the liberation of impressionist sensibility achieved by Bruegel.

The most characteristic work by Herri met de Bles is the *Copper Mine* (Uffizi). Rocks have lost their asperity and the artist's concern with atmosphere has softened significant forms. A plethora of motifs and the multiplication of picturesque details tend to impair the unity of the composition. Patinir's strong, rich color has dwindled into a more or less somber scheme of brown and yellow ochre. Born about 1480 at Bouvignes, Herri met de Bles is believed to have been Joachim Patinir's nephew; he enrolled in the Antwerp Guild in 1535 under the name of Herri Patinir. He spent the last years of his career in Italy; in Venetia to begin

Peeter Huys (1519-1584).

The Temptation of St Anthony, 1577. (30×37″) Mayer van den Bergh Museum, Antwerp.

with, then (according to Lanzi) at Ferrara, where he died about 1550 in the service of the Dukes of Este. He was given the nickname of "La Civetta" because "he put in all his works a little owl, sometimes so well hidden that we are at much pains to detect it" (Van Mander).

The only painting whose attribution to Jan Wellens de Cock (d. Antwerp 1526) is fully documented is the small *St Christopher* panel in the Von Bissing Collection, Munich. Painted with minute care in light blues and ochres, it clearly derives from Patinir. The woodcuts ascribed to Cock show that he did much to propagate Bosch's influence at Antwerp; an influence that reached its full flowering in the art of his son Hieronymus Cock (c. 1507-1570), who acted as a connecting link between Bosch and Bruegel. No sooner was he admitted to the Guild of Painters (in 1545) than he went to Italy. During his stay in Rome (1546-1548) he was much impressed by the success of such local print merchants as Ducetti, Lafreri and Antonio Salamanca, and on his return to Antwerp "he abandoned painting and set up as an art dealer" (Van Mander). Hieronymus Cock's establishment, "At the Sign of the Four Winds," became the headquarters of a team of brilliant engravers and his name appears on all the best prints made in the Netherlands between 1546 and 1570. His influence on the art and taste of the time was great. Guicciardini mentions him as being "the finder and publisher of the works of Hierosme Bos" *(sic)*. His brother Matthys Cock (1509?-1548) specialized in landscape painting, and Lampsonius apostrophized him in glowing terms. "You, Matthys, were so skilled a landscapist that I doubt if our age has ever seen your like." What little is known of his œuvre shows that he combined reminiscences of Patinir with a thorough understanding of Venetian landscape art, and apparently he influenced Bruegel. K. G. Boon has recently attributed to him the drawings in the *Album Errera* (Musées Royaux, Brussels). These drawings—seemingly early works—tend to support the attribution to Matthys Cock of the *Landscape* (whose "atmosphere" is distinctively that of the Meuse Valley) in the National Gallery, London, successively ascribed to Patinir, Mostaert and Bruegel.

Cornelis Massys (c. 1500-c. 1580), Quentin's son, belonged to the same generation and qualified as master at Antwerp in 1531. His *St Jerome in a Landscape* (Antwerp), initialed and dated 1547, gives a good idea of his style. He exploits the plastic possibilities of the panoramic method to the utmost. Admirably composed in terms of a color scheme of various shades of brown, dappled with patches of soft green and diversified with nuances of pale blue and ochres, this small work illustrates the vogue in the mid-16th century of the "microcosm picture." Cornelis Massys also dealt with popular subjects deriving from Bosch and German little masters. From 1531 on, he frequently had engravings made of his paintings. Balthazar and Cornelis Bos did likewise, thus promoting a genre soon to be ennobled by Pieter Bruegel's genius. Other painters took over Bosch's iconographical formulas verbatim —but the mystical impulse was losing strength, creative fantasy dwindling into mere *diablerie*. The "droll" picture was coming into favor; whimsy and the desire to tell a story were supplanting painterly aspirations. Exemplified by the works of Gillis Mostaert (c.1534-1598), Frans Verbeeck of Malines (c. 1495-1570) and Frans Crabbe van Espleghem (d. before 1561), this minor trend of Flemish painting was redeemed from mediocrity by Jan Mandyn (1502-c. 1560) and Peeter Huys (1519-1584).

Bruegel: Man's Place in the Universe

Pieter Bruegel (c. 1525-1569). Hunters in the Snow (detail), 1565. Kunsthistorisches Museum, Vienna.

Bruegel: Man's Place in the Universe

IT would be hard to name any painter since the days of Fouquet who was so "complete" an artist as Pieter Bruegel; who had so keen a sense of form and a synthetic vision so compulsive that he could impart not only to the protagonists in his compositions, but even to their smallest elements, an impressive monumentality. His entire œuvre bears the imprint of an active participation in the spirit of his age. For when he broke the long silence of the Gothic epoch and ushered in the painting of modern times with bursts of Gargantuan laughter, the ribald humor of the peasantry, and when he cast off the yoke of a long religious tradition, it was because he "descended from the world of the eternal to plunge into the here-and-now" —because, in a word, he could *live himself into* the objects that met his eye. Thus his mind was broadened and enriched by contacts with the realities of experience and for this reason his highly personal art expresses all the more dynamically the very spirit of the Northern Renaissance. None the less, though Bruegel's work stands out so strikingly against its background, we cannot help feeling that had Bruegel never lived the natural course of painting from the 15th to the 17th century would not have been deflected. For even the most evolutionary-minded art historian can hardly claim to see in him a vital link in a chain, an essential intermediary. His elimination from the scene would deprive us of one of the great landmarks of art history, but would not involve the patent break of continuity that would result from the absence of men like Leonardo, Dürer or Quentin Massys. And while this tends to accentuate his profound originality it also, paradoxically enough, brings out even more clearly his universal caliber.

A supreme expression of the genius of Flanders and to some extent an heir of Hieronymus Bosch, he cut an isolated figure in the heart of the 16th century, standing as he did outside the movement that was orienting Flemish art, under the auspices of Italian dialectic, towards the Baroque age. True, he adopted none of the specific formulas and attitudes of the Renaissance; neither its mythological themes nor its deference to classical antiquity, neither its architectural settings nor its preoccupation with anatomy. Nor was he interested in the portrait celebrating an individual personality, or with the gaze inviting the spectator's attention. Nor, finally, with investigation of the space dimension for its own sake. And yet he expressed, more powerfully than any other Flemish artist, the very spirit of the age of humanism; less, perhaps, by assimilating the basic principles of the Cinquecento than by his conception of man viewed not as an individual but as an embodiment of mankind, and by giving a new coherency to his relations with the scheme of things. Bruegel was in fact a discoverer of those aspects of the universe in which human elements play an active part: scenes of life changing with the season and the hour, everyday occupations, crowds in arms or merrymaking, field sports and children at play. Freed from the obsession of the static mirror held up to life, he replaced an ideological eternity by the eternity of nature; time arrested by time in flux: the time in which men live, suffer and die, as nature herself lives, grows and dies, transmitting to new generations her indomitable rhythms. This discovery of the vital rhythms of all existence linked up with that of humanism and relegated the paintings of Van Eyck's age to the plane of fictions sublimated by religious faith. It is with this in mind that Lionello Venturi says that Bruegel triumphantly inaugurated modern art.

For this contemporary of Veronese and Tintoretto rates infinitely higher than the "droll painter" *(Viezen Bruegel)*, the primitive humorist "skilled in drawing amusing things, good

Pieter Bruegel (c. 1525-1569).

Children's Games, 1560. (46½×63⅞") Kunsthistorisches Museum, Vienna.

to make us laugh"—the role to which the ages of Rubens, Watteau and Ingres assigned him. And he ranks no less above the artist in clogs ("peasant Bruegel"), the rough-hewn genius of peasant stock and the drab, unlovely incarnation of the spirit of his race (an uncouth spirit, needless to say) and of his milieu (thick-witted, by all accounts), that at the beginning of this century some Flemish writers and art historians who should have known better thought fit to see in him.

For though Bruegel sometimes dressed up as a peasant so as to share in the junketings of the countryfolk and (as his first biographer Carel van Mander, writing in 1604, informs us) often "amused himself scaring people with ghost stories and queer noises," he was neither the clown nor the boor that some would have us think. And even if much remains obscure in his life story, this much is certain: not only his works themselves but also his friendships, the circles in which he moved, speak for his having been a man of high intellectual stature who kept abreast of the movements of the élite of the age, an age of moral and social ferment and philosophic controversy. An independent-minded man, a mocker of authority, an intimate of such enlightened spirits of the day as Ortelius, Plantin, Goltzius and Coornhert, and also (it is thought) an adept of a sect of religious reformers; a patriot, member of the Flemish "Resistance," and lastly—and above all—a painter in the fullest sense of the term, Pieter Bruegel was the living symbol of both the culture and the philosophy of a momentous phase of European history.

Pieter Bruegel (c. 1525-1569).

The Fight between Carnival and Lent, 1559. (46½×64¾") Kunsthistorisches Museum, Vienna.

Though in the absence of written records there is no certain knowledge on the point, it is generally assumed that he was born about 1525 "in a small village whose name he adopted as his patronymic and transmitted to his descendants." Even so, the exact location of his birthplace remains uncertain, some believing it was the village of Bruegel north of Eindhoven, others that it was Groote Brögel in the Limburg Campine. Charles Bossus claims to have located Bruegel's birthplace in this part of Belgium, at Ooiwarstnest (Stork's Nest). According to Gustav Glück he was educated at Bois-le-Duc and there became acquainted with the work of Hieronymus Bosch—a tempting hypothesis but quite uncorroborated. Personally I am inclined to think that his "discovery" of Bosch's fantastic creations was more or less fortuitous.

For actually his career began only with his move to Antwerp when he was seventeen or eighteen. It was only natural for young Bruegel to feel drawn to the great cosmopolitan city and flourishing trade center which, while Bruges, still rooted in the past, was slowly dying of inanition, had succeeded in breaking the régime of a parochial economy and given free scope to the new forces of capital and individual enterprise. Antwerp was now the headquarters of German, Italian, Spanish and Portuguese bankers who had flocked to the city from all the provinces of the Empire of Charles V, finding that there they could enjoy the completest freedom and turn to lucrative account the most fully developed economic system known to the age. Besides an active trade in spices from the East, in wheat from the North and in French wine, a thriving picture market had grown up in Antwerp. Works of all sizes

and descriptions flowed in from Flanders and abroad to the market held on the Kerkplaats adjoining the Cathedral, and in 1540, when the space available there proved insufficient, the market was transferred to one of the upper galleries of the Stock Exchange. In his *Descrittione di tutti i Paesi Bassi*, published at Antwerp in 1567, Ludovico Guicciardini tells us that works were often purchased there "sight unseen," before they had been delivered to the dealers. Daily some five thousand picture merchants discussed prices and settled between them the market value of their wares. Whole shiploads of pictures were embarked at Antwerp for dispatch to Spain. We can well imagine the delight and wonder of the young artist at finding himself in this veritable painters' paradise whither he had come to secure his patent of "free master" of the Antwerp Painters' Guild—which, like the city, had now modernized its regulations.

According to Van Mander, Bruegel was apprenticed to Pieter Coeck whose daughter he later married. Besides being a skilled Romanist painter and a man of exceptional erudition, Coeck was the translator of Vitruvius' and Serlio's treatises on architecture. On his teacher's death, which took place suddenly at Brussels in 1550, Bruegel joined the staff of the painter-engraver Hieronymus Cock, also a man of culture, who had recently opened a new publishing house, "At the Sign of the Four Winds," for the production and sale of prints. Cock's establishment soon became a leading humanist center, a place where literary men and intellectuals forgathered, where dealers and collectors met. Here Bruegel had frequent opportunities of seeing not only the works of the great Italian masters but those of Bosch and other painters in the popular autochthonous tradition, whose wide diffusion was ensured by the energetic publisher. It is no derogation of his genius to admit, like Louis Lebeer, that the prints designed

Pieter Bruegel (c. 1525-1569).

The Fight between Carnival and Lent (detail), 1559. Kunsthistorisches Museum, Vienna.

Pieter Bruegel (c. 1525-1569). The Fight between Carnival and Lent (detail), 1559. Kunsthistorisches Museum, Vienna.

by Bruegel, executed by one or other of his usual engravers (Philipp Galle, Frans Huys, Jan Wierix, Pieter van der Heyden, Pieter Perret) and published by Cock, help us better to understand the origins, general conceptions and even the technique of many of his paintings. And as a matter of fact it is thanks to some of these prints and drawings that we know of Bruegel's journey to Italy in 1552 and his residence in Rome the following year. They are no less interesting for the light they throw on his formative years, since they show that, far from being hypnotized by the genius of Michelangelo or by the majestic ruins of the classical age, he was enraptured by the natural beauties of the countryside. Turning to account his exceptional powers of observation and breaking loose from all traditional restraints, he revivified the art of landscape. The *River in a Hilly Landscape* (Louvre) and the *Ripa Grande in Rome* (Chatsworth) have the charm of impressionist art at its purest, such is the lightness, spontaneity and vibrancy of these drawings. True, when he is dealing with the Alps his line loses something of its simple forthrightness; but what it loses in spontaneity it gains in breadth and intensity, earth, sky and water merging into a romantically majestic vision of the scene. It is an interesting point that in the course of his travels, which took him, after halts in Lyons and Vienne, from the North of Italy to Sicily by way of Rome and Naples, he struck up friendships with the Bolognese geographer Scipio Fabius and the Roman miniature painter Giulio Clovio (who collaborated in one of his works). But more to our present purpose is the fact that, in transposing his landscapes to the north, he took over some Italian compositional schemes and that these had a decisive influence on his style. Thus De Tolnay has aptly pointed out that in his drawings he often employs the dynamic rhythms found in the Venetian landscapes of Campagnola and Titian, and also the organization of space in "linear volutes" practised by Piero della Francesca, Baldovinetti and Pollaiuolo in their depictions of the Tuscan countryside.

On his return to Antwerp late in 1553 "Maestro Pietro Brugole" became one of the pillars of the House of Hieronymus Cock, and for two years or more devoted himself to "inventing" compositions which he left it to others to engrave (the only known etching by his own hand is *Hunting Wild Rabbits*, 1556). In the famous *Large Landscape Series*, published in 1555, he combined Alpine reminiscences with motifs of the Flemish countryside; but such is the organic unity of these composite productions that they seem like representations of real landscapes. Here the human figures are mere onlookers and give the impression of contemplating the scene with philosophic detachment—a foretaste of that smiling skepticism which was henceforth to be one of the characteristic traits of Bruegel's *Weltanschauung*; confronted with the infallible logic of nature, man is conscious of the limitations of all human endeavor. However there were as yet no indications of the new direction his art was soon to take. In 1556, again at the instance of Hieronymus Cock, he embarked on several series of drawings to be converted into prints, chief of which was the sequence of the *Seven Deadly Sins* (Anger, Sloth, Pride, Avarice, Gluttony, Envy, Lust). In these he no longer had "motifs" capable of quickening his sensibility but "subjects" of a didactic order which gave him opportunities of railing (always with a double-entendre) against the follies of "The World Turned Upside Down." Was it because he had entered into some arrangement with his dealer that he consented thus to revert to a vein already exploited by Hieronymus Bosch? That may well be so and we can easily believe it was this commission, prompted by the success of a specific genre, that led him also to borrow from Bosch's imagery a number of fantastic elements: hybrid monsters, obscene creatures, grotesques and *diableries*. To illustrate the punishments that vice entails he drew, like Bosch, on the colorful repertory of old popular proverbs, transposed verbatim into graphic terms. It has been rightly pointed out that the layout devised by Bruegel for these prints—that of a central motif acting as a *point de repère* for the various narrative elements—was to serve him in good stead in such paintings as the *Fight between Carnival and Lent, Dulle Griet* and the *Triumph of Death*.

When taking the folly of mankind for his theme, Bruegel plunged into the polyvalent, perilous realm of signs and symbols, and in so doing he was led to subordinate data of optical experience to the sole guidance of the intellect—with all the risks entailed. This incursion into the world of Hieronymus Bosch quickened his innate skepticism and gave a new edge to his wit. The popular proverbs which he "illustrated" throughout his life were merely incidental to that wider theme which for ever fired his genius: the human comedy as a whole. Thus, discarding the lingering traces of archaism that persisted in the morphology of Bosch, Bruegel turned his back on the unreal and deliberately entered the world of everyday actuality. Begun in 1559, the series of the *Seven Virtues* (Faith, Hope, Charity, Justice, Prudence, Fortitude, Temperance) marks this turning point in his artistic career. The allegory serves merely as a pretext for an incisive picture of the mores of the populace, fettered by conventions as futile as they are preposterous. A pretext, also, for bringing on the scene a host of figures to whose poses and attitudes he imparts plastic and psychological values in equal measure. They are of the characteristic Bruegelian type: broad-backed, short and stocky, and their elliptical structure gives only the faintest hints of the latent geometrical scheme that has gone to their making. This generalization was the result of Bruegel's close and constant contacts with reality, of a persistent practice of drawing from nature. He embarked on a series of studies *(Peasants, The Pilgrim, Team of Horses)* so evidently done from the life that the inscription *naer't leven* ("from the life") was quite superfluous. The liveliness and spontaneity of the drawing in these studies testify to a quite exceptional sensibility, unimpaired by the constant will to synthesis that makes itself felt across the closely analytical treatment of details. The theory advanced by Axel Romdahl that in some cases Bruegel made use of wooden lay figures rests on very slender grounds and, to my thinking, has no weight.

Pieter Bruegel (c. 1525-1569).

Dulle Griet ("Mad Meg"), 1564? (45¼×63⅜″) Mayer van den Bergh Museum, Antwerp.

Pieter Bruegel (c. 1525-1569). Dulle Griet (detail), 1564? Mayer van den Bergh Museum, Antwerp.

Pieter Bruegel (c. 1525-1569). Dulle Griet (detail), 1564? Mayer van den Bergh Museum, Antwerp.

Pieter Bruegel (c. 1525-1569).

The Tower of Babel, 1563. (44⅞×61″) Kunsthistorisches Museum, Vienna.

Bruegel was about thirty at this time. He was now at the height of his powers and had mastered a technique and style that justified him in giving free rein to his painterly instincts, his feeling for the magical properties of color. Except for the *Riverine Landscape* (Stuyck del Bruyère Collection, Antwerp) dated 1557, his earliest signed pictures—*The World turned Upside Down* (Berlin, signed and dated 1559), better known as *Netherlandish Proverbs*; the *Fight between Carnival and Lent* (Vienna, signed and dated 1559); and *Children's Games* (Vienna, signed and dated 1560)—were treated in a style closely resembling that of his graphic works. Their content might be described as a figurative anthology, the derisive imaging of a world gone crazy in the throes of a collective fever. Here Bruegel brings off the feat of creating works whose technique and execution are thoroughly modern in spirit and which none the less keep to the visual approach of the Gothic *imagiers*. Renouncing the grandiose vision of the Renaissance artists which, starting from a single, unvarying, immobile point of sight, penetrates deeply into space, he represents these fables as they would be seen by a number of spectators, viewing them from different angles. In a host of episodes—soldiers' pranks, peasant dances, mountebanks doing their turns, mock fights, ludicrous incidents of daily life—he conjures up bustling crowds of small, typical, yet always personalized figures. All disport themselves upon a single plane like that of the medieval tapestries, and there is no attempt to graduate them in perspective. The third dimension is merely *implied* by a system of diagonals acting as lines of force (and prefiguring Baroque pictorial

construction) that build up the formal structure of the composition and serve as its unifying principle. Bruegel's color schemes (in which by a curious alchemy of contrasted warm and cool tones, instinctive but unerring, he evokes clangorous sonorities) reinforce this general harmony, which is ensured, supremely, by the unity of thought governing a diversity of details. In this respect he resembles Rabelais of whom it was said that he "combined in his work the boldest drolleries of all ages and all lands." And, again like Rabelais, he synthesized "all the railleries against the ancient social order that had been accumulating for centuries." Customs and morals had been rudely shaken in this age of drastic changes, the populace at large had lost its bearings and was hard put to it to cope with new conditions of existence that played havoc with its most venerable beliefs and practices. In the form of light, topical imagery, Bruegel gave utterance to the tragedy of the times and voiced an ancient wisdom racy with the ribald humor of old-time Flanders.

Deeply involved in the everyday life of his countrymen, Bruegel could not remain indifferent to the events which were soon to steep the Netherlands in blood. As early as 1533 the conduct of the Spanish troops sent by the Emperor Charles V "to take part in the war with France" had led to a nation-wide movement of revolt and this gained strength when Philip II outraged public opinion by increasing the powers of the inquisitors in their campaign against the Calvinist heresy (1556). Bruegel took sides; the painter of scenes of popular life became a champion of the Resistance. In *Two Monkeys* (Berlin, signed and dated 1562)

Pieter Bruegel (c. 1525-1569).

The Procession to Calvary, 1564. (48¾×66⅞″) Kunsthistorisches Museum, Vienna.

we have a hardly veiled allusion to the plight of the Flemish provinces; chained in a dark archway, the two animals have their backs turned to the delightful panoramic view of the port and City of Antwerp lightly veiled in mist. In the guise of a biblical theme that superb picture, the *Battle of the Israelites and Philistines* (Vienna, signed and dated 1562), evokes the hated presence of the foreign soldiery. The setting of the scene is grandiose, a skillfully ordered reconstitution of the artist's memories of the South. Signed and dated the same year, the *Fall of the Rebel Angels* (Brussels) derives its morphology from Bosch's world of bizarre forms, its purpose being to denounce human folly, incarnated in the hideous hosts of Hell launching feverish, foredoomed attacks on the bright invincible Archangel.

Meanwhile the situation was deteriorating, from the Spanish point of view, the opposition gaining in strength and growing bolder. Huguenot preachers were holding services in the open, and in *St John the Baptist Preaching* (Budapest, signed and dated 1566) we have a discreet tribute to their courage. The country was flooded with pamphlets printed at the headquarters of the underground Calvinist movement; there were tavern brawls between patriots and Spanish soldiers; hundreds of suspects were arrested, tortured, burnt at the stake. The *Procession to Calvary* (Vienna, signed and dated 1564) depicts the preliminaries of one of those public executions which strung up the nerves of the populace "beyond all that the temper and condition of the people could endure" and in this tragic scene of hundreds of Flemish workers rounded up by Spanish mounted troops, nature plays her part in the human tragedy. Clad in her springtime finery at the starting-point of the procession, she gradually loses all her verdant splendor as the crowd moves on towards the bleak desolation of the fatal hill. Touches of local color, forcefully yet discreetly indicating the bright red of the soldiers' tunics, implement Bruegel's amazingly skillful technique in his handling of the soil, which forms a sort of backcloth dappled with myriads of small, starry patches of green, brown and pink, no longer rendered with the minute precision, the smooth enamel finish and glossy greens favored by the Primitives, but disseminated as the artist's fancy took him. Here we have the beginnings of a technique of "becoming," of incessant mobility, tellingly conveyed by a host of tiny figures fanning out in all directions and filling the entire picture surface with sparkling, tremulous life. Upon a stormy sky a bird is wheeling, a bird of ill omen, one of those sinister carrion crows that haunt places of execution. But it also has a plastic value and as a focal point, high in air, suggests the infinite depths of space—giving the same effect of fathomless immensity as does the bird flying above the frozen ponds in *Hunters in the Snow*. In the foreground of the *Procession to Calvary* the group of mourners —St John upholding the Virgin, attended by the Holy Women—shows, incidentally, the persistence of that Gothic formalism which had lingered on into the art of Massys; here both theme and style seem out of keeping with the intense dramatic actuality of the scene.

So as the better to mask his indignation with the turn of events Bruegel resorted, once more, to Boschian "dialectic" in his *Dulle Griet* (c. 1564, Mayer van den Bergh Museum, Antwerp); here an indictment of Spanish tyranny is partially concealed by the archaism of the subject and its illustration of the popular saying "If you go to Hell, do so sword in hand." As Minnaert has ably demonstrated, we have here a free interpretation of one of the folk tales relating to the ogress Gridr (a personification of Hell in the Eddas); in old German legends she bears the name of Schwarze Gret, "Black Margaret," while in the Low Countries she was known as "Margriet" or "Griete." Through a teeming throng of the monstrous creatures, bred of the atavistic fears and dark imaginings that haunt the mental underworld, Dulle Griet, a gigantic, gaunt-faced harridan, strides boldly forward. Carrying the long, rapier-like sword wielded by the giants of mythology (the "magic staff" of the Eddas), wearing a helmet and breastplate, her eyes flashing fire, she towers above the myrmidons of Hell, while from her gaping lips issues the song of the eternal tyrant, *wil je niet je moet wel* ("whether you like it or not, you *shall*!"). She is carrying baskets crammed with miscellaneous loot and seems quite indifferent to the havoc she has spread around her, lit up on all sides by the glare of distant fires. It is clear that this apocalyptic figure, center of gravity of the composition, is charged with a symbolic meaning; as Minnaert has pointed out, she stands

Pieter Bruegel (c. 1525-1569). The Procession to Calvary (detail), 1564. Kunsthistorisches Museum, Vienna.

for the spirit of oppression and wanton cruelty then let loose in Flanders—elemental malevolence without a spark of human pity. The two monkeys miserably penned behind prison bars reinforce the artist's message. The miseries of the Occupation are the firstfruits of the "Disasters of War," and *Dulle Griet*, an anticipation of *Guernica*, has a like dramatic intensity. When Philip II prescribed a stricter enforcement of his Edicts (October 1565) he ordered that executions should no longer take place in public, so as not unduly to outrage public opinion. But when 60,000 citizens were condemned to death there was general consternation, and in 1566 a group of great nobles founded a national league which was promptly joined by wealthy merchants, by members of the lesser nobility and by the working class. The signatories to the "Compromise" of April 5, 1566, bound themselves to expel the Inquisition and to secure the abolition of the Edicts, and this nation-wide resistance movement was acclaimed at a famous banquet where, dressed in beggars' garb, the company shouted with one voice "Long live the Beggars!"

The Beggars (Louvre, signed and dated 1568) is an obvious allusion to the Calvinist revolt. It shows five pathetic cripples holding a clandestine meeting in a corner of a field swept by an April shower, each of them symbolizing a different social class; the soldier has a shako, the prince a cardboard crown, the peasant a cap, the bourgeois a béret, the bishop a paper miter, and all but the soldier wear a white smock to which foxtails are attached—the foxtail (an attribute of beggars) having been adopted as their badge by the signatories of the Compromise. While the Beggars were hatching their plots, popular unrest was steadily increasing in all parts of the country, which was passing through an alarming crisis due both to the prevailing political anarchy and to catastrophic economic conditions, for industry had come to a standstill and there was widespread unemployment. A furious burst of iconoclasm in 1566 was accompanied by a tidal wave of destruction; bands of fanatical rioters roamed the countryside burning down churches, looting monasteries, slashing pictures and mutilating statues. Philip took prompt action and on October 30, 1566, the Spanish regiments stationed in Lombardy were dispatched to the insurgent provinces. In the *Massacre of the Innocents* (c. 1567, Kunsthistorisches Museum, Vienna, and Baron Descamps Collection, Brussels) we see the Duke of Alva's troops at their bloodthirsty task. The picture contains, Van Mander tells us, "several scenes that are exact representations of what actually occurred, such as a family of peasants imploring a brutal soldier to spare a child whom he has captured and is about to kill, the lamentations and anguish of the mothers and other incidents straight from the life." The setting of this gruesome scene is a small Brabantine village, half-buried under frozen snow, and the glacial stillness of nature acts as a foil to the brutal violence of the foreign soldiers, who are mounted on fiery thoroughbreds depicted with a mastery worthy of Pisanello.

Thousands of men, women and children were butchered in those tragic years, whose horrors Bruegel has so poignantly and powerfully recorded in one of his most gripping works, a masterpiece of its kind, the *Triumph of Death* (Prado). There are no more monsters; only a company of human beings, gathered together on a barren hillside, whose sun-scorched slopes are rendered in a scale of warm reddish-browns. They are being hunted down on all sides by the invincible battalions of Death. Collective massacres, tortures and hangings, cartloads of skulls, trumpet-blowing skeletons, gibbets and gallows, fires and shipwreck, smoking ruins, flashes of apocalyptic light—all are here, integrated in an amazing synthesis by the genius of an inspired magician of the brush. Yet the true tragedy lies within—that secret anguish which, as André Lhote has rightly observed, makes its latent presence felt across the gorgeous counterpoint of plastic form and color. Among the moderns Salvador Dali and Yves Tanguy certainly owe something to this great Flemish visionary who, across the light mists veiling the *Magpie on the Gallows* (1568, Darmstadt), addressed a final, deeply moving remonstrance to the forces of oppression. He made many other works inspired by the Resistance, but (Van Mander tells us) "as some were too biting and sharp, he had them burnt by his wife when he lay on his deathbed, fearing they might get her into trouble."

Bruegel settled in Brussels in the summer of 1563, soon after his marriage with Maria Coeck, daughter of his first teacher, and moved into a studio in the Rue Haute, in the old

Pieter Bruegel (c. 1525-1569).

Hunters in the Snow, 1565. (46×63¾″) Kunsthistorisches Museum, Vienna.

working-class district inhabited for the most part by weavers. This was for him a period of relaxed effort; he spent much time roaming the environs of the city, charmed by the beauty of the sandy foothills and the soft light of the Brabant countryside. It was in this setting he composed that grandiose pastoral symphony, *The Seasons* (1565), commissioned by a wealthy Antwerp burgher, Niclaes Jonghelinck who, though passionately devoted to Italian art, was one of Bruegel's warmest admirers. No doubt he had particularly appreciated the dovetailed pictorial construction, the delicate precision, the glints of gold and silver in Bruegel's *Tower of Babel* (Vienna), painted in 1563, which he promptly bought. In this picture Bruegel used the biblical theme as a pretext for yet again denouncing human folly, that leitmotiv of all his work. De Tolnay claims to have detected the structure of the Coliseum in the Tower, but its proximate sources are unknown to us, except for a miniature in the Grimani Breviary. It is surprising, none the less, to find in it the exact form of one of those circular ziggurats whose remains have been unearthed by modern archeologists in the region of Sumer. In another version, smaller than the Vienna painting and now in the Boymans Museum, Rotterdam (former Van Beuningen Collection), the style is more fully evolved and it can probably be dated to about 1567.

The series of *The Seasons* originally consisted of six large panels illustrating the successive occupations of the months of the year (in pairs). *Hunters in the Snow* (Vienna, signed and dated 1565) represents December and January; *The Dark Day* (Vienna, signed and dated 1565), February and March; *Haymaking* (Prague), June and July; *The Harvesters* (Metropolitan

Pieter Bruegel (c. 1525-1569).

Hunters in the Snow (detail), 1565. Kunsthistorisches Museum, Vienna.

Museum, New York, signed and dated 1565), August and September; *The Return of the Herd* (Vienna, signed and dated 1565), October and November. The panel illustrating April and May is lost. Bruegel portrays man in his basic relations with the natural world, but from an angle of vision that, overruling the hierarchy of appearances, brings out the full significance of his labors. Though sometimes he shows his figures side-face, he oftener shows them in back view, engaged in arduous, uphill struggles with the tasks assigned them. Sometimes we see a man toiling up a mountainside, but it is no longer the Cross that he is bearing, nor Calvary he is ascending. He is a type-figure, anonymous, a symbol of human effort—an incarnation of humanity pressing towards some goal that may be unattainable, but which man for ever, indefatigably, seeks, despite the obstacles set up by natural forces. Thus Bruegel gave expression to the spiritual trends of his time in universal terms. It matters little whether he drew inspiration from illuminations in the Grimani Breviary or the Hennessy Book of Hours. His intensive study of nature may equally well have been prompted by the humanism of Marsilio Ficino or Leonardo da Vinci. Be this as it may, these pictures of the Seasons, as seen by typically 16th-century eyes, represent a new conception of landscape, "sensitized, individualized," and no longer relegated (as Bosch still had relegated it) to a transcendent immobility. Each of these scenes stems from the synthetic compositional formula of the early landscapes engraved in 1555 and mingles aspects of the Flemish plain with Alpine scenery, while colors, values and execution are everywhere adapted to the basic theme—the "idea" of the season in question. This central concept makes its presence felt in every detail: calm or turbulent streams, dry or rain-soaked earth, bright or lowering skies, slumbering or wind-tossed fields, clear or fogbound air, slow or agitated gestures—all the colors of life—and those of death. For each of Bruegel's landscapes is a living creature on which Nature imposes the ineluctable rhythms of her eternal recurrences.

Hitherto Bruegel had subordinated the human element to the old medieval conception of its function, plastic and spiritual, as a microcosm. In these landscapes, for the first time, the human figure bulks larger and is given a certain prominence relatively to a given space echeloned in depth; thus, in a world organized in terms of an underlying hierarchy, appearances were now beginning to prevail. But a change was soon to come in the relations between the elements of this subtly balanced schema, and nature, viewed as a scene unfurling itself before the eyes of a spectator (in the manner of the panoramic "traveling" shot of the cinema), recedes into the background. The human figure is brought forward, given the monumental proportions of the "close-up," and several of Bruegel's last works illustrate this new relationship between man and his environment.

The *Land of Cockaigne* (Munich, signed and dated 1567), which may well pass for a protest against the academic *tours de force* of Bruegel's Romanist contemporaries, brings off a striking pictorial paradox, the figures being treated in foreshortening on a vertical plane tending to project them towards the spectator. Three persons, a knight, a peasant and a student,

Pieter Bruegel (c. 1525-1569).

Hunters in the Snow (detail), 1565. Kunsthistorisches Museum, Vienna.

Pieter Bruegel (c. 1525-1569).

The Wedding Banquet, c. 1568. (44⅞×64⅛″) Kunsthistorisches Museum, Vienna.

lie stretched on the ground like spokes of a wheel around a central tree-trunk; they have fled from the Spanish Reign of Terror so as to bask the hours away in a fabulous land of idleness and luxury. Like this picture, *The Birdnester* (Vienna, signed and dated 1568) illustrates a Flemish proverb: "The man who knows where the nest is has the knowledge, but the man who takes it has the nest." Standing out against a delicately rendered, sunlit landscape prospect, a burly peasant, placed well in the foreground, is pointing with his finger to the young birdnester scrambling up a tree. This small picture was a prelude to those large scenes of rustic life which earned for the master of the *Triumph of Death* his reputation as a painter of the peasantry: the *Wedding Banquet* and *Peasant Dance* (both in Vienna, painted c. 1568). In his *Schilderboeck* Van Mander tells us that Bruegel never wearied of studying the customs, junketings, dances and love-making of the countryfolk and "had a rare gift for depicting them with his brush, sometimes in oils, sometimes in tempera, being equally proficient in both mediums... It was amazing," Van Mander continues, "to see how clever he was in giving his peasants precisely the right costumes and rendering their attitudes, their gait, their ways of dancing." The care he took to secure complete accuracy as to costumes, gestures and attitudes is evidenced by the numerous preliminary drawings that from 1559 onwards he made *naer't leven*, from models called in to pose for him, and by the notes of the colors he inscribed on these sketches. Such was his faculty of abstraction, surprising for the times, that he reduced these figures to the elementary geometrical forms preconized by Cézanne: spheres, cones and cylinders. Here again, in accordance with a practice he had been gradually developing from the time of his earliest encyclopedic compositions, Bruegel

Pieter Bruegel (c. 1525-1569).

Peasant Dance, c. 1568. (44⅞×64⅝") Kunsthistorisches Museum, Vienna.

arranged his figures in back view or side-face, the better to stress these basic forms. The sculpturesque density imparted to them by this drastic synthesis (like that which gives Giotto's figures their full-bodied plasticity) does not in any way diminish the expressive quality of their attitudes; indeed these produce almost the effect of snapshots and are more natural than the attitudes of the figures in the works of his contemporaries at Antwerp, Pieter Aertsen and Joachim Beuckelaer. Large, monumental shapes, suavity in the modeling, plastic values conveyed by filled and empty spaces, an harmonious balance of masses, richness and vigor of the color rhythms—all have the effect of sublimating even the most trivial incidents of everyday life on to a universal plane. For despite the Baroque and Italianizing tendencies of the age Bruegel remained supremely classical and he created the modern type of *tableau de mœurs*, as with the *Storm at Sea* (Vienna, c. 1568) he created the first seascape in its own right. This small panel (painted at the time of the great Atlantic voyages) was at once a marine equivalent of Patinir's earliest landscapes without figures and a lyrical counterblast to the many works of the period conforming to the laws of mathematics and pure Reason. The sky hangs almost black above a storm-tossed sea and ships are struggling against huge, murky billows, lit with vagrant gleams of light. In the foreground a whale is opening its jaws towards a barrel floating on the waves. We owe the most probable explanation of the scene to Ludwig Burchard; the whale, playing with a barrel thrown overboard by sailors so as to divert its attention and enable their ship to escape, symbolizes the man who, for the sake of trifles, lets slip his true chance of salvation. In Bruegel's art even those paintings which on the face of them seem freest and most fanciful always carry metaphorical allusions.

Bruegel (c. 1525-1569).
The Birdnester, 1568. (23¼×26¾″) Kunsthistorisches Museum, Vienna.

At the close of a career which—be it noted—spanned a bare decade (his first known picture, *Riverine Landscape* in the Stuyck del Bruyère Collection, Antwerp, is dated 1557), Bruegel gave full expression to his philosophy of life—a philosophy in which indignation had triumphed over irony, skepticism over faith. Signed and dated 1568, the *Parable of the Blind* (Naples) may be described as his last word on the human predicament. Its lesson is that blind confidence darkens counsel and spells disaster for the man who has it; every abeyance of the reasoning faculty is fatal to the critical spirit. Bruegel shows us six poor wretches with empty eye-sockets, their livid faces turned towards the sky, leading each other down a slope at the end of which is a deep ditch into which the man in front has fallen and where the others soon will join him. These tragic figures are aligned in single file on a diagonal that, like a strident cry, traverses and unifies the composition. Nevertheless the setting is a stretch of country near a Brabantine village (identified as Pede Sainte Anne near Brussels), bathed in the gentle light of spring, and not a breath of wind ruffles the shining peace. Here for the last time Bruegel points the contrast between the elemental calm of nature and the vanity of human effort.

After the plastic tension of the *Parable* comes a restful composition, *The Misanthrope* (Naples, signed and dated 1568). Here the polemical intent that always lay behind the Bruegelian dialectic has yielded to a quieter mood, and the technique, too, is more "impressionistic." Indeed we are tempted to read into this last work a gesture of renunciation—all the more so since it appears to be unfinished. After so often seeking to justify the collective vocation of the individual contending with a world of sheer absurdity, he now shows us the somber figure of the Misanthrope in mourning for a lost ideal. Wearing a long grey-blue cloak, his head buried in a cowl-like hood, he is nursing his grievance against the world as he enjoys —if enjoyment it can be called—the congenial solitude of a countryside to all appearances deserted. "Because the world is so faithless I am going into mourning." But while he goes his would-be lonely way an oafish dwarf has crept up behind him and is stealing his purse. The world is even more "faithless" than our sage had thought! Thus in the bleak light of a dying day, the man who had depicted with unflagging fervor the joys and tragedies of Flanders in that troubled age, passes discreetly from our view, cut off in his prime, disillusioned by the inexorable futility of man's lot on earth.

Pieter Bruegel (c. 1525-1569).

Peasant Dance (detail), c. 1568. Kunsthistorisches Museum, Vienna.

From Massys to Mannerism

Quentin Massys (1466-1530).

Lamentation over the Dead Christ, detail: The Sepulchre, 1511. Musée Royal des Beaux-Arts, Antwerp.

From Massys to Mannerism

THE year of Pieter Bruegel's death, 1569, also witnessed the publication by the Flemish cosmographer Gerardus Mercator of the first map on "Mercator's projection." During this period, the latter half of the 16th century, humanism was at its zenith. Except in the field of the portrait, Bruegel had explored all the possibilities of that humanist art for which the times were ripe. His fine sense of color enabled him to realize that color had constructive, not merely ornamental values and, by the same token, he achieved a pregnant fusion of archaisms and the new conceptions of the age. But Bruegel, as we have said, was a case apart, unique of his kind.

We must now go back a little and trace the artistic evolution of this somewhat baffling century in which one world was dying and another coming to birth.

That the Renaissance reached the Low Countries so belatedly is due to the fact that economic conditions such as those which had fostered its early flowering in Northern Italy did not develop in the Netherlands until the beginning of the 16th century. For capitalism arose not in Flanders but in the great commercial centers of Tuscany and Venetia where, during the 14th century, the successful practice of investment had opened men's eyes to the power that comes of accumulated wealth. And the notion of individualism was a direct result of the rise of capitalism; the wealthy man now stood out from the common herd, and from his dominant position complacently surveyed both worlds—the old and the new.

There thus developed a new scale of values, fundamental to the spirit of the age, among which the traditional concepts of time and space, hitherto independent of each other, were integrated into a single system. Only yesterday the measure of space was the sky, and that of time, Eternity. In the Ghent Altarpiece of Jan van Eyck we have a symbolic world where many processes of time are represented side by side; oranges of the South flowering simultaneously with northern apple trees, prophets and martyrs advancing heavenwards simultaneously across the same vast green carpet. That ineffable peace which pervades the masterworks of the Flemish Primitives also derives from a unique moment of time arrested in space: a brief pause in the eternal flux enabling the craftsman's eye and hand to apprehend the "thing in itself" and so to achieve that meticulous precision which, as Huizinga points out, was in the last analysis, no more than "one of the ultimate forms of the development of medieval thought," always preoccupied with "the need of converting every religious notion into a clearly defined image." For only when the gaze itself is stationary, can it detect the secret movement of the universe and relations between objects, and thus discern a scale of magnitudes making it possible to situate the data of visual experience in an ordered hierarchy. Seconded by the scientific discoveries of the period, this faculty of the individual eye was now to modify forms of nature as apprehended by the mind and a new method of investigation came into being, an approach that, striking through the screen of medieval abstractions, enlarged the field of mental activity and stimulated the interest of man in man, of men in nature, and of art in life itself. Not that the new "realism" necessarily led to a truer, more faithful image of the visible world. All it actually did was to express a new aspect of the visible, owing something no doubt to classical antiquity, but neither more nor less "true" than in the past. What happened was simply that a new convention, soon to discover its appropriate terminology, replaced its predecessor and made good a different system of equivalences.

In Flanders this metamorphosis took place by slow degrees. For it came in conflict with local traditions, with the well-established disciplines of the studios, with the highly influential Chambers of Rhetoric (literary guilds which still preserved a completely medieval character) and with the draconian regulations of the trade-corporations. But perhaps the greatest obstacle was the influx of wealth into the Low Countries and all that this entailed. If, round about the year 1500, we find a crystallization of the modes of pictorial expression taking place and with it a movement towards archaism sponsored at Bruges by Adriaen Isenbrant, at Brussels by Colin de Coter and at Antwerp by the Master of Frankfort, this was not due to a nostalgic yearning to return to the great tradition of Flemish art. Though these tendencies have been regarded by some critics as a reaction against Memling's "mawkishness," and though traditional elements gained ground in Flanders at the very time when Italianism was coming to the fore, this reactionary trend, in our opinion, corresponded to a radical change in the social frame of reference. For the picture, whose *raison d'être* had hitherto been its religious message, and its proper destination a religious edifice, was now becoming, in the hands of the new-rich burghers, a "collector's piece," a luxury article, an "investment." Less and less often painted to order, it was being mass-produced; oftener than not—now that the great masters of the North were enjoying Europe-wide renown—with an eye to the export market. As a natural result, this intensive production of unbespoken works of art led to the replacement of strict adhesion to religious values by a cult of "the beautiful." And it is an interesting point that, if we look for premonitory signs of these changes of contemporary taste, we find them in Gothic mannerism—whose evolution, as it so happened, stopped short at the cult of form for form's sake.

At Bruges this reversion to the past is manifest in the art of Adriaen Isenbrant, Jan Provost and Ambrosius Benson, while a group of painters at Antwerp (none of whose names are known) refined on the style of Van Eyck and his immediate successors. In the works of the Master of the Antwerp *Epiphany*, the Master of the Antwerp *Crucifixion* and in those of that sophisticated artist Jan de Beer, we find a strongly agitated line, elongated forms, and affected gestures which completely fail to suggest movement; these parodies of life merely emphasize its absence, while the excessive use of ornament is no less symptomatic of a relapse into the formulas of medievaldom. But with the coming of the Renaissance there developed a tendency to broader, simpler gestures, appropriate to the generous impulses of humanistic thought—a trend that reached its apogee in the art of Quentin Massys.

While Gerard David brought the "Golden Century" of Flemish painting to a close at Bruges, Quentin Massys opened up at Antwerp ("*patria* of all Christian nations") vistas on the new age that was dawning. Though he shrewdly capitalized on the glorious heritage of his predecessors and even struck Sir Thomas More as being "the renovator of ancient art," he counts for far more than an artist of the transition; there was no real hiatus in Flanders between the reign of the dukes of Burgundy and that of the Spanish kings. Massys acted as a vital link between two ages and, broadly speaking, bridged the gulf between Van der Weyden and Rubens. In his art we feel that the age-old belief in man's total subjection to the cosmos is losing ground. He reflected the change that was coming over religious sentiment, voiced the new freedom of thought, and interpreted the ideology of the new middle class. Moreover, he pioneered the trend towards a much wider choice of subjects, superseding the set program of religious themes that had prevailed since the time of Van Eyck. Massys aims at establishing a sort of dialogue with the spectator, whose attention the figures seem to be inviting. And once he feels that he has caught the spectator's interest, the artist proceeds to charm him with the rediscovered glamour of "ideal beauty" and deploys a range of expressions stylizing an equal range of psychological realities. He also took over, if sparingly, some of the Italian idioms that had made their way to Flanders and with them reinforced the national genius; thus, without changing anything of the past, he gave a new direction to Flemish painting. Closely associated with the great humanist movement of the period, his art is as it were a plastic equivalent of the conceptions of Erasmus, of whom, like Dürer and Lucas van Leyden, he was an exact contemporary.

The tradition that Massys was trained as a blacksmith before he turned to painting may possibly be true. The charming decorations in wrought iron above a well facing the portal of Antwerp Cathedral may have been his work and thus bear out Van Mander's statement. In any case his father was a worker in iron and the Joos Massys who made a new clockface for the tower of St Peter's Church was almost certainly his brother. Though he was born in 1466 at Louvain, his parents came originally from Grobbendonk, a village in the Limburg Campine to the north of Louvain, where there was a priory affiliated to the Congregation of Windesheim. In his youth he kept in touch with his native countryside and it was there that in 1486 he married Alyt van Tuylt, daughter of a rich landowner. Canon Prims has made out a plausible case for the theory that Massys received his early training at the Grobbendonk priory. "In the monasteries of this Order the scribes did not confine themselves to copying manuscripts, but illuminated them as well." And Georges Marlier suggests that contacts with the Grobbendonk illuminators may well have led to his choice of a vocation. "In which case," he continues, "there is at least a grain of truth in the story related by Van Fornenbergh in the 17th century, to the effect that Quentin, the blacksmith's son, learnt as a child the art of painting by making colored pictures in the manner of the book illuminators." This seems all the more probable since (as Marlier further points out) the spirit of Massys' art "has much in common with the edifying works produced by certain ascetic writers such as Jan Storm and Jacob Roecx at the priory of Grobbendonk." According to Van Mander, Massys was "well-read and a skilled musician," and this, too, bears out the view that he was in close touch with the local monks. Be this as it may, there are good grounds for believing that at some time during this early period he practised art at Louvain in the entourage of Dirk Bouts.

It was, however, at Antwerp that Massys established himself—a city which, though now the leading business center of the western world, had as yet no artistic tradition. He qualified as a master in the Guild of St Luke in 1491. In 1504 the Lusitanian painter Eduardo o Portugès visited his studio. When his wife died in 1507 he was left with two young sons, Jan and Cornelis, both of whom became painters. In the following year he married Katharina Heyns, by whom he had ten children. In 1509 Don Manuel, an envoy from the king of Portugal, gave him a commission for a large altarpiece representing the *Seven Griefs of the Virgin,* for the Madre de Deus convent at Lisbon (it is now in the museum of that city). Between the years 1513 and 1517 the same Portuguese "agent" gave him another order for an equally large triptych for the monastery of Santa Clara at Coimbre; the two wings have survived and are now in the local museum. His long-standing friendship with Joachim Patinir (dating apparently to well before the latter's arrival in Antwerp in 1515) led to a fruitful collaboration between them. He appears also to have been on friendly terms with Jan Provost and, from 1515 on, with Gerard David. Though intimate with Pieter Gillis (also known as Aegidius), secretary to the municipality, through whom he became acquainted with Erasmus (in 1517), he seems to have refused to assume any official post in the Painters' Guild. In 1519 "Mestre Quintino" bought a house in the Rue des Tanneurs; Dürer, in the diary he kept during his journey to the Netherlands in 1520-1521, briefly notes that he visited it but does not speak of meeting its owner. Friedländer suggests that Massys deliberately avoided Dürer out of shyness or pride. It is perhaps more reasonable to surmise that some urgent task had called him away from Antwerp at the time—an hypothesis to which his seeming absence at the wedding of his friend Patinir, in the same year, lends color. In 1521 Massys bought another house, in the Rue des Arbalétriers which, we are told, he furnished "exactly to his taste" and decorated "with mural paintings in the Italian manner." On Patinir's death in 1524 he acted as guardian of his friend's two daughters. Holbein called on him, on his way to England in 1526. Massys died on September 30, 1530. A print engraved by Jan Wierix after a self-portrait shows a refined-looking man, sensitive and kindly.

One of his earliest works is a *St Christopher* (Antwerp) presumably painted at Louvain about 1490, and, despite an obvious reference to the right wing of Dirk Bouts' *Adoration of the Magi* (Munich), the style seems ill-assured. A delicate sensibility, instinct with devout religious feeling, pervades the *Salvator Mundi* (Antwerp) where the face, presented frontally, is framed in rich brown shadows, and still more notably the *Virgin in Prayer* (Antwerp) in which the Madonna's head droops gracefully under the weight of a richly wrought crown of gold. In an early *Virgin and Child* in a private collection in Switzerland, though he still conforms to Gothic tradition, Massys strikes a more personal note. The Virgin is shown standing in front of a low garden wall; behind her stretches an exquisitely rendered landscape, while the slim, supple figure, with long golden hair rippling over a cloak widely outspread on the ground, recalls the style of the Master of the Legend of St Lucy. In this work we see a happy fusion of the real with the imaginary. It contains in embryo all the Madonnas that Massys was soon to paint in a broader manner, tinctured with Italian influences. The Lyons *Virgin and Child with Angels* (there are replicas in Count Seilern's Collection, London, and the Duke of Newcastle's Collection, Clumber Park) was ascribed successively to Rogier van der Weyden, Memling, Gerard David and even to Eduardo o Portugès before Henri Focillon assigned it to Massys. Here the traditional religious message of the theme is blurred by a plethora of ornament: putti, rinceaux, colonnettes, sumptuous marbles and so forth. For the time being the artist has limited himself to the more superficial aspects of Renaissance art. But when at the close of his career we see the Madonna represented as a very human young mother (1529, Brussels, Berlin, Louvre), holding a plump, well-fed Child who is kissing her on the lips, the spirit of the Renaissance has effectively banished that of the religious "myth." (Gerard David, in his *Vierge à la soupe au lait*, c. 1520, painted after his arrival in Antwerp, moved in the same direction.) Particularly striking in these Madonnas of his last period are their delicate tonal effects, the melting softness of the colors and the idealization of faces, which have much of the spell-binding beauty we find in Leonardo's and Luini's figures. The feminine type now favored by Massys, a fair-haired, demurely winsome young woman, is seen at its best in the famous *Magdalen* (Antwerp).

Through what channels did Massys acquire his knowledge of Italian painting? The problem is far from having been adequately solved. This much seems certain, however, that Leonardo's influence, so evident in the *Madonna with the Red Mantle* (Brussels), both in the composition (a pyramidal mass centered on the figures) and in the technique (a presence glimmering forth through light veils of *sfumato*) cannot have taken effect before 1491. Leonardo's *Virgin of the Rocks* was not finished until 1499 and his *Virgin and Child with St Anne*, from which a *Virgin and Child* ascribed to Massys (in Poznan Museum) so unmistakably derives, was completed only in 1506. Neither the prints nor the tapestry cartoons he may have seen could have transmitted to him such specifically painterly influences; thus there are good reasons for believing that at the beginning of the century Massys made the journey to Italy and thus prepared himself for handling large-scale works.

In 1507 the Confraternity of St Anne at Louvain commissioned him to make a triptych (now in Brussels Museum) for their altar in St Peter's Church. Signed and dated 1509, it illustrates the *Legend of St Anne*, a theme that had been popularized by a recent book by Johannes Trithemius, *De laudibus sanctissimae Matris Annae tractatus* (Mainz, 1494). A work of large dimensions, it constitutes a landmark both in the evolution of Massys' style and in that of Flemish painting in general. Clearly the painter was here taking stock of his new resources. Yet we cannot but feel that his means did not fully match his aspirations, and the spectator is left with the impression of a task inadequately coped with. There is an evident disharmony between the ambitious magnitude of the work and the fragility of the colors, whose extreme delicacy and limited range do not measure up to the scale of the figures.

This altarpiece may have suffered from the ravages of time, but Leo van Puyvelde assures us that it has not undergone any cleaning since it was made. This confirms its "experimental" nature; for the first time a Flemish painter, instead of using pure, saturated colors, rings the changes on tonal values such as translucent blues, olive greens, pale lilacs, while another of his technical innovations is the use of broken tones in the folds of garments (a purplish red tinted with pink). The composition, too, breaks with the structural verticalism of earlier days and is organized in diagonals, while the breadth and emotive boldness of

Quentin Massys (1466-1530).

Lamentation over the Dead Christ, 1511. (102½ × 107½") Musée Royal des Beaux-Arts, Antwerp.

attitudes and gestures impart flexibility to the symmetrical layout. Moreover, by entering into the psychology of his figures the artist creates meaningful associations between them, so that they seem less like subjects of a "golden legend" than like living human beings participating in some real event. In the center are the Virgin and Child and St Anne; seated on either side, with their children, are Mary, wife of Zebedee, and Mary Salome. The scene is enacted under the watchful eyes of their respective husbands, standing behind a balustrade: St Joseph, Joachim, Alpheus and Zebedee. All fifteen figures have a marvellous serenity and, their eyes half closed, seem lost in tranquil meditation. They are spaced out in front of a Brunelleschian portico and disposed in three triangular schemas, that is to say following the arrangement used by Leonardo some ten years earlier in the *Last Supper* in Santa Maria delle Grazie, Milan. Though the artist's obvious concern with architectonic order and formal beauty and the rolling landscape tinged with blue in the far distance give an Italian accent to the composition, the work as a whole is pervaded by a very human, typically Flemish sense of intimacy, almost, one might say, the atmosphere of a family reunion.

In the Antwerp *Lamentation over the Dead Christ* (there are variants in the Matthiesen Gallery and the Frank T. Sabin Collection in London, and in Count de Pret's Collection in Castle Vordensteyn at Schoten) Massys dispenses with the artifices of dialectic, and the realistic tone of the work is more in keeping with the Flemish temperament. This large triptych was commissioned in 1508 by the Antwerp Carpenters' Guild for their chapel in the Cathedral. It was completed on August 26, 1511, and the sum paid for it was used by the artist for the purchase of an annuity in the name of his two eldest sons. The altarpiece leapt into immediate fame; both Philip II and the Queen of England signified their willingness to purchase it, but their offers were politely declined. Van Mander rightly spoke of it as an "outstanding work" and in fact it has always been regarded as the painter's masterpiece. At once a final echo of the 15th century and a brilliant prelude to the Flemish Renaissance, it might be described as an anthology or summation of an art on which a whole lineage of disciples was to thrive for several decades.

A rocky landscape spans the picture like a backcloth, pierced on the right by a small cavity: the entrance of the sepulchre that is being hastily made ready. This backcloth imposes a strictly planimetric presentation of the nine lifesize figures grouped around Christ's body, which stretches horizontally along the bottom of the composition. The figures have a quite remarkable robustness, and indeed represent a wholly novel conception of plasticity. Both technique and execution reveal the changes brought about by a new way of seeing and an altered sensibility: changes speeded up no doubt by the more realistic style of preaching that had now come into vogue. There is in fact a close parallel between the evolution of the devout literature of the age and that of its art. These broken, blended tones are very different from the vivid colors of the Primitives, while figures have little of the sharpness of definition characteristic of the age of Rogier van der Weyden. Given exceptional density and weight, the bodies are those of living, active specimens of humanity seen under the stress of poignant emotion—no longer arabesques or empty silhouettes. St John's deeply moving face foreshadows the type of portraiture we find in Massys' *Erasmus*. So natural are these gestures of compassion and attitudes of grief that the action is transposed on to the terrestrial plane and in this revelation of human suffering are intimations of the new style that (in the side wings of the triptych) marked, beyond a doubt, a turning point in Flemish art. Indeed the *Martyrdom of St John* becomes a frankly secular scene, such is the pre-Bruegelian realism of the plebeian executioners, which strikes a telling contrast with the aristocratic elegance and equivocal graces of the company in *Herod's Feast*.

Linking up with this major work are several other panels of a remarkable maturity of style. The *Adoration of the Magi* (Metropolitan Museum, New York) might be described as an exact symbiosis of the three panels of the Antwerp triptych, combining as it does the wistful pathos of the Virgin (but rendered here with well-nigh abstract aloofness), the pomp and splendor of the three Kings (stressed with mannerist insistence) and the ribald exuberance of the crowd whose leering, boorish faces so strikingly recall some of Bosch's peasant types. This work belongs to the period of syntheses through which Flemish art was passing, and we agree with Grete Ring and E. P. Richardson in dating it to about 1526. Reminiscences of Bosch as well as the bulkiness of the figures intensify the expressionism of the *Ecce Homo* (Prado). Lastly, contrasting with the dynamism of these compositions, we have the *Three Marys at the Tomb* (Lisbon) where, in the foreground of a landscape veiled in dusk, the fine psychological restraint in the rendering of the women has all the poetic quality we found in the Antwerp *Lamentation*.

Along with the social changes that were taking place, the ground had been prepared for esthetic innovation, and the advent of the genre picture facilitated a transition from the sacred to the secular. Thus a disruption of the "liturgical poem" had become inevitable and it was Massys who, with the rising tide of Lutheranism, led the way.

Quentin Massys (1466-1530).

Lamentation over the Dead Christ, detail: St John, 1511. Musée Royal des Beaux-Arts, Antwerp.

Quentin Massys (1466-1530).

The Magdalen, c. 1525. (17¾×11½″) Musée Royal des Beaux-Arts, Antwerp.

At the time when Lucas van Leyden, then quite a young man, painted the highly original *Game of Chess* (Berlin), Massys was creating a prose version of the St Eloi (Eligius) theme: the famous *Money Changer and his Wife*, dated 1514, once owned by Rubens and now in the Louvre. Its sentimental appeal, elegant sophistication and flawless execution called forth a host of replicas. Apparently it was inspired by the great *St Eligius* of Petrus Christus (1449, Robert Lehman Collection, New York), unless it derived from a lost work by Jan van Eyck showing a money-changer making up the day's accounts with his clerk. But Christus gave his money-changer (or goldsmith) all the grave dignity of a prelate. Massys, when treating the theme, brings out its moral significance by the subterfuge of a double portrait. For there is a meaningful contrast between the attitude of the banker, absorbed in weighing the gold coins, and that of his wife, so dazzled by the wealth they represent that her attention has wandered from the pious book before her. The new influx of wealth was tending to depreciate religious values—whereas there should have been an equipoise, as was suggested by an inscription which still figured on the frame of the picture in Rubens' time: *Statura justa et aequa sint pondera* ("let the scales be true and the weights equal").

Once opened up, this vein of social criticism soon took a satirical turn, in the spirit of the most caustic passages in the *Praise of Folly*. The *Ill-sorted Couple* (Countess de Pourtalès Collection, Paris) shows us one of those old men who, Erasmus writes, "have hardly human faces, who stammer, dodder and—crowning folly—fall in love with young girls, over whom they make bigger fools of themselves than the most inexperienced youngster." *The Usurers* (Palazzo Doria, Rome), *Two Old Men Praying* (Private Collection, Lisbon; replica in the Palazzo Doria, Rome), *Sharpers' Deal* (Van Maerlant Museum, Damme) and the so-called *Ugly Duchess* (National Gallery, London) also contain grotesque figures deriving more or less directly from Leonardo's drawings. However, writes Friedländer, "what was for Leonardo merely a caprice of the pen was taken seriously by the grave-minded Fleming." And this cult of ugliness can be no less irritating than the willful distortion of form, for it often degenerates into the worst type of expressionist caricature.

His portraits show that Massys kept in close touch with the leading humanists. Except in the *Portrait of a Man* (Metropolitan Museum, New York) and the *Man with a Pink* (Art Institute of Chicago)—both early works, as is proved by the impersonal approach, bright tones and green, translucent backgrounds—Massys ranks as the initiator of the humanist portrait in the Low Countries. The diptych, now dispersed, one panel of which contains the portrait of the famous humanist Pieter Gillis or Aegidius (Earl of Radnor's Collection, Longford Castle; replica in the Royal Museum, Antwerp) and the companion panel that of Erasmus (Galleria Nazionale, Rome) who seems to be conversing with him, is particularly revealing on this point. Georges Marlier has aptly described this diptych, which brings home to us the painter's personal refinement no less than that of his two sitters, as "the poem of a fourfold friendship." "Fourfold" because it was commissioned by Erasmus in 1517 for presentation to their common friend Sir Thomas More. "Pieter Gillis and I," Erasmus wrote to Thomas More on May 30, 1517, "are having ourselves painted together and we shall send you the picture as a present from us both." In 1515 the future Lord Chancellor of England had met Pieter Gillis, who held the post of secretary to the Antwerp Municipality, and it was to him that he dedicated his *Utopia*, printed at Louvain in 1516, under the superintendence of Erasmus. No company was more agreeable to him, wrote More in the forefront of his famous book, than that of "one Peter Gyles, a citizen of Antwerp... For it is hard to say whether the young man be in learning or in honesty more excellent... towards his friends [he is] so kind-hearted, so loving, so faithful, so trusty, and of so earnest affection, that it were very hard in any place to find a man that with him in all points of friendship may be compared."

In his portrait of Aegidius Massys brings out the attractive personality of his sitter, while giving him the astute look of a man never misled by appearances. Shown half-length, turned to the left, the Antwerp humanist is wearing a black cap and a voluminous cloak with a marten-fur collar, whose dark mass stands out against the reddish-brown wainscoting of his study. In his left hand he holds a letter from More, while the fingers of his right hand rest on a book bound in red. Other books, strewn on a shelf behind him that is carried over on to the panel which shows Erasmus lost in thought, act as a psychological link between the figures. Erasmus is seated at his desk, wrapped in a dark green, almost black mantle; he has paused, pen in hand, to collect his thoughts before continuing to write his *Paraphrase of the Epistle to the Romans*. The dazzling white of the pages of the manuscript is stressed by the bright red of a blotting-pad. Here the fluid modeling strikes a contrast with the hard precision of Holbein's and Dürer's portraits of Erasmus.

Massys made several portraits of men of learning, theologians, lawyers, scientists, all of them rendered with the same lifelikeness, the same facility, and always—and above all—with the same remarkable power of revealing the sitter's inmost self. The *Portrait of Canon Stephen Gardiner* (Liechtenstein Collection, Vaduz) is an exceptional case; treated in the Italian manner, it is more sharply defined, more forcibly direct—in a word, more "calligraphic" than the other portraits. L. Reis-Santos suggests that the order for the *Portrait of an Old Man* (Musée Jacquemart-André, Paris) may have been given to Massys by Erasmus with a view to presenting the picture to Giovanni de' Medici who took the name of Leo X on his elevation to the papacy in 1513, since the portrait bears this date and may well be a likeness of Cosimo de' Medici—a view supported by its marked resemblance to (amongst others) Pontormo's portrait of Cosimo (Uffizi). But we cannot follow the learned curator of Coimbre Museum in maintaining that this picture constitutes a peak-point in the painter's œuvre; its plastic quality is of a low order, its style mannered and unconvincing. Quite possibly it was inspired by some Leonardesque caricature. Very different is Massys' last "portrait," instinct with exquisitely rendered shades of feeling; I have in mind the gaunt but divinely serene face of the Savior in *Christ Blessing* (Winterthur). Here all is inwardness; vibrant beneath the tranquil countenance are the spiritual anxieties of the age, and the figure shines out, radiant with an inner light, through veils of shade and color.

Massys exercised considerable influence on his own age and the next. His striking discoveries, his innovations in the field of color seconded by exceptional technical proficiency, the fluid rhythms and the substantiality of his figures, his suave modulations and realistic tensions, furnished a stylistic repertory on which his disciples or heirs drew freely according to their tastes and tendencies.

Coming after the magisterial researches of J. de Figueiredo, the "Flanders, Spain and Portugal" exhibition held at Bordeaux in 1954, though limited in scope, served to confirm the influence of Massys on the art of several Portuguese painters: Frei Carlos, the "Flamengo de Lisboa," Garcia Fernandes, Francisco Henriques, Cristovao de Figueiredo, Gregorio Lopes and Eduardo o Portugès. It is much to be hoped that a fully comprehensive exhibition of all the key works will be organized in the near future, enabling us to form a clearer picture of the relations (still somewhat ill-defined) between the artists of the Iberian Peninsula and the Northerners. The Bordeaux exhibition anyhow performed one very useful service: it enabled Georges Marlier to throw new light on the hitherto shadowy personality of Ambrosius Benson, a Hispano-Flemish master active in the first half of the 16th century, whose work he was the first to appraise and catalogue in a well-documented monograph (1957). A *Pietà* (Kleinberger Galleries, New York) ascribed to Benson is particularly interesting in that the faces have an unusual suavity, while the composition as a whole is a thinly disguised variant of that used by Massys in his *Lamentation over the Dead Christ* (Antwerp).

Among the members of the Antwerp group who showed most intelligence and sensibility in interpreting the more poetic aspects of Massys' art, the Master of the Mansi Magdalen holds pride of place. In the *Magdalen* after which he is named (now in Berlin, formerly Marquis Mansi Collection, Lucca) the artist—whom Friedländer proposed to identify with a certain Willem Meulenbroec, enrolled as "pupil of Massys" in the Antwerp Painters' Guild in 1501— the idealized figure of the saint is modeled with tender feeling. Her graceful form stands out against a landscape background done in various shades of brown and interspersed with oddly shaped rocks—reminiscences of Patinir and Dürer. The Master of the Morrison Triptych, so called after an altarpiece representing the *Virgin and Child* in the Hugh Morrison Collection,

Quentin Massys (1466-1530).

Portrait of Canon Stephen Gardiner. (28¾×23⅝″)

Collection of the Prince of Liechtenstein, Vaduz.

Jan de Beer (c. 1480-c. 1535).

The Adoration of the Magi, c. 1510. (23⅝×16⅝″) Musée Royal des Beaux-Arts, Ghent.

London, has been the subject of a study by Friedländer. The figure of the Virgin, which has affinities with Massys' and Memling's Madonnas, is given a hybrid setting composed of Gothic and Renaissance elements, and Massys' influence is perceptible chiefly in the execution.

Rogier's grandson Goswyn van der Weyden (died after 1538) borrowed no less from Massys than from Bosch. Massys' own son Jan (1505-1575) began by taking over his father's popular themes, which he handled with satirical gusto and caustic wit, before specializing in *scènes galantes* in the manner of the School of Fontainebleau. Like him, several other artists—Marinus van Reymerswaele, Jan Sanders van Hemessen, Peeter Huys, Pieter Aertsen and Joachim Beuckelaer—continued to exploit the realistic vein, making no secret of their intention to keep Flemish genre painting to the path mapped out by national tradition.

Although Flemish art was inadequately represented, the large-scale exhibition illustrating the "Triumph of European Mannerism" held at Amsterdam in 1955 was of help towards defining an art conception that is both complex and elusive. But however readily our modern sensibility accepts in a general way the "mannerist" idea, it is well to formulate a scale of values enabling a balanced estimate of what that somewhat vague idea embraces. For, despite the efforts of contemporary critics to see in Mannerism a distinctive, self-sufficient style, we cannot fail to note that, looked at from an international viewpoint, it contains some of the most perplexing anomalies of all 16th-century art. Is it not a fact—a fact that if we are honest with ourselves we are bound to recognize—that the Renaissance shattered the majestic organic unity of the medieval world? At the close of his brilliant historical synopsis, Henri Pirenne makes it clear that after the early 16th century the European social order, disintegrated by the force of events, fell far short of that grandiose homogeneity, due to the acceptance of a common faith and the selfsame Christian ideal, which characterized the Middle Ages. So it was that painting (always adjusted to the modalities of the age the artist lives in and only partially conditioned by his personal aspirations) now lost the absolute unity of a single supreme style. The fragmentation of culture and the dispersal of art centers, ideological conflicts and religious differences, the clash of ancient myths and Holy Scripture—all alike led, in that period of spiritual unrest, when thought was winning its freedom and the Western World becoming "internationalized," to a proliferation of very diverse tendencies and that intermingling of art currents which by general consent is given the name of Mannerism.

Mannerism—style *in extremis*—combines restless experimentalism, symptom of a culture's growing pains, with those successive refinements which are the aftermath of great creative epochs. At various stages art develops a "manner" based on formulas borrowed verbatim from the past. But meanwhile the forward-looking artist, seeking new fields to conquer, refashions the forms that he takes over, investing them with strange enchantments. Imagination, given free rein, supplants direct observation. A taste for artifice, a more or less pronounced intellectualism and an urge to break up classical order and proportion (while retaining its underlying structure) lead the mannerist artist to transform nature into ornament. Hence a feverish, overwrought art combining extreme literalism as to details with an overall effect of purest fantasy; and this conflict lies at the source of the "excesses" of Mannerism.

Under all its various forms it acted as a prelude to the great flowering of Baroque art. In point of fact nothing was less spontaneous than this sudden intoxication with forms that were outcrops, so to speak, from the masterpieces of the recent past. When Mannerism swept over Europe, from Antwerp to Lisbon, from Rome to Prague, from Florence to Amsterdam, by way of Fontainebleau, it imposed on each of these art centers specific idioms, conditioned by local creative trends. To Flanders falls the credit—if credit it be—of having given rise round about 1500 to the first wave of Mannerism. The Antwerp mannerists, whose leader, that exquisite artist Jan de Beer, we have already mentioned, stemmed directly from the late 15th-century Flemish masters. On the theme of the *Adoration of the Magi*, so rich in decorative possibilities, they embroidered—if in terms of a much narrowed vision—ornamental beauties vying with those of flamboyant Gothic, which still held its own in architecture. Their concern with the organization of space is evident, as is their taste for novel effects. It is interesting to see how they relegate the architectural vestiges of an earlier age to the background and bring to the fore, like portable stage scenery, Renaissance porticos with composite pillars and decorations that seem made of papier-mâché. The presentation of the figures, their strangeness, their affected poses and arbitrary colors reinforce the "magical" atmosphere of these small pictures. We find a similar pictorial language, magnified to the scale of larger pictures, in the works Friedländer ascribes to the Master of 1518 (better known as the Master of the Abbey of Dilighem). Its curiously taut drawing, thin, angular forms, narrow heads, slotted eyes, rhetorical gestures and a lavish use of ornament give an unforgettable quality to the *Legend of Mary Magdalen* (Brussels).

Throughout the century of the Reformation we can feel a strain of restlessness in the art of Flanders, as though it were always striving towards the Baroque style vocational to it. For it was not in the nature of the Flemish sensibility to express itself classically, and all that the Renaissance style, as fashioned in Italy and stabilized in France, induced in the Low Countries was no more than the echo of a formula. The first wave of Flemish Mannerism (whose indebtedness to German art must not be overlooked) linked up with Italian Mannerism, which in fact, conjointly with Cranach and Dürer, it had itself done much to stimulate in Tuscany. And it was now to give rise to a Mannerism of an international type, though largely determined by the *genius loci*.

Joos van der Beke, better known as Joos van Cleve, was of all Antwerp mannerists the most akin to Quentin Massys. Neither the place nor date of his birth is known. But the very special nature of his sensibility and the fact that throughout his career he kept in contact with Germany lead us to believe that the name he made famous may properly be taken at its face value and that he hailed from the ancient city of Cleves on the Lower Rhine. Though the presence at Genoa of an *Adoration of the Magi* (Church of San Donato) and a *Nativity* (Galleria Balbi) cannot definitely prove that he lived for any length of time in Italy, there is no reason to question the commonly held view that he was in Genoa anyhow during the period when that city was under the control of Philip of Cleves, Lord of Ravensteyn (1501-1506). His arrival in Antwerp is proved by his having qualified as a master in the local Guild of Painters in 1511. Judging by the style of his earliest dated works—the wings of a triptych(1507) in the Louvre and the *Portrait of a Man* (1509) in the Koetser Collection, London—we may surmise that he was born somewhere around 1480. That in his thirties his reputation was already well established is proved by the fact of his being appointed Dean of the Antwerp Guild of Painters in 1516 (this appointment was twice renewed, in 1520 and 1525). It is thought that meanwhile he made a brief stay in Cologne. He seems to have been as closely associated as Quentin Massys with Joachim Patinir and there is no doubt about their collaboration. Thus Van Mander speaks of a *Virgin* by Joos van Cleve "to which Patinir added a charming landscape background." Between 1530 and 1535 he worked in France and there are grounds for thinking that he then went to England to paint (in 1536, at the same time as Holbein) his portrait of Henry VIII (Hampton Court). On November 10, 1540, he signed his will, witnessed by the painter Pieter Coeck, and died shortly after.

Joos van Cleve was known over a long period as the Master of the Death of the Virgin, the name assigned the author of two altarpieces illustrating that theme (Cologne, dated 1515, and Munich). The stylistic affinities of these two works with an *Adoration of the Magi* (Detroit) bearing the initials J. B. (i.e. Joos van der Beke); with an *Adoration of the Shepherds* (Naples) signed Jo. B. Cleve; and with the wings of an altarpiece, the *Passion of Christ* in the Church of Our Lady at Danzig, initialled "J. B.", have made it possible to co-ordinate this painter's œuvre and to regard him as a central figure of the mannerist movement.

Already there were intimations of Baroque emotionalism in the deeply moving *Death of the Virgin* (Bruges) painted by Hugo van der Goes at the close of his career, but these tended to be neutralized in the moral unity of the picture context. Van Cleve, however, in his *Death of the Virgin*, presents the theme theatrically, in the manner of his German contemporaries. In the Munich version the twelve apostles gathered around the deathbed in an agitated group are giving unrestrained expression to their emotion and if St John is shown placing a taper in the hand of the dying Virgin, this is merely to indicate a plastic *point de repère*. Every

Jan Gossart (c. 1472-1533/36).

The Adoration of the Kings, c. 1505. (69¾×63½″) By Courtesy of the Trustees, National Gallery, London.

figure, whether presented side face, in back view or in full face, serves as a pretext for a feat of stylistic legerdemain. The artist conceives the figures both as vehicles of rhythmic arabesques and as spatial referents; but their spacing is so badly calculated that he fails to bring this off and, thrust indiscriminately upon our gaze, they produce a bewildering effect. Van Cleve's incisive line stresses the distraught vehemence of gestures borrowed, one would think, from the protagonists of German Mannerism. Nevertheless his deliberate, painstaking execution tends to stabilize the agitation of the forms, and this careful craftsmanship stems unmistakably from a long tradition indigenous to Flanders. Noteworthy among the apostles' faces is that of an old man who also plays the part of one of the Three Kings in the Adorations and the part of Joseph in the Holy Families Van Cleve so often painted; and it is not going too far to say that in the face of this old man, with his square head, sparse curly hair, heavy eyebrows and aquiline nose, the artist created a prototype.

His three versions of the *Adoration of the Magi* mark three stages of Van Cleve's artistic evolution. What catches our attention in the first (Dresden) is the unco-ordinated mass of details reflecting the incertitude and extreme mobility of the early phase of Mannerism. Painted about 1510, it seems to have greatly impressed the local purveyors of "Epiphanies" at Antwerp. A larger *Adoration*, also in Dresden, was commissioned about 1520 for a church at Genoa. Better balanced and less tightly executed, the composition hinges on a central axis and the Virgin's face is handled in the Lombard manner. But the strongly mobile rendering of the kneeling king's cloak, in billowing folds, conflicts with these classicizing tendencies and gives the style a curious ambivalence. In the Detroit *Adoration*, however, movement is at an end, the artist has achieved a serene equilibrium, a spacious peace. Perhaps we see Van Cleve at his best in his portraits, whose fine spareness of color does away with the shrill discordant tones that disfigure some of his big religious compositions.

Jan Gossart's attitude shows more detachment from the past, though he too relies on it to some extent. He was the first court painter in 16th-century Flanders. His sensibility, his predilections and the whole moral tenor of his work were largely determined by the circumstances of his birth, for he came of an aristocratic family and from his earliest youth had opportunities of admiring the work of vanguard artists in the royal collections. He played the part of an intermediary between Italy and the Northern Lowlands, and it was owing to the influence he had on Jan van Scorel and Lucas van Leyden that Dutch art assimilated many procedures of the Italian Renaissance. "He was one of the first," Van Mander writes, "to make known to Flanders the true method of composing and executing religious works peopled with nudes and mythological figures, which so far had not entered into the practices of the country." Though Friedländer, Glück and Duverger tend to restrict the scope of Gossart's influence, Van Mander's statement seems fully justified in the light of the known facts. There is no doubt that Gossart was the pioneer of Roman humanism in the Low Countries and that its secularizing tendencies were congenial to his temperament. It therefore fell to him to acclimatize on Flemish soil the body of conventions, based on a strictly logical chain of discoveries, that had shaped the course of Italian painting, amongst them being the use of circular rhythms, perspective based on architectural geometry, "close-ups," anatomical foreshortenings and sculpturesque modeling. These were complemented by a thorough knowledge of antique art and Gossart had no difficulty in reconciling them with certain Germanic influences, most potent of which was that of Dürer. But despite a full assimilation of these so to speak extraneous factors, the Flemish side of his temperament makes itself felt in the density of his colors, his faultless craftsmanship, his penchant for analysis and, last but not least, a pre-Rubensian sensuality.

Though some authorities believe that Jan Gossart was born at Maubeuge, it seems more probable that he was born about 1472 in the castle of Wijck-bij-Duurstede, near Utrecht, and came of a family stemming from the Hainaut. He is thought to have been the son of Jacques de Maubeuge who held the post of intendant to the Bishop of Utrecht, David of Burgundy, between 1470 and 1490. Equally problematic is the question of his early training. Stylistic, historical and iconographical data lend color to the theory that he served his apprenticeship at Ghent in the entourage of Gerard Hoorenbout (or Horebault), who has been tentatively identified as the illuminator of the Grimani Breviary, on which (if this view is correct) Gossart may have collaborated. The first authenticated date is 1503, in which year the records of the Antwerp Guild of St Luke contain an entry to the effect that Jennyn van Hennegouwe (i.e. Jan of Hainaut) obtained his degree of master. Henceforth he went by the name Jan van Mabuse (Flemish for Jean de Maubeuge). After 1507 there is no further mention of him in the Antwerp records, doubtless because he now was constantly traveling in the service of princes to whose households he was attached.

Jan Gossart (c. 1472-1533/36).

The Agony in the Garden, after 1509. (33½×24¾") Kaiser Friedrich Museum, Berlin.

On her appointment as Regent of the Netherlands in 1507, Margaret of Austria had taken up residence at Malines, where the relative simplicity of her palace was tempered by the presence of the art treasures she had brought to it from her castle at Pont-d'Ain in the Bresse region east of Lyons. Gossart was a *persona grata* at her court, and it was there that he won the patronage of Philip of Burgundy, a highly cultivated prince with humanistic leanings and "Grand Maistre d'Hôtel" of the Archduke Maximilian. Philip spoke Latin fluently, "had a truly kingly appreciation of the arts," and had even made a name for himself as an amateur painter and goldsmith. This enlightened prince played a considerable part in the Flemish Renaissance. Sent on a diplomatic mission to Pope Julius II, he left Malines on October 26, 1508, taking Gossart with him. His secretary Gerard Geldenhauer, a man of learning and friend of Erasmus, says that Philip enjoyed nothing more than gazing at the monuments of ancient Rome, and that he had drawings made of them "by the highly esteemed painter Jan Gossart." Some of these pen drawings, all of which bear traces of Gothic Mannerism, have survived: *The Coliseum* (Berlin), the *Resting Apollo* (Venice), the *Runner extracting a Thorn from his Foot* (A. Welcker Collection, Amsterdam) and an interpretation of the *Dying Gaul* (Frankfort). The triptych representing the *Holy Family, St Barbara and St Catherine* (Lisbon) and another *Holy Family* (Wedells Collection, Hamburg) contain reminiscences of the archaizing style of Goswyn van der Weyden, the Master of Frankfort and the Master of Hoogstraeten. In them we find the restricted vision, formal affectation and meticulous finish distinctive of Antwerp Mannerism. Yet such is their excellence that Friedländer feels justified in singling out Gossart as the true founder of Mannerism. But this superiority is not necessarily a sign of anteriority. Gustav Glück inclines to the view that Gossart, when endowing his works with the flexibility, harmony and organic unity which are the apanage of exceptional talent, was drawing inspiration from the earlier masters named above.

All these qualities are seen to fine advantage in the large *Adoration of the Kings* (London) painted about 1505 for the Abbey of St Adrian at Grammont in East Flanders. It is the earliest work bearing his signature: "IENNI[N] GOSSART" is inscribed on the embroidered trimming of King Balthazar's turban and also on the black attendant's collar. The action takes place in a "romantic" setting: the ruins of a building, spaced out in geometric recession up to a narrow archway framing a distant prospect. The broken pavement with weeds growing in the interstices, the damp, fissured walls and general air of decrepitude answer to the taste for all things ancient that had suddenly developed in the North after the publication in 1499 in Venice of the *Dream of Polyphilus*. We have here an archaizing rhetoric resembling that of the poems of a certain Jehan Lemaire des Belges, Margaret's court historian, whom Gossart may have met in Italy.

He was in Rome at the same time as Erasmus, up to June 22, 1509. Thus he may well have seen Michelangelo at work on the ceiling of the Sistine Chapel, Bramante on St Peter's and Raphael on the Stanze of the Vatican. On his return he produced that amazing *Agony in the Garden* (Berlin), which displays a freely ranging creative imagination, liberated perhaps by the artist's contacts with Latin "humanities." To appreciate its remarkable originality we need only compare it with Italian versions (Mantegna's or Bellini's) of the same theme. Christ is shown kneeling at the foot of a rocky knoll. It is a sultry summer night and the sky is filled with lowering clouds, through a break in which a shaft of moonlight strikes down on the Savior's face (which here has an extraordinarily young, almost boyish appearance). The figures of the sleeping apostles in the foreground are lit by vagrant gleams of cold, hard light, which both give the scene fantastic overtones and provide possibilities for unusual effects of chiaroscuro.

The large *St Luke painting the Virgin* (Prague), commissioned for the chapel of the Guild of Painters in the Cathedral of St Rombaut at Malines, was completed in 1515. Gossart reverted to one of Van der Weyden's favorite themes but handled it in a very different mood. All its religious implications have been drained away; indeed St Luke looks like a humanist painter enraptured by the mundane charms of an elegant young woman. Here Gothic formalism is combined with the spirit of the Renaissance, and the impeccable relations between figures and setting are a perfect illustration of the new way of seeing. Motifs treated with illusionist realism, volumes rich in tactile values, and subtle alternations of light and shade are located in monumental space rendered with superb assurance, if with a certain affectation. From 1510 on Jacopo de' Barbari had been attached to the court of Margaret of Austria and was working along with Gossart for Philip of Burgundy. Towards the end of 1515 both artists were asked to decorate the castle of Suytburg in Zeeland, one of the prince's residences.

Jan Gossart (c. 1472-1533/36).

Danaë, 1527. (45×37½″) Alte Pinakothek, Munich.

Bernard van Orley (c. 1488-1541).

Portrait of Dr Georg van Zelle, 1519. (15½×12⅝″)

Musées Royaux des Beaux-Arts, Brussels.

Jacopo died in 1516, and Gossart was left to finish the decorations single-handed. The theme set the painters being a "glorification of the nude," mythological nudities were obviously called for, and in any case they answered to the taste for classical subjects which had gradually been gaining ground in the Netherlands.

Neptune and Amphitrite (Berlin) inaugurated this new style. Dated 1516 and signed "Joannes Malbodius" (the latinized form of his name), it is the largest extant fragment of this sequence, which must have been of an impressive size and to which perhaps also belong the small panels of *Salmacis and Hermaphrodite* (former Van Beuningen Collection, Vierhouten) and *Hercules and Deianira* (dated 1517, Barber Institute, Birmingham). All the nudes are modeled with remarkable vigor, though anatomical elements are treated in a mannerist spirit. The fact that behind these figures we can sense the presence of prototypes (figures in Dürer's and Jacopo de' Barbari's engravings) or that they derive from antique statuary is of little moment; in the result, as Glück has pointed out, they reveal a personal, highly effective style imbued with an idealism neither specifically Italian nor exclusively Germanic.

Danaë (Munich), painted in 1527, is even more clearly inspired by that "ambivalent spirit of the Renaissance" which has been spoken of in connection with the interpretations of the story of Lucretia brought into fashion by Massys, Van Cleve, Gossart himself and some anonymous masters. Confined in a small pillared niche in the classical style, and wearing the blue garment usually reserved for Virgins, Danaë is welcoming the heaven-sent light of deliverance, and the lambent shower of gold rippling over her bare, quivering shoulders has plunged her into an ecstasy of love. Particularly effective is the contrast between the cold, classical austerity of her temple-prison and the warm, intensely human beauty of the young girl's half-naked body. Here, masterly technique and a range of cool, clear colors dispel any taint of sensuality that might have impaired the balance of this remarkable work, perhaps the culminating point of Gossart's œuvre.

Gossart was also a very fine portrait painter. He treats his sitters (Amsterdam, Berlin, Hampton Court, Paris) in a less austere, more sensitive and relaxed manner than that of Anthonis Mor, Pieter Pourbus, Willem Key and Nicolas de Neufchâtel. With a view to creating an appropriate atmosphere, Gossart makes the most of accidents of light; he suggests volumes by cast shadows and a skillful disposition of values softening transitions from darks to lights, and often employs bluish shadows to bring out the modeling of faces.

When in 1517 Philip of Burgundy acceded to the bishopric of Utrecht, Gossart accompanied him and a suite of rooms was placed at his disposal in the castle of Duurstede. There he had several pupils, among them the young Dutch painter Jan van Scorel. On his patron's death in 1524 he entered the service of Philip's son Adolph of Burgundy, Lord of Veere and Flushing, and moved to Middelburg, where in 1527 he was joined by Lucas van Leyden. The two artists made many festive expeditions together in various parts of the Netherlands. Gossart died between 1533 and 1536 after a full, rewarding life in the course of which he had won for the Flemish provinces an outstanding place in the chronicles of High Renaissance art.

Bernard van Orley was born in Brussels about 1488. He came of a family of painters, hailing from Luxemburg, and received his early training from his father Valentin van Orley. In 1516 he supervised the weaving of Raphael's tapestries illustrating the Acts of the Apostles and in 1518, succeeding Jacopo de' Barbari, was appointed court painter to Margaret of Austria. In this capacity he made many portraits of the imperial family and court officials. Together with several members of his family he was involved in 1527 in a charge of heresy. After the death of Margaret, the new Regent of the Netherlands, Mary of Hungary, confirmed him in his post of court painter (1532). When he died at Brussels on January 6, 1541, he was laden with honors and deluged with orders for pictures. Among the major works to which he owed his reputation was a magnificent series of stained-glass windows, designed for the Collegiate Church of Sainte-Gudule, Brussels, and the brilliant decorative sequence known as *Les Chasses maximiliennes* now in the Louvre.

Though Van Orley is commonly regarded as the leading figure of Brabantine painting in the first half of the 16th century, his talent has in our opinion been considerably overrated.

At no time (except in his mural decorations) did he achieve that happy balance between perfectly organized form and expression stepped up to its maximum intensity which is a criterion of real genius. With him the "new art" of the period secured a foothold in the School of Brussels, hitherto dominated by the influence of its founder, Rogier van der Weyden. But whereas Massys had reinvigorated a semi-moribund tradition, Van Orley did little more than pander to contemporary taste, as is evidenced by his "motto," *Elx sijnen tijt* (Let each man be of his time). He confined himself to reinterpreting traditional themes, or themes taken from the *Golden Legend*, in the language of the Renaissance. But he had less a genius for assimilating the content of Italian syntax than a talent for devising a merely verbal, encyclopedic synopsis of its elements. His triptych, *The Virtue of Patience* (Brussels), commissioned by Margaret of Austria in 1521 for the castle of Hoogstraeten, sums up his style. We find an exuberant profusion of ornamentation combined with a carefully contrived, pre-Baroque disorder achieved by means of all the devices then in vogue for indicating spatial recession: gestures and attitudes rendered in foreshortening and architectural elements—all borrowed from the works of Raphael and Signorelli.

This triptych, like the *Last Judgment* (1525, Antwerp), goes far to confirm the view advanced by Friedländer, Van Puyvelde and Lavalleye, who discount the theory of a journey to Italy as the source of Van Orley's "Italianisms" and put them down to influences operating at second hand, by way of Italian prints and cartoons that had found their way to Flanders, coupled with the presence at Margaret's court of so many connoisseurs and artists infatuated with Roman art. True, he always kept to the typically Flemish use of strong, rich, saturated colors. But, as Jacques Lavalleye observes, "Orley's addiction to decorative effects prevents him from achieving, even in his color, Gossart's full-bodied resonances, for he never succeeds in making the most of oppositions of light and shade (as Gossart did), with a view to giving depth to his compositions or additional vigor to forms."

The next generation took relatively little interest in the political turmoil and religious controversies which the spread of Calvinism had intensified in the Seventeen Provinces and the Liége region in particular. Militant intellectualism gave place to pacifist erudition; Justus Lipsius ousted Erasmus. Like the philologians who took over the style of the ancient classics, painters who followed the fashion took their stand on Roman classicism and brought the mannerist movement to its culminating point. On the whole, their work, as compared with the exceptional achievement of Pieter Bruegel, goes far to prove that in the last analysis Flanders was basically as allergic to classical art as Italy was to Gothic. True, such artists as Lancelot Blondeel (1496-1561) at Bruges, Michel Coxcie (1499-1592) at Malines, Lambert Lombard (1505-1566) at Liége, Frans Floris (1516-1570) at Antwerp and Pieter Coeck (1502-1550) at Brussels compel our admiration, such is the breadth of their culture, the diversity of their interests and so gallant their attempt to combine native individualism with cosmopolitanism. But in their efforts to reconcile forms deriving mainly from Raphael and Michelangelo with a realism racy of the soil, they were led to travesty Christian themes or to fall back on the allegories of pagan mythology. The ingenuity of the pictorial construction fails to compensate for their lack of imagination, still less for their technical shortcomings. Indeed, the sole interest of their copious production lies in their unavailing attempt to introduce the time dimension into space—an attempt that Rubens was soon to validate by intimately associating color-movement with the overall movement of the picture.

At Antwerp, however, a number of painters still kept to the basic principles formulated at the beginning of the century in the art of Massys; that is to say, turning their back on Roman formalism, they followed the path mapped out by the teachings of Erasmus. Zealous partisans of the Reformation, forthright in their execution, they drew inspiration from the life around them, while turning to good account traditional forms. So it was that Flemish Mannerism found a new mode of expression, diversified with popular accents, in which direct observation of nature breathed new life into the dry bones of Gothic Mannerism.

Such was notably the case with that curious artist Marinus van Reymerswaele. He is mentioned by Guicciardini as one of the most eminent painters of the Low Countries, while

Van Mander describes his manner as "more hard than agreeable"—a very apt comment and testifying to a singularly "modern" critical sense. What strikes us most today is this artist's keen feeling for inanimate objects and his peremptory rejection of the contemporary cult of an "ideal beauty." His painting was the product of a ruthlessly analytic, bitterly pessimistic mind, and the vehement, highly strung expression in which Marinus excelled was largely the outcome of his religious convictions. The originality of his art lies in a strongly agitated line reinforced by strident colors. He transposes nature, already roughly handled by mannerist esthetic, on to a strangely artificial plane—an ultra-realism hitherto unknown. This fine painter oriented the genre piece towards a somewhat exclusive range of subjects by specializing in two or three themes borrowed from Quentin Massys: *Weighers of Gold* (Dresden; Bargello, Florence; Madrid, Munich, Nantes), *Money Changers* (Antwerp, London, Munich), *St Jerome in his Study* (Antwerp, Berlin, Madrid, Stockholm, Vienna).

Most of these works fall between 1521 and 1542, though his artistic activity must have covered a much longer period. The date of his birth is unknown, but he is recorded as having enrolled in 1509 in the Antwerp Guild, as an apprentice, under the name of Marinus Claeszoon van Romerswaelen (this is the name of a small town in Zeeland that was swallowed up by the sea in the 17th century). It is also known that he was arraigned at Middelburg in 1567 for having taken part in the destruction of a church, and condemned "to follow the procession clad only in his shirt, a taper in his hand, and thereafter to be banished from the town for a term of six years." Thereafter all trace of him is lost. His works bear the

Marinus van Reymerswaele (c. 1497-c. 1570).

St Jerome in his Study, 1541. (30¾×42¼") Musée Royal des Beaux-Arts, Antwerp.

The Monogrammist Hb (second half of the 16th century).

The Prodigal Son. (50¼×61¼″) Musées Royaux des Beaux-Arts, Brussels.

imprint of fanaticism and a strong moral purpose. This is seen (and felt) at its most emphatic in his many pictures of St Jerome, patron saint of the biblical humanists, whose complete works Erasmus had published in 1516 to the great chagrin of Luther. This theme both acted as a connecting link between medieval symbolism and biblical erudition and pointed the way to the "Vanitas" picture popularized by Calvinism throughout 17th-century Europe. Marinus van Reymerswaele's *St Jerome* derives from a prototype by Quentin Massys (Vienna) which is also said to have inspired the *St Jerome* painted by Dürer at Antwerp in 1521 (now in Lisbon). The saint is seated at his table in his cell, a massive figure with the menacing air of a Hebrew prophet, a piercing gaze, hook nose and gaunt face seamed with wrinkles, and a beard that almost looks false, so peculiar is its shape. A bleak light stresses the forms of worn old books and curling sheets of yellowed paper, of a guttered candle and the skull—*memento mori*—to which the saint's bony fingers, like talons of a bird of prey, are directing our attention, as if to remind us of the brevity of life and the vanity of all material things, doomed ineluctably to pass away.

Of much interest is the unidentified painter known as the Monogrammist of Brunswick, since instead of signing his famous *Banquet of the Poor* he merely initialed it: S.J.M.V.

(The deciphering of the third letter is problematic; it might be "H" or "A".) Obviously intended as a piece of social criticism, this work (Herzog Anton Ulrich Museum, Brunswick) may probably be dated to about 1550. Friedländer and Van Puyvelde believe the monogram contains the initials of Jan Sanders van Hemessen whose name figures in the Antwerp records between 1519 and 1548. In 1551 Van Hemessen (whom Van Mander describes as a "very curious" painter) sold all his belongings and moved to Haarlem, a Calvinist center where Flemish refugees could count on a hearty welcome. Guicciardini mentions him in 1567 as an artist who had lately died. A *Bacchus and Ariadne* (Edinburgh) hitherto catalogued under the name of Sebastiano del Piombo has been found, after a recent cleaning, to bear the inscription *Johannes Hemessen pingebat Florentiae*. This at once explains his affiliations with Italian Mannerism and enables us to trace the origin of his fondness for monumental effects and the heroic nude (*St Jerome*, Lisbon and Hampton Court; *Susanna and the Elders*, Dr Franco de Cesare Collection, Barcelona). But his style is no less clearly marked by the spirit of the Reformation. Thus he transposes both scriptural and mythological subjects on to the plane of everyday life and converts them into genre scenes, often containing more or less overt "tracts for the times." Some fifteen such works, signed and dated between 1531 and 1556, are extant. They are characterized by an arbitrary treatment of colors, by a massive interpretation of volumes (stressed by very harsh effects of light and shade) and by an exaggerated emphasis on muscular development, gesture and facial peculiarities. The fundamental incompatibility between his urge to express mobility and the means employed leads

Pieter Aertsen (1508-1575).

Peasant Interior, 1556. (55¼×78") Mayer van den Bergh Museum, Antwerp.

to what is in effect a parody of movement. Still these grotesque aspects of his art should not blind us to its exceptional plastic qualities and their historical significance. For they point the way to the new realism that Caravaggio and the French masters of the 17th century were to bring to its full flowering.

But the time was not yet ripe for the association of an art on heroic lines with Flemish naturalism; it was left to Jordaens to effect that synthesis. Van Hemessen's contemporary Pieter Aertsen prudently refrained from trying to combine esthetics that, as things stood, seemed clearly incompatible. And, since he always kept nearer to real life and the facts of visual experience, he succeeded in overcoming the anomalies inherent in Van Hemessen's hybrid style and expressing the spirit of Baroque with superb assurance.

Aertsen was of Dutch origin. A peasant painter, known as "Lange Pier" (Long Peter) owing to his stature, he "had countrified manners and never put on airs." He was born in 1508 at Amsterdam and, so Van Mander tells us, made a trip to the famous Château de Boussu in the Hainaut (burnt down in 1555) when he was only eighteen in order to see the collection of pictures it contained. Thence he went to Antwerp where, to begin with, he lodged with his compatriot Jan Mandyn. He became a free master of the Painters' Guild in 1535, was admitted to citizenship of Antwerp in 1542 and married Kathelijne Beuckelaer, aunt of his pupil Joachim Beuckelaer. He soon developed, Van Mander goes on to say, "a broad, vigorous style; he had no qualms about tackling all kinds of subjects and soon made a great name for himself. When he painted kitchens stocked with a variety of foodstuffs, all was so true to nature that one fancied one was looking at the real things. By assiduous practice in this genre he became more skillful in his handling of colors than any other painter of his time, or any time." Aertsen began by using a highly personal palette in which salmon pinks, bluish or olive greens, blue shading off into grey predominated. His lively brushwork, frank execution, and skillful handling of expressive values might seem to point the way to a technique instinct with the very breath of life. But the "nature" of which Van Mander speaks still was viewed at a remove, across the screen of Mannerism; objects were transposed into an unreal world and the seeming dynamism behind the multiplicity of motifs was still of a conventional order. Only when *direct* contact with reality had been established, could the still life, for which Aertsen had prepared the way, come into its own.

The new style of living was taking effect on painting, subjects of pictures being given a new clarity and actuality. Renouncing the ambiguity of parables, Aertsen set out to make the content of his paintings directly accessible and comprehensible by means of a dialectic based on contrasts of volumes and masses. What most impressed contemporaries was his practice of putting inanimate objects—fruit, meat and vegetables—well in the foreground of a religious or other figural composition. This reversal of the traditional hierarchy of values fell in line with a type of composition invented by Jacopo Bassano in the decade 1530-1540, which had repercussions on Italian painting and led up to the Spanish 17th-century *bodegones*.

Aertsen also made a new and closer approach to reality by the use of the "close-up." He magnified the humble lives of servants and housewives by portraying them as large, full-length figures surrounded by household objects and in the act of making some familiar gesture. Moreover he enriched these scenes by handling light and color in the Venetian manner, color infusing light with warm vitality and light acting as the constructive element of the entire composition (*The Milkwoman*, 1543, Lille; *Servant Girl*, 1559, Brussels; *The Cook*, 1559, Palazzo Bianco, Genoa; *The Kitchen*, 1562, Stockholm). These last works belong to the painter's Dutch period and were made soon after the famous *Peasant Interior* (Mayer van den Bergh Museum, Antwerp), last of his Antwerp works. In point of fact this picture should more properly be named the *Aertsen Family*, since it was a group portrait made in April 1556 to commemorate a birthday. The persons figuring in the group have been identified by Mlle Simone Bergmans. The man in the center lifting a pitcher to his lips is the painter himself (this is borne out by Van Mander's description of him); his daughter is the girl leaning forward to baste the roast, the young man behind her being her suitor, and finally the boy seated beside the hearth is the hero of the day, young Pieter. In this colorful little scene,

Joachim Beuckelaer (c. 1535-1574). The Egg Woman, 1565. (49⅝×32″) Musée Royal des Beaux-Arts, Antwerp.

an incident in the daily life of a simple home is set to the rhythms of the still life. Now that the colors have been brought out by judicious cleaning, we can see how ably Aertsen has moderated that excessive dynamism which gives Van Reymerswaele's and Van Hemessen's works their air of febrile agitation. And though still conforming to mannerist esthetic, he practises the unflinching objectivity that is his Netherlandish birthright.

Although Joachim Beuckelaer was trained by his uncle in the painting of fruit, vegetables, fish, meat and game and other still-life motifs, his pictures met with less success in his lifetime, and he was reduced to working by the day for Anthonis Mor (better known as Antonio Moro), who had him touch up his portraits. Born at Antwerp about 1535, he became a master in 1560 and, though he died young (in 1574), he left a large body of work, dating from 1561 (*Vegetable Market*, Stockholm) to 1574 (*Fish Market*, Antwerp). While making Aertsen's methods his point of departure, he pressed them to preposterous lengths—paradoxical both plastically and psychologically—going so far as to create theatrical medleys of figures and still lifes and even to place a market scene in the midst of a Renaissance palace with the biblical incident that is ostensibly the subject of the picture located far back, under an archway (*Fish Market and Ecce Homo*, 1570, Stockholm). This picture is a curious combination of academic classicism with mannerist artifice; yet the plenitude of forms is such that we tend to overlook the flagrant discrepancy between its decorative and its realistic elements. Stylistically, it points the way to the Baroque naturalism of the following century, as found in the works of Jordaens and Snyders. Movement has already seeped into the inner structure of forms, while masterly pictorial construction goes far to justify the emphasis on purely ancillary motifs, as for example in *The Egg Woman* (Antwerp), signed and dated 1565, where the color-light relation resembles Aertsen's.

Since Aertsen and Beuckelaer were active over about the same period and died within a year of each other, we are apt to forget that master and pupil belonged to different generations. Both drew inspiration from the same sources and there was once a tendency to confuse their works. Modern critical research, however, has made clear the differences between them. The strict objectivity of the Dutch genius was distasteful to Beuckelaer and he gave rein to an innate Flemish lyricism. His technique, too, owed more than Aertsen's did to indigenous tradition. On the other hand, his broader, more modern vision gave his art a definitely Baroque turn and he invented rhythms that were soon to reach their climax in the tidal movement of Rubens' mighty compositions. Thus it is difficult today to see why the large *Prodigal Son* in the Royal Museum, Brussels, inscribed with the monogram "Hb", should have been attributed to Beuckelaer. A piquant mixture of popular idioms and urbanity, it is out of keeping with the tone and temper of the Antwerp milieu. A clean-cut geometrical layout distributes the picture space between the still life in the foreground and the zone in which each figure "holds the pose." The execution is relatively tight and the color scheme (purplish reds, browns, greys and yellow ochre) somewhat unusual. Though the picture has been damaged and undergone tasteless repaintings in certain parts, it has a charm all its own and was evidently the work of an international-minded artist active in the second half of the 16th century. It contains a glimpse of a wooded background done in the Venetian manner, some countrified servant girls of a universal type and an elegant couple dressed in Fontainebleau fashion. Manners and customs were changing with the years—and painting, indefatigably, keeping pace with them.

The Humanist Portrait

Master of the Antwerp Family Portrait.
Portrait of the Van Gindertaelen Family, 1559. (77¼×49⅝″) Musée Royal des Beaux-Arts, Antwerp.

The Humanist Portrait

IT would seem that modern critics have said the last word on the art of the Renaissance and the modalities of thought distinctive of the period. Illuminating perspectives have been opened up and our insight into the subject goes far deeper than it did a hundred years ago. Yet we must beware lest, as a result of this enlargement of our knowledge, we tend to underestimate the stature of pre-Renaissance man. Humanism has been described as one of those rare moments of historical equilibrium when man seems to discern "an eternal answer to the question set him by his consciousness of that spark of being which is his morsel of Eternity." Reflected in the mirror of world history, both the grandeur and the limitations of the Renaissance are becoming apparent. Nevertheless the modern tendency to extend the scope and stress the achievement of the Humanist movement cannot invalidate Henri Focillon's description of the earlier, medieval conception of man as the "true expression of western European civilization." The glory of the Renaissance and its fervor are immortalized in the stones of the great cathedrals. As for the Van Eyck portrait, the 16th century confined itself to dissipating its grandiose enigma.

The practice of studying the march of history in terms of centuries, purely conventional slices of time, may seem arbitrary. Yet we have no alternative to using this convenient yardstick when the content of a portrait forces it on our attention; Jan van Eyck's effigy of Canon van der Paele belongs to a specific period of time no less clearly than do the portraits of Erasmus by Dürer, Holbein and Massys and those of Helena Fourment by Rubens. Men, it seems, tend always to adapt their style of life to its historical context and the same holds good for works of art. These are infallibly "dated" by the moving hand that brings them into being. Only in cases where that gesture eludes us do they seem to lie "outside time"—sometimes outside space as well.

Flemish portraiture was the product of an urge no less compulsive than that of its Dutch equivalent. There is, however, no common denominator between the portraits of the Reformation era and those painted under the régime of the Dukes of Burgundy. Among the "revivals" we shall deal with later, only the art of Quentin Massys linked up effortlessly the present with the past. At this stage Flemish portraitists seem frankly retrogressive, incapable of competing with their German and Italian contemporaries. The glorious achievements of Holbein and Titian won Europe-wide renown. And pending the time when Rubens restored to the court portrait a splendid universality, Anthonis Mor alone (following in the path of Gossart) succeeded in raising it to an international level.

As depicted by Van Eyck and Van der Weyden (and by Fouquet, too), 15th-century man appears to be immersed in the cosmos, rapt in adoration of the supreme power; his hands are always clasped in prayer or parted only to point towards, or grasp, some symbol. His invariable air of gravity derives less from his contemplative attitude than from the intensive scrutiny to which he is subjected as he yields himself to the painter's searching gaze and this intimate communion is seconded by an amazing technical proficiency. Like the sculptor-priests of India and Egypt, Van Eyck was the spokesman of a community that insisted on his making an image perfect in its kind, at once good to look upon and convincing. Each work was a feat of craftsmanship, conforming to the high standard set by the Guild to which he belonged. Exact analysis of physical appearance is carried to such a pitch as to reveal, beneath appearances, the profoundest secrets of a personality. The sheer technical perfection

Jan Cornelisz. Vermeyen (c. 1500-1559).
Portrait of Chancellor Jehan Carondelet, c. 1530. (22⅝×32″)
Musées Royaux des Beaux-Arts, Brussels.

of the portrait ensured the rendering of character and an illusion of reality. Indeed it seemed impossible to better, if the sole aim were to achieve exact resemblance. But times were changing and new values emerging. The 16th century witnessed the extinction of the feudal system and by the same token freed man from the thrall of mysticism. And in so doing liberated his personality. "You can determine your own nature according to your free will, whose power I now bestow on you." These words Pico della Mirandola puts into the mouth of the Creator. "I have placed you in the center of the universe, to enable you to see more clearly what takes place in it. You can shape yourself as you will; you have the power of sinking to the level of the brutes, but also of being reborn in a higher, nay, a divine order if you think fit." This new conception of the dignity of man led to the emergence throughout Europe of a new type of portrait: one which no longer served uniquely to celebrate the generosity of a donor or a royal betrothal, but immortalized the memory and renown of a prince, a statesman, a humanist or a wealthy merchant. For Van Eyck's motto *Als ixh xan* ("As best I can"), Bernard van Orley (anticipating Daumier) substituted *Elx sijnen tijt* ("Let each man be of his own time").

Thus objective analysis was now replaced by introspection. The exact science of the Primitives was sacrificed to the expression of values deemed extrinsic to mere likeness: those of the human being conscious both of his inner self and of his place in society. The sitter no longer holds a pose or meditates, but is engaged in action, illustrated or implied. The painter aims not so much at physical resemblance as at engaging in a subtle dialogue with the man before him and is more anxious to parade a distinctive "manner" and to make good his personal ambitions than to vie with the painstaking craftsmanship of his predecessors. And in the process something was lost to art, but something gained.

We need not, therefore, be surprised that Renaissance humanism, while starting out from traditional formulas, inaugurated the independent portrait. This isolation of the figure from a context led to changes in the manner of its presentation, while the fashion of the day determined its austerity or elegance; and the ethos of the century, its style. Whereas the Italians sought after monumental or decorative effects, Flanders retained that taste for cosy intimacy which led to the evocations of home life we find in the group portraits of Frans Pourbus the Younger, Frans Floris and Martin de Vos. Here the figures are usually placed against a neutral ground: brown, green or dark grey, as the case may be. They are bathed in their own atmosphere (Jan Vermeyen, *Portrait of Chancellor Jehan Carondelet*, c. 1530, Brussels) or given a setting appropriate to their occupation and social status (Bernard van Orley, *Portrait of Dr Georg van Zelle*, 1519, Brussels). A transition from the sign to the thing signified is under way, and in the case of accessories symbolic values are giving place to

Willem Key (c. 1515-1568).

Portrait of a Man. (17¼×14")

Musées Royaux des Beaux-Arts, Brussels.

direct, easily comprehensible allusions. Thus inkwells, scissors, writing-desks, books and the like quite simply stress the humanist associations of such portraits as Quentin Massys' *Erasmus* (Galleria Nazionale, Rome) and *Aegidius* (Collection of the Earl of Radnor, Longford Castle), and Jan Gossart's *Portrait of a Jurisconsult* (Galleria Doria, Rome). Always, however, the emphasis is less on the sitter's milieu than on his personal character, his inmost self (Nicolas de Neufchâtel, *Portrait of the Mathematician Neudorf and his Son*, 1561, Munich; replica at Lille). This individualization is effected not only by the sitter's gaze, but by the set of his lips and movements of his hands (Anthonis Mor, *Mary Tudor*, 1554, Prado). With the new spirit of the century facial expression, too, was changing. The human gaze was losing that otherworldliness which in the portraits of an earlier age make it seem to be focused on abstract space and held by some transcendent vision; it is now both a reflection of the man's inner life and also directed towards the outside world, observing and appraising it. It is significant that now the color of the model's eyes determines the color scheme; indeed the whole formal structure of these portraits is determined by the gaze, which acts as the physical and moral center, pivot of the composition.

While in other branches of art Baroque tendencies were gaining ground, the 16th-century Flemish portrait kept to its own path and to the disciplines of classical art. Many years ago Heinrich Wölfflin observed that in these works the composition, built up in terms of horizontals and verticals, is always architecturally ordered and compact. Even when giving an agitated rhythm to costumes (as in Gossart's *Knight of the Golden Fleece*, Berlin), mannerist sensibility never impairs the balance or the frank actuality of these portraits, and ornamental elements are disposed with mathematical precision (as in Mor's *Mary Tudor*, Prado). Intensity of saturated local tones complements an interplay of values, while a bold use of thick or translucent shadows, tinged with brown or blue, shows that here too the artist seeks to establish a relationship between light and color, and thus, while softening the modeling, he reinforces volumes and imparts plastic density to the face (Frans Floris, *Man with a Red Cap*, Munich)—a technique that Rubens and Jordaens were to bring to perfection. A broader vision makes itself felt in the amplitude of forms, which implements the attitude of proud self-confidence struck by the model. Often, too, a completely frontal position invites a frank, direct colloquy between the figure and the beholder (Van Orley, *Portrait of Canon Jehan Carondelet*, c. 1512, Munich).

In the early 16th century, however, a painter of the School of Brussels (name unknown) kept to the austere, meditative portraiture of the Flemish Primitives. This was the so-called Master of the Magdalen Legend, to whom we owe those enigmatic likenesses, painted in an elegant, somewhat precious style, of *Philip the Fair* and *Joanna the Mad* (Wilkinson Collection, Paris). His clean-cut, incisive line affiliates them to that remarkable portrait of Philip the Fair which is assigned to Juan de Flandes, an artist about whom we still know too little and who passed all his active life in Spain, dying at Palencia shortly before 1519. His portraits have something of the relatively abstract style of Jean Perréal. He employs pale, translucent colors, pinks, mauves, greyish shadows faintly kindling into blue, usually setting them off against a greenish background. Among the works ascribed to him are two beautifully executed portraits, *Girl with a Rosebud* (Thyssen Collection, Lugano) and *Child with a Dead Bird* (Brussels), in which Leo van Puyvelde thinks he can identify the face of Margaret of Austria. Delicately wrought and stripped of all non-essentials, these works have a rare distinction; it is as if all the grosser material elements of bodies had been fined away. A similar stylization is found in the productions of Master Michiel, a painter of Baltic origin (Tallinn, 1469-1525) who studied at Bruges in 1484, was attached to the Court at Malines from 1502 to 1505, and in 1516 entered the service of the Emperor Charles V. His style, as we see it in the *Portrait of a Woman* (Vienna), shows the influence of Memling associated with that of the Master of Moulins. The Master of the Brandon Portraits, on the other hand, who was active at Bruges about 1510 and also worked in England at the court of Henry VIII, employed the more fluent rhythms of Dutch painting in his portraits. His *Man with a Pink* (The Hague) contains a decorative surface arabesque foreshadowing the broken rhythms of Mannerism.

Anthonis Mor (c. 1517-1576).

Portrait of Mary Tudor, Queen of England, 1554. (43×33⅛″) Prado, Madrid.

Thus there developed round about 1500, under the auspices of royal courts, an international type of portrait with tendencies towards idealization of the sitter. And, welcoming as they did Renaissance influences, these painters went far to emancipate portraiture from the thrall of Gothic formulas. Many fine artists forgathered in Margaret of Austria's palace at Malines: Jan Mostaert, Jacopo de' Barbari, Jan Gossart, Bernard van Orley, Jean Perréal and Jan Vermeyen. One effect of these direct contacts between artists was to create a new concatenation of influences—promoted on a different plane by rich merchants and bankers of the day, by humanists and engravers. Meanwhile, though her eyes were turned towards Germany and Italy, Flanders was seeking for a style congenial to herself.

A new type of portrait took form, then, centering on expression, its aim being to strike a balance between physical and psychological reality, between depictions of new, meaningful attitudes and an arrangement of the content that made the portrait spatially self-contained and autonomous. Hence a progressive unification, imposing on forms an ever stricter cohesion. The first exponent of this pictorial *ars poetica* was Quentin Massys. All the same, while following the Master of Frankfort in treating the portrait as a genre theme, he still employed the perspective effects favored by the Primitives, from which Joos van Cleve, Jan Gossart and Ambrosius Benson were to break away, pointing the way to a drastic reform of the art of portraiture. This was effected by Anthonis Mor (better known to posterity as Antonio Moro), that great painter whom Holland claimed as her own in view of his birthplace, and Flanders as having launched him on his brilliant career. Born about 1517 at Utrecht, he qualified as a master at Antwerp in 1545 after studying under Jan van Scorel. He was active successively at Brussels, Rome, Lisbon, Madrid and London, and died at Antwerp in 1576. Official portrait painter to the princes and grandees of the House of Habsburg, he viewed with lofty detachment the tragic happenings in the Netherlands and maintained a calm pre-eminence over the period whose catastrophes and horrors Bruegel (who, as it so happened, never made a portrait) depicted with such burning indignation. For there were two sides to the medal, and we cannot doubt that Bruegel's was the nobler choice. Still, unlike as were their viewpoints, the testimonies of these two great artists combine to give a faithful picture of the age.

Dated 1544, Mor's earliest work was the double portrait of *Canons van Horn and Anthonis Taets* (Berlin), which has much in common with the portraits painted by Van Scorel for the Confraternities of the Holy Sepulchre at Utrecht and Haarlem, though—and this shows Gossart's influence—forms are given more painterly modulations and more amply rendered. On his arrival at Brussels in 1549 Mor painted his portrait of *Antoine Perrenot de Granvella* (Vienna). A landmark in the history of Netherlandish painting, this work, based on a schema taken over from Titian, inaugurated the modern portrait. The model is portrayed standing, half length, against a neutral dark-grey ground. The painter seems to have sized up his sitter at the first glance and the portrait reveals with total fidelity the character of the Cardinal-to-be, a man athirst for honors, haughty, supremely sure of himself. Light, integrated into color, is the unifying principle, holding forms together and giving the figure a fine compactness and a ruthless verisimilitude. The unbending dignity and strangely haunting gaze of Philip II, of the Duke of Alva, and of Mary Tudor are rendered no less convincingly. Court decorum and the type of costumes worn give these official portraits a rather somber gravity appropriate to the Spanish conception of good breeding. Even the portraits of ordinary citizens painted by Mor towards the close of his life have traces of this reserve, tempered however by a more frankly human approach and more relaxed execution.

These last works link up with the portraits of Willem Key (c. 1515-1568), who made a point of handling them, Van Mander tells us, "with care and giving them a smooth finish." This can be seen in the *Self-Portrait* recently discovered in Holland (private collection). The portraits by his nephew Adriaen Thomasz. Key (1544?-1590?) keep closer to Anthonis Mor's style; the face is usually turned in such a way that the right eye comes exactly in the center of the portrait, while the ear stands out against the neutral ground—a layout enabling effective contrasts of light and shade. Touches of diaphanous brown on the pink flesh tints bring out the modeling of the cheeks. One of this artist's mannerisms is his practice of binding

Frans Floris (1516-1570).

Portrait of the Van Berchem Family, 1561. (51¼×88½″) Musées Vuyts-Van Campen et Baron Caroly, Lierre.

the lower eyelid with a streak of bright color; another (in his male portraits) of emphasizing the tiny wrinkles at the outer corner of an eye. We find still greater freedom of execution, allied with suppler compositional schemes, in the portraits of Frans Floris (1516-1570) whose very real qualities as a portraitist have tended to be overlooked in the light of those rather flashy "Romanist" compositions which were so much admired by his contemporaries. The *Portrait of an Old Woman* (Caen), signed and dated 1558, is remarkable for the bravura of the execution; the *Falconer* (Brunswick) signed and dated the same year seems to be a companion picture, and in it we find the same exuberant virtuosity, the same feeling for the weight and density of a human body. Form is apprehended as a totality and this sense of solid bulk predominates despite the inner dynamism that animates it. In the *Van Berchem Family* (Lierre) all these tendencies are seen to perfection, together with a wide range of subtle psychological differentiations. This work was a new departure; the many figures, though still treated as independent units, are purposefully grouped. Here we have a beginning of the portrait group in the Southern Low Countries, foreshadowing both Frans Hals and Rubens.

In the portraits made by Pieter Pourbus (1523-1584) close, methodical observation tends to supplant intuition, form to supersede expression. His art was in fact a throwback in the evolution of the Flemish portrait. These archaizing tendencies are evident in his *Jean Fernagut* and *Adrienne de Buck* (Bruges), both signed and dated 1551. Devoid of weight, untouched by any external light, these figures have the frail transparency of alabaster. Faces are molded in a uniform, pinkish impasto, of an enamel-like smoothness. Only in one of his last works, the *Portrait of Jan van der Gheenste* (Brussels), signed and dated 1583, does the modeling show any vigor. It is not surprising that the charming group portrait of the *Van Gindertaelen Family* (Brussels) was formerly ascribed to this painter, who had more feeling for graceful arabesques than for his *matière*. Recently, however, when an exhibition of Flemish portraits took place in Paris in 1952, A. B. de Vries suggested that this work might well be a production of the studio of Dirck Jacobsz., a portrait painter active in Amsterdam in the second quarter of the 16th century—an attribution that has been recently confirmed to some extent. Paul Philippot has shown that it belongs to a whole group of portraits made at Amsterdam in 1554 and 1559, whose style relates them to a specific painter whom he proposes to name the Master of the Antwerp Family Portrait. Similarly a series of sober, forceful, yet elegant portraits have been grouped with some other works in a highly individual style that are attributed to that expert painter of the Antwerp bourgeoisie, the Master of the 1540s.

Born at Bruges in 1545, Frans Pourbus died in Antwerp at the early age of thirty-six. From his father he inherited a close-knit, compact technique which he adapted to a more modernistic conception of the portrait (*A Member of the Smidt Family*, 1573, Brussels). His portraits have density and depth, and combine Anthonis Mor's virtuosity with Frans Floris' freedom of expression. The *Wedding of the Painter Hoefnaegel* (1571, Brussels) reminds us of the keen interest in music and conversation that characterized the age of the Renaissance, and also shows that middle-class life was now by way of developing a new "style." Each of the persons represented has a slightly affected elegance, as if he or she were posing for posterity. There are some twenty of them placed on either side of a diagonal that does not affect the static quality of the scene, held together by well-marked linear rhythms. But the painter's vision is constricted and the execution ill-assured in places. It is to be hoped that some day a careful cleaning will restore their pristine brightness to the colors—bluish greens, ochres and greys—and bring out the original rendering of space, obscured in the picture's present condition by the bituminous ground.

The portraits of Martin de Vos, born at Antwerp about 1531, are more expressive and more adroitly composed. True, the attitudes in his double portrait of *Gillis Hoffmann and his Wife* (1570, Amsterdam) are still rather stiff, and in the *Anselme Family* (1577, Brussels) the arrangement of the figures is still conventional. But with a view to creating an appropriate atmosphere, the artist has had the ingenious idea of placing in the middle ground a table on which some objects are grouped around a charming bunch of flowers. This enables him to diversify the scene with notes of lively color, while harmonizing them with the bright hues of the children's clothes. Faces are modeled in a glossy, unctuous impasto, lightly clouded with diaphanous shadows. The parents are appropriately sedate, the children playful. Still the forms of all four have a somewhat excessive stability and are rigorously self-contained; there is something here of academic classicism. However, when Martin de Vos died in 1603, Rubens had already gone to Rome, and the stage was set for a second Golden Age of Flemish painting.

Imaginative Landscape

Jacob Grimmer (c. 1526-c. 1592).

Landscape with a Castle (detail), 1592. Musées Royaux des Beaux-Arts, Brussels.

Imaginative Landscape

IN the second half of the 16th century a drastic and decisive change came over landscape painting and it was the Flemish painters who made this new approach to scenes of nature. Their influence spread throughout Europe during the period when, for political and religious reasons, so many of them had to leave the home country and take refuge in Italy, Germany and France. The two traditional tendencies—that of idealized, decorative landscape, and that of landscape based on nature observation—lingered on for differing lengths of time. But the only positive effect of their survival was to enrich with reminiscences or curious details the new landscape art in which these conflicting elements were fused together. The foundations of this art, in which landscape pure and simple became the sole *raison d'être* of the picture, were laid soon after Bruegel's death by Gillis van Coninxloo.

When tracing the origins of the various kinds of landscape found in the works of the Primitives, a distinction is usually drawn between, firstly, the imaginary landscapes used as backgrounds of religious compositions and reflecting the ideas and emotions these were intended to evoke, and, secondly, the landscapes in illuminated books, less ambitious works in which we often find colorful details of everyday life treated realistically. Needless to say, neither approach ruled out the other and in fact they were often combined by artists practising both forms of art, the miniature and large-scale painting. Nowhere do we find them so closely intermingled as in the Flemish School. None the less, from the end of the 15th century on, under the influence of the Italians and Leonardo da Vinci in particular, there developed a tendency in Flanders to locate figures in dreamlike landscapes full of strange, fantastic forms: beetling crags and jagged rocks, quite out of keeping with the flat monotony of the Flemish plains. Thus in the hands of such original artists as Bosch and Patinir, Renaissance idealism found a new outlet. While starting out from the descriptive, realistic elements which still were giving the works of Gerard David their familiar, immediate appeal, they added mystical, romantic overtones that were something new in Flemish art. Bosch and Patinir set no bounds to their imagination, no scene of chaos could be too horrific when it came to creating a setting for the Temptation of St Anthony or a vision of divine reprisals on the wickedness of man. Instead of Italian perspective which organizes space in terms of prominent figures, they give us a panoramic vision and a limitless recession which absorbs the human elements and dominates the entire composition. The artist deliberately resorts to an asymmetrical layout, one side of the picture consisting of a mass of towering crags which acts as a buttress or *point d'appui* for a landscape prospect stretching either in depth or laterally across the picture. Within this open space the various elements are arranged according to a scale that gradually diminishes in recession, a sequence of planes echeloned at narrow intervals and usually spanned by bridges, roads or rivers. The effect of fragmentation that might otherwise result is counteracted by the convention of "the three dominant colors": reddish or greenish brown in the foreground, an expanse of green in the middle distance, and a grey or bluish skyline in the background. But these distinctive, "local" tonalities are shaded off into each other in each successive zone and, blending, implement the harmony of the whole. Sometimes, however, one of these dominant colors submerges the others to such an extent that the entire landscape is pervaded by it; sometimes, too, vast, almost uniform expanses are lit with flashes of lightning or the glow of distant fires, intensifying the eeriness of a near-abstract vision of nature.

Abel Grimmer (c. 1570-c. 1619).

Summer, 1607. (13×18½″) Musée Royal des Beaux-Arts, Antwerp.

With Pieter Bruegel we have the impression of returning (if in respect of details rather than of the picture as a whole) to more familiar aspects of the outside world. Some, indeed, have thought to detect in his landscapes, flat, patterned by hedgerows and dotted with cottages, literal depictions of the part of Flanders in which he spent his youth. On close inspection, however, a Bruegel landscape is found to be not local, but *composite*. Obvious reminiscences of countries he had visited in earlier days—notably of his journey across the Alps and of his travels in Italy, recorded in a series of drawings made on the spot— were incorporated many years later in homelier landscapes. True, the seascape in Vienna contains a distant view of towers and buildings identified by some as features of the Antwerp coastline; nevertheless the rendering of the ships floundering in heavy seas with their sails slackly bellying despite the raging gale is at a far remove from reality. On the other hand, Bruegel gradually scaled down his landscapes to man's measure by the ever-increasing prominence he gave to human figures. In this respect his artistic evolution has considerable interest; the early works, executed with much precision, but with loosely spaced out figures, are followed by more and more tightly knit compositions. Though in order to produce an effect of depth he had recourse, up to the end of his career, to long recessive vistas and sharply demarcated gaps revealing distant prospects—memories perhaps of the Alpine passes—he tended more and more to construct his pictures laterally and to place their various elements at an almost equal, relatively short distance from the eye of the spectator. Thus he ended up by bringing the horizon much nearer, with the result that, after him, there was no longer any question of leading the eye through a maze of distant meanders, and henceforth the

Abel Grimmer (c. 1570-c. 1619).

Autumn, 1607. (13×18½″) Musée Royal des Beaux-Arts, Antwerp.

painter who sought to penetrate the heart of nature stepped right into it, as it were, on the very threshold of the composition. Hence the new importance of the foreground, where a dark framework of thick, over-arching foliage throws into prominence brilliantly illuminated tracts beyond: sunlit glades, clearings, gaps in the forest. The practice of etching, in high favor with 16th-century painters, did much to promote an active interest in the structural elements of landscape, and especially in trees and plants.

When we seek to trace the highly complex evolution of Flemish landscape painting at the turn of the 16th century, its chronology (dubious at best) is of very little help. And, similarly, any attempt to study these painters by "schools" involves misleading simplifications. Though groups of artists flourished in certain localities, their members (even in the case of the Flemish colonies abroad) were always independent-minded. On the other hand family tradition played a very important part and there are several cases of generations of painters who transmitted their "trade secrets" from father to son, while intermarriages sometimes brought together different "dynasties" of artists. Thus, for example, we find survivals of certain minor elements of the Bruegelian tradition (which in the 17th century seemed out-moded) forming part of the technical repertory of genre-painting. For these reasons it seems best to deal first with artists who, closely or at a remove, reveal influences of the great 16th-century masters, Patinir and Bruegel, and to follow up this trend well into the 17th century —until the emergence of that major innovation, the genre picture. We shall have to look far back to trace the antecedents of the outstanding 17th-century master, Rubens, and this chapter will be largely devoted to a study of artists who may rank as his forerunners.

In his own time Bruegel was regarded as a little master entertaining enough in his way but hardly to be taken seriously. The painters who followed in his footsteps in the second half of the century tended to whittle down his message and thus contributed to the narrow view formerly taken of his genius. Yet many of these men were excellent artists, though they lacked the native brilliance of the master and, as compared with him, seem unadventurous. First was Jacob Grimmer, a pupil of Matthys Cock, who qualified at Antwerp as a master in 1547. Grimmer spent his whole life in that city; after his death, about 1592, his son Abel (born c. 1570) continued to work on his father's lines and lived in Antwerp until 1619. Both painters had a keen eye for anecdotal details and made a practice of filling out their pictures with little groups of unconnected figures. Jacob Grimmer's large views of the immediate neighborhood of Antwerp have much to tell us of the life of the time and the recreations of the citizens, on river banks or, in winter, on the frozen canals. Though he renders architectural features with meticulous precision, he gives them a dreamlike quality by bathing the entire scene in a single dominant tone, blue for instance. Abel Grimmer, more attracted than his father by the rural aspects of Bruegel's art, reverted to the traditional themes of the Seasons and Months. In the *Four Seasons* (Antwerp) we have a quite original interpretation of the subject. His use of expressive distortions furthers a construction in terms of volumes, rare in his time and redeeming the banality of the theme. What is more, this painter has a feeling for significant outline and converts his figures, stripped of all non-essentials, into type silhouettes. Organized in clean-cut schematic patterns, his compositions are enlivened by the use of bright, cool hues and have a quite delightful freshness and simplicity.

We find a freer, less schematic treatment of space in the small, sophisticated compositions of the Valckenborgh brothers. It is surprising that their works should bear so strong an imprint of their place of origin, considering that circumstances forced them to spend so much of their lives abroad. Born at Louvain some time before 1535, Lucas van Valckenborgh worked as an apprentice at Malines in 1560 and was enrolled as a master in 1564, but was obliged to fly to Liége (in 1566) as a result of his adherence to the Reform movement. After moving to Aachen, he entered the service of Archduke Matthias of Austria and followed his patron to Linz. In 1593 he settled at Frankfort, where he died in 1597. His brother Marten, born at Louvain in 1535, worked for a time at Antwerp, then moved to Aachen to escape persecution. After a brief return to Antwerp, he too settled at Frankfort, where he died in 1612. In Lucas van Valckenborgh's early views of the countryside around Liége his chief concern is with panoramic effects. The foreground opens out like a screen, revealing a wide valley, every detail of which is recorded with extreme precision, sometimes with a certain harshness. Bruegel's influence appears a little later in Lucas' choice of subjects (e.g. *Winter Landscape*, 1586, in Vienna and the *Tower of Babel*, 1594, in the Louvre). In his mature period he imposed unity on his compositions by a judicious use of nuances and skillfully contrived sequences of recessive planes in tender greys, greens and blues (brown rarely figures in his uniformly light-hued palette). Tree-trunks are done in small touches flicked on with the tip of the brush, leaves in graduated tones of green, and distant prospects are suffused in a delicate, ethereal blue. Figures are robust, their movements rendered with a convincing naturalness. Some tiny landscapes in gouache testify to Lucas' technical proficiency. His brother Marten shows much skill in his arrangement of masses and planes echeloned in deep recession along the course of winding rivers. Sometimes we glimpse a light-flooded vista through a gap in the leafage, sometimes a tree stands out in lonely eminence from a smiling countryside, while sudden contrasts of light and shade diversify the scene. Notable is Marten's fondness for the picturesque—he had an eye for topographical curiosities and the quainter aspects of country life— and no less notable his use of color as the unifying principle of his compositions. Keen observers of nature though they were, the Valckenborghs did not aim at reproducing literally what they saw but at interpreting the general effect produced by variations of light. In such a work as the *Demoniacs of Gerasa* (1597, Brussels) Lucas envelops the whole scene in a soft grey haze through which local colors hardly show, thus anticipating the monochrome landscapes which thirty years later were to make the name of the Dutch painter Jan van Goyen.

Hans Bol, born at Malines and an exact contemporary of the Valckenborghs, practised a closely detailed realism foreshadowing Jan Bruegel's. Though he, too, traveled in Germany and resided in various Dutch towns (he died at Amsterdam in 1593), he kept to the art form for which he had a natural bent, the miniature, and specialized in meticulously faithful pictures of urban and village life, peopled with tiny figures. Some charming illuminations by his hand (*Book of Hours of the Duc d'Alençon*, Bibliothèque Nationale, Paris) are extant. The gouache method enabled him to paint in small, well-defined touches of bright, gay colors, standing out against each other and giving a kaleidoscopic sparkle to the picture surface.

There is a close affinity between Hans Bol and Jan Bruegel, Pieter's younger son, who, born in 1568, was a mere child when his father died. Jan kept much more closely to the tradition of the Flemish miniature painters and engravers than to his father's. According to Van Mander the orphan boy was educated by his maternal grandmother, a popular miniaturist, who taught him the watercolor technique; the effect is seen in the remarkably fluid texture of his paint. He later studied at Antwerp and then went to Italy, staying at Naples (1590) and Rome (1593-1594) where he made the acquaintance of Cardinal Federigo Borromeo who enrolled him in his service at Milan in 1595. On his return to the Netherlands in the spring of 1596 he settled in Antwerp after a brief stay in Holland. Henceforth his career was one of unbroken success; he was one of the most famous painters of the day and was deluged with commissions until his death in January 1625, when he and three of his ten children died in the plague epidemic then sweeping Europe.

Lucas van Valckenborgh (before 1535-1597).

Landscape. (9⅜×13″) Musée Royal des Beaux-Arts, Antwerp.

Usually known as "Velvet" Bruegel, Jan won his reputation by the brilliance of his color and the daintiness of his brushstrokes. His earliest pictures produce a patchwork effect; it was not until his stay in Italy that he learned to modulate his colors by blending one into the other. His style came to maturity between 1605 and 1610 when he broke with the convention of "the three dominant colors," not by an extended use of monochrome but, on the contrary, by a well-ordered polychromy, with touches of pure color placed side by side and harmonizing to the happiest effect. Jan Bruegel had a good eye for the telling detail, for the picturesque aspects of the world around him. Many extant drawings (the *Chariots* sequence in Dresden, analytical studies of flowers and petals, designs of birds and insects) show his concern for scientific accuracy. This repertory of minutely observed forms is sometimes rather arbitrarily introduced into compositions already complete in themselves; nevertheless, unity is ensured by the soft atmospheric light bathing the scene. His intricate landscapes studded with small figures going about their rural tasks do not seem overcrowded like those of Hans Bol, since air circulates freely between the picture elements. Streams with moving boats wind their tranquil way across brightly lit open spaces, flanked by clumps of trees. One of his favorite motifs is a windmill perched on a hill-top, silhouetted against a cloudy sky. Obviously Jan Bruegel was familiar with the larger, more ambitious works of his contemporaries, but he was very little influenced by them, only borrowing a few of their accessories. Within its narrow

Hans Bol (1534-1593).

Country Fair. (19⅝×25″) Musée Royal des Beaux-Arts, Antwerp.

Jan Bruegel (1568-1625).

Village Scene, 1608. (8¾×13″) Galleria Sabauda, Turin.

compass his art is always personal, genuinely inventive; he was, moreover, the originator of a new genre, flower painting, which became more and more popular throughout the 17th century. He had the knack of arranging flowers in eye-catching bouquets and what had hitherto been only a minor decorative element now became a subject in its own right. Rubens, who was a personal friend of Jan Bruegel and thought highly of his work, had him paint the wreaths of flowers around his *Virgin and Child* (Louvre and Munich).

Jan Bruegel played a considerable part in the cultural activities of his age, notably in those of such professional groups as the Chamber of Rhetoric known as "the Wallflower," the Painters' Guild, and the Society of Romanists (i.e. Flemish painters who had studied in Rome). He appears to have been a wealthy man; between 1604 and 1619 he bought no less than six large houses at Antwerp. In 1609 Archduke Albrecht and his consort Isabella, Regents of the Southern Low Countries, invited him to their court at Brussels and commissioned four pictures and eleven "large compositions with many figures in landscapes," and Bruegel remained in favor with the rulers over a large number of years. Several letters from him to his first patron, Cardinal Borromeo, have survived and show that he was a man of parts, intelligent, shrewd, genuinely kind-hearted, always ready to put in a good word for younger artists (in particular Frans Snyders), arrange for them to visit the sumptuous collections of his patrons and find a market for their pictures. Jan Bruegel's style was so faithfully copied by other landscapists that we sometimes have difficulties in distinguishing their works from his. Among them were Abraham Govaerts and Anton Mirou who, after undergoing the joint influences of Coninxloo and Momper, were gradually won over to the meticulous perfection of Velvet Bruegel. The tradition was carried on by his son Jan Bruegel II and a host of lesser men. As late as the beginning of the 18th century we find two painters, Pieter Bout and Theobald Michau, still keeping to the Velvet Bruegel style.

It is hard to discover a common measure between Pieter Bruegel's genius and profound humanity and the art of the minor landscapists who imitated him during and after his lifetime. Still, we find something of his breadth of vision in a few contemporary painters who, gifted with a very real originality, found in his message a starting-point for a new approach to nature: the "Baroque landscape" which Rubens was to bring to perfection. Many of them went abroad: Coninxloo to Frankenthal, then to Amsterdam; the Bril brothers to Rome, Roelandt Savery to Austria, then to Holland, and Jacques Foucquière to Paris. Each, as it happens, became the leader of a school in his adoptive country, thus giving an international status to an essentially Flemish art; for, however much affected by foreign influences, these artists remained basically faithful to the tradition of their native land.

Gillis van Coninxloo may rank as the initiator of this enlargement of the artist's vision of nature. Born at Antwerp in 1544, he was apprenticed at an early age to Pieter Coeck, completed his training under Lenaert Kroes and Gillis Mostaert and, after stays in Paris and Orleans, qualified as master painter at Antwerp in 1570. In 1585, as a result of the politico-religious troubles, he had to take refuge in Zeeland. Soon after, he migrated to Frankenthal and resided there until 1595. Finally he settled in Amsterdam, where he became the head of a large colony of refugee artists and died in 1606.

In his lifetime he was admired for his "modernism." Van Mander saw in him the best land-scapist of his period and Lampsonius described him as "the leader of our landscape painters." Discarding traditional techniques and conventions of the past, he abandoned, *inter alia*, the method of composition in coulisses and the three-color division of space and integrated the successive planes into an overall color harmony. In his early works at Antwerp he favored the bird's-eye perspective employed by Bruegel in the landscapes of his last phase, but showed at the same time much originality in an ingenious distribution of lights and shadows and in the unusual intensity of his colors.

Though later in life Coninxloo confined himself to wooded landscapes, peopled with hunters or shepherds, the true dramatis personae are not these rather hackneyed figures, but the trees themselves, which he treats not as mere staffage but as nuclei of vibrant personalized life. With loving care he depicts each tree in detail, from its huge twisted roots to the branches striking out from the gnarled trunk and its thick crown of leafage, and weaves the leaves into sumptuous decorative patterns extending to the top of the picture in alternating zones of light and somber verdure, while in the shadowy recesses of the forest everything assumes fantastic shapes. As time goes on, he simplifies his composition and gives increasing pro-minence to foregrounds framing the central theme with masses of exotic vegetation. An opening in the middle or on the side, generally of little depth, gives on an expanse of shimmering sky, dotted with birds and insects. Sunbeams falling on dark clumps of foliage form inter-ludes of brilliant light and leaves are evoked, rather than depicted, by small luminous patches. Coninxloo sweeps on his color boldly in broad, fluid brushstrokes and in rendering detail confines himself to essentials. Painted sometimes on wood, sometimes on canvas, his pictures have exceptionally large dimensions (for the period), corresponding to the breadth of the artist's initial conception.

The romanticism of Coninxloo's style developed during his stay at Frankenthal in Germany and Elsheimer may have been affected by it in his early phase. There is no question, however, of his influence on other Flemish landscape painters. Pieter Schoubroeck and Frederik van Valckenborgh—both of whom, like Coninxloo, sojourned in Germany—took over his more striking effects, but failed to achieve the flexibility of his style. Kerstiaen de Keuninck, of whom little is known except that he was born at Courtrai in 1560 and lived at Antwerp until 1635, pressed to extremes some of Coninxloo's idiosyncrasies during his stay in Germany. He has a predilection for dramatic effects, nature in her most tempestuous moods, the bursts of livid light accompanying a storm in the mountains, when streaks of angry red, grey or brown mottle a lowering sky. Outlined against the light are tangled masses of undergrowth, and uprooted trees thickly draped in creepers strew the foreground. His execution is rapid, forthright; in the foreground he lays on his colors thickly, whereas distant forms are rendered in delicate, translucent touches.

Other painters fell in line with Coninxloo at the end of his life in Holland; amongst them Carel van Mander (best known today as "the Vasari of the Flemish painters") and David Vinckboons, both resident at Amsterdam. All the same we find traces of Italianism in their landscapes, due no doubt to Van Mander's stay in Rome, and they take more pains to harmonize their figures with the setting. It was Roelandt Savery who, with his pantheistic exaltation of vegetable and animal life, came closest to the master. Nevertheless his sensitive awareness of the mystery underlying all the forms of nature led him to create a purely imaginary world, which he rendered with a precision sometimes reminiscent of Jan Bruegel.

Born at Courtrai in 1576, Roelandt Savery is thought to have been trained by Jacob Savery (perhaps his elder brother) at Amsterdam. He spent his life traveling back and forth between the Low Countries and Austria. At Prague, while attached to the court of Rudolf II in 1604, he made a number of drawings of the animals in the Emperor's zoo. On the death of his royal patron he returned to Amsterdam, in 1612; then, in 1614, after entering the service of the Emperor Matthias, he worked in Vienna, Salzburg and Munich. In 1618 he returned to the Netherlands, staying for a time in Haarlem, then settling at Utrecht where he died in extreme poverty in 1639. Savery's art differed considerably from that of his contemporaries. He saw the world through the medium of a poetic, highly imaginative temperament, and his landscapes, teeming with exotic animals, have a curiously dreamlike quality.

Joos de Momper (1564-1635).

Miraculous Deliverance of the Emperor Maximilian I. (46⅜×68¼") Musée Royal des Beaux-Arts, Antwerp.

Alexander Keirincx (1600-1652).

Landscape with Stag Hunt, 1630. (26¾×35⅝″) Musée Royal des Beaux-Arts, Antwerp.

contemporary Dutch landscapists, his forms became more static, his horizons veiled in tenuous mist, while he simplified his color schemes almost to the point of monochrome, using a palette ranging from light brown to grey and reminiscent of Van Goyen's.

Alongside these lyrical effusions and passionate responses to natural beauty there flowed a calmer current, that of a lucidly composed and tranquil type of painting, pointing the way to the classic formula of French landscape art. This tendency was represented by Paul Bril, an almost exact contemporary of Coninxloo. Born at Antwerp in 1554, Bril went to Rome in 1574 and lived there until his death in 1626. His early efforts to Italianize his art (e.g. his frescos, painted from 1585 to 1600, in the Vatican, in Santa Maria Maggiore and Santa Cecilia, notably on the ever-popular theme of anchorites braving the perils of nature at her wildest) are of less interest than his return to the Flemish tradition, applied however to new motifs: scenes of the Campagna, seascapes and views of Mediterranean seaports. The Flemish artists now flocking to Rome maintained close contact with their native land and through the intermediary of Adam Elsheimer (who settled in Rome at the turn of the century), Bril learnt of the latest developments of Coninxloo's art and the leading part he now played in the school of Frankenthal. Bril's synthetic turn of mind led him to dispense with naturalistic details— he paints leaves, not individually, but in bulk—and also to give his forms the sharply defined contours of objects seen in southern sunshine, while his sure eye for color helped him to bring out the haze of broken lights that hovers on the sea. Skillfully planned in well-marked rhythms,

Peter Paul Rubens (1577-1640).

Landscape with Atalanta's Hunt (detail), c. 1620. Musées Royaux des Beaux-Arts, Brussels.

his landscapes have a fine serenity. Bril's style was imitated by Jacques Foucquière who, having settled in Paris in 1621, produced, to the order of Louis XIII, a great number of landscapes containing views of French towns. But it was in Rome itself that Paul Bril seems to have influenced two of the most famous French painters of the century. Poussin took over his method of pictorial construction in depth by the use of successive planes alternating on either side of a diagonal axis that runs across the picture, while Claude Lorrain brought his "atmospheric" style to a perfection that has overshadowed Bril's achievement in this field.

But it was left to an artist whose whole life (except for two problematic but probable journeys to Italy and the Tirol) was spent in Flanders to give these new conceptions of landscape the panoramic sweep of Patinir's vision. Joos de Momper, born at Antwerp in 1564, was admitted to the local Painters' Guild at the early age of seventeen. Along with Tobias Verhaecht and Adam van Noort (subsequently Rubens' teachers) he took part in making the decorations for the state entry of Archduke Ernest in 1584. Though he had some pupils, filled several posts and prospered at the outset of his career, he later fell on evil times and was heavily in debt when he died in 1635. His output was immense and we learn from records of the time that he employed specialists in figure painting for inserting the small figures of riders, hunters and gipsies that animate his big compositions. For he was interested above all in landscape, his prime concern being to give it an overall depth that prolonged the field of vision, but without any dispersal of the picture elements. With this in mind he builds his composition in staggered planes, sloping down towards valleys whose curves produce the effect of distance. When painting a picturesque tract of mountainous country interspersed with waterfalls and grottoes, he does not linger over anecdotal details but stresses the majestic volumes of the mountains. An adroit manipulation of light leads the eye along a sequence of coulisses abutting on a spacious, brilliantly illuminated zone in the background. Momper's color is less saturated than that of his contemporaries. He transposes natural hues into a high-pitched color scheme in which a pervasive golden-yellow flushes into blues and greys. The pearly greys of his winter landscapes are broken here and there with touches of light brown. But in general Momper reserves brown for the "screens" he places in the foreground, so as to diffuse beyond them a golden, sometimes russet glow, preceding the light blue tint of the background. So personal is one of his procedures—his habit of edging the projections of rocks with a thin line of bright color—that even unsigned works can promptly be identified as his. Another distinctive trait is his practice of defining the outlines of trees located in the background with small yellow dots, with the result that clumps of such trees acquire a peculiar shimmer, recalling that of some Pointillist canvases.

Several Antwerp painters, Tobias Verhaecht amongst them, followed in Momper's path, but their imitations of the master were conspicuous only for their painstaking precision, their narrow vision, the relative feebleness of their reproductions of his light effects. The one exception was Gysbrecht Leytens, whose remarkably successful works were long assigned to a hypothetical Master of the Snowscapes. Though his foregrounds are rather harshly rendered and he took little pains over his distant prospects, he skillfully adapted his color orchestration to the atmospheric conditions of the season and diversified his compositions with lively notes of red or pink struck by the figures dotting the snowbound landscape.

That charming landscapist Lucas van Uden derived the essential features of his art from Momper. A collaborator and friend of Rubens, several of whose works he engraved and some of whose landscape backgrounds he is believed to have painted, Van Uden has a predilection for vast stretches of flat country whose successive planes he sets out in a broad, boldly stated rhythm. His landscapes are bathed in an evenly diffused light suggesting atmosphere, exceptional prominence being given to the sky. The scene generally unfolds itself before us horizontally and one of Van Uden's mannerisms is to space out across the middle distance rows of trees whose rounded masses, painted in bright colors and fringed with light, stand out sharply against the background. His admirable etchings show a sensitive appreciation of the natural charm of the Campine and Brabantine countryside, which he renders with a fine simplicity and forthrightness.

Rubens and Living Forms

Peter Paul Rubens (1577-1640).

Portrait of an Old Woman (so-called Portrait of the Artist's Mother), c. 1616-1618. (19⅜×12⅝″) Alte Pinakothek, Munich.

Rubens and Living Forms

THERE once was some uncertainty as to the birthplace of Peter Paul Rubens. He himself believed that he was born at Cologne whither his family fled in the face of Spanish persecution. The year of his birth, 1577, witnessed the culmination of the "Spanish fury," involving the sack of Antwerp and the massacre of over six thousand citizens. In the mid-19th century, thanks to the researches of a Dutch scholar, R. C. Bakhuizen van den Brink, the mystery shrouding Rubens' birth was cleared up and it is now known that he was born at the small Westphalian town of Siegen. Records have also been uncovered throwing light on the erratic life of his father Johannes Rubens, a man of learning who, after fleeing his native Antwerp, finally settled at Cologne in 1568. There he became legal adviser to Anne of Saxony, wife of the Prince of Orange, William the Silent. But, as the result of an indiscretion with his patroness, he was thrown into prison and narrowly escaped the death sentence. After two years, however, he was released (1573), thanks to the generous endeavors of his wife, Maria Pypelincx, but only to be ordered to remain, much against his will, in Siegen, where Maria gave birth to two children, younger of whom was Peter Paul.

In 1578 the family was permitted to return to Cologne and, after the death of Johannes Rubens in 1587, moved to Antwerp, which greatly harassed city was now, under the humaner rule of the Regents Albrecht and Isabella, enjoying a period of recuperation and even a measure of independence. In his early teens, Paul attended a Grammar School whose headmaster, Rumoldus Verdonck, was an excellent Latinist, and there acquired the rudiments of a solid classical culture which he steadily enriched throughout his life. But even at this early age he was irresistibly drawn to painting and, fortunately enough, Antwerp was one of the rare cities where, to quote Ludovico Guicciardini, artists were esteemed "important, praiseworthy and useful citizens." None the less there is much difficulty in determining under whom he studied in his 'prentice years; chroniclers of the period seem to have paid less attention to this point than to the vicissitudes of the Rubens family in their years of exile. Some have assumed he was a pupil of Tobias Verhaecht, on the strength of an inscription (probably apocryphal) to that effect on one of his engraved portraits. All we know for certain, since it is vouched for by a statement made by Rubens' nephew, Philip, to the Parisian art historian Roger de Piles in 1676 or 1677, is that he studied under Adam van Noort (whose daughter became the wife of Jordaens) from 1591 to 1598; then under Otto van Veen, who was so enamored of all things classical that he changed his name to "Vaenius." Nothing definite is known of Van Noort's oeuvre—various works have been attributed to him, but on the slenderest of grounds—and on the strength of the productions of his other pupil and son-in-law, some have sought to see in him a champion of Flemish naturalism. On this view the youthful Rubens is assumed to have drawn inspiration from two widely different sources: both from national tradition and the most extreme forms of humanist art. Actually, however, none of his early work has come down to us; all we know is that at the age of twenty-one he qualified as a "free master"—meaning that he had demonstrated his technical proficiency to the satisfaction of the Guild. Painters of the day were often trained in some specialized branch of art, but apparently this was not so with Rubens, who even at this early age seems to have had a broader outlook and a wider technical range than most of his contemporaries.

In 1600, at the age of twenty-three, he went to Italy and, after a short stay in Venice (which has given rise to many legends), joined the household of Vincenzo Gonzaga, Duke of Mantua, whose wife was a member of the Medici family. There can be no doubt that Venetian painting was one of the formative elements of Rubens' art. He may have already become acquainted with it at Antwerp, where many Venetian paintings were to be seen in private collections. That he had a thorough knowledge of the works of Titian, Tintoretto and Veronese is plain to see throughout his œuvre; indeed he made no secret of his cult of Titian, thanks to whom (as he put it in a letter) "painting had acquired its perfume." But though he made copies of some of Titian's major works, interpreting them in a strikingly original manner, this was only much later in his career, during his second diplomatic mission to Spain—a singular caprice, when one thinks of it, much as if Matisse in full maturity had taken to making free copies of Delacroix's larger pictures. In any case it is clear that Rubens was equally well acquainted with the leading works of Mantegna, Leonardo, Raphael, Michelangelo (he made drawings of the frescos in the Sistine Chapel), Caravaggio, Annibale Carracci and Correggio; for time after time we find reminiscences of these masters in details of his compositions. However, this merely goes to show that Rubens was one of those universal-minded, versatile artists who have no qualms about taking from others what may serve their turn, but without attaching over-much importance to such borrowings.

The ducal palace at Mantua was adorned with enormous frescos by Mantegna and Giulio Romano, and among the members of the court were such famous figures of the age as the composer Claudio Monteverde, the Flemish portraitist Frans Pourbus the Younger and, a little later, Galileo. Thanks to his position at the court, Rubens had opportunities of widening his experience by frequent travel, and he was often absent from Mantua either on diplomatic missions for the Duke or in the interests of his art. His first stay in Rome lasted from July 1601 to April 1602 and in the course of it he made three rather ponderous religious paintings for the Church of Santa Croce in Gerusalemme (now in the chapel of the hospital at Grasse in Provence). In 1603 a diplomatic mission brought him to Spain, by way of Florence, Pisa, Leghorn and Alicante, one of his assignments being to present King Philip III with copies of Italian pictures. Some had been damaged in the course of the journey and the skill with which Rubens repainted them was much admired at Madrid. Despite his youth and the limited funds at his disposal, he made a brilliant success of the Spanish visit and not only won the friendship of Philip's minister, the powerful Duke of Lerma, whom he painted on horseback (Count Valdelagrana Collection, Madrid), but produced a good impression on the King, who commissioned him to paint a series of half-length figures of Apostles (Prado).

On his return to Mantua, he painted for the Gonzaga family tomb in the local Jesuit Church the altarpiece of *Vincenzo Gonzaga and his Consort kneeling before the Trinity*. In the portraits of the donors, posed in the same way as the Archduke and Infanta in the considerably later *St Ildefonso Altarpiece* (Vienna), we find a wealth of colors and a remarkable freedom of expression. The compositions on the side panels, *The Baptism of Christ* (Antwerp) and *The Transfiguration* (Nancy), are eclectic productions, their themes inspired by Michelangelo and Raphael and treated in the spirit of Tintoretto. In 1605, when at Genoa, he made several portraits and studied with keen interest the architectural features of the city (at Antwerp in 1622 he published a book describing the palaces of Genoa). Meanwhile he obtained permission from his patron to pay a second visit to Rome, where he stayed until the end of 1608. Without enrolling in any of the local associations of Netherlandish painters, he kept in touch with individual artists, in particular with Elsheimer, but he also devoted much of his time to archeology and made many drawings from the antique. For the new church of the Oratorian Fathers, Santa Maria in Vallicella, he painted a gigantic picture, *The Virgin adored by Saints and Angels*; since this turned out to be too large he made a reduced version in three panels, meanwhile trying, but without success, to persuade the Duke of Mantua to buy the original. This truly magnificent work is now the pride of Grenoble Museum. Rubens brought the picture with him to Flanders and probably retouched it before placing it above his mother's tomb in St Michael's Church. In October 1608, on the receipt of alarming news about his mother's health, he abruptly returned to Antwerp, after excusing himself to the Duke of Mantua for his precipitate departure. Rubens never went back to Italy.

Peter Paul Rubens (1577-1640).

The Rape of the Daughters of Leucippus, 1618. (87½×82⅜″) Alte Pinakothek, Munich.

of the Redeemer but with all the sins of the world. So powerful is the diagonal thrust of the central scene that it spreads into the side wings of the triptych, while details of garments and leafage are magnified to colossal proportions. Painted almost certainly in a single burst of creative ardor, this great work was followed shortly after by the very different *Descent from the Cross*, commissioned by the Confraternity of Arquebusiers, September 16, 1611. This second work is as reposeful as the other was turbulent, and in it the artist secures an effect of grandeur by the sheer plenitude of volumes, without a trace of grandiloquence.

Peter Paul Rubens (1577-1640). The Drunken Silenus (detail), 1618. Alte Pinakothek, Munich.

The color scheme of dull red, deep black and blackish greens has an exceptional density; planes are smooth, compact and lusterless. As patron of the Confraternity of Arquebusiers, St Christopher had to figure on the exterior of the altarpiece when closed. On the inside Rubens depicts the persons who shared in carrying the body of the Dead Christ; the grandiose *Descent* occupies the central panel, with the *Visitation* on its left and, on the right, the *Presentation in the Temple*. But these two scenes, treated in a very different spirit, have no real affiliation, esthetically speaking, with the central composition, which was completed and set up on September 12, 1612, whereas the wings were added nearly two years later, the consecration of the altarpiece as a whole taking place on July 20, 1614. Charming as are the lateral scenes—notably the *Visitation*, in which the Virgin wears a large typically Flemish hat, the action is located in the open air, and the atmosphere is almost homely—it is the central scene that shows the master at his splendid best. The body of the Savior forms a diagonal swerving off leftwards from the vertical, and is not, as in so many "Depositions," stretched tensely along the upright of the Cross, but a pale white form sinking into the whiteness of the shroud held out to receive it. The movement is full of subtle nuances, developed with a fluency and naturalness striking a new note in Flemish art. Nothing could be more effective than the contrast between the limp, pallid flesh of the dead body and the monumental figure of St John who, clad in red, clasps in a strong embrace the Master's sagging form. In this beautifully balanced painting, one of his most "classical" compositions, Rubens achieved a perfect synthesis of all that was best in the works he had seen in Italy.

He seems to have lost little time dallying with the allurements of Baroque and quickly settled down to a calmer, more careful style—doubtless better suited to the taste of his patrons. To this transitional period, preceding the great efflorescence of his art in 1618-1620, belongs a group of static compositions relatively sparing of details and wholly religious in tone—Virgins with angels or surrounded by garlands of flowers (these latter executed in collaboration with Jan Bruegel)—as well as various portraits, landscapes and scenes of rural life, rendered with meticulous precision and a fine smoothness of surface effect. While careful to avoid expressive distortions and over-emphasis, Rubens shows a remarkable insight into the characters of his models. We cannot but be struck by the just balance of tones in such portraits as that of Hendrik van Thulden (Munich). Though he may seem to confine himself to the outward features of his sitters and to refrain from probing into their inmost selves, a wonderfully human warmth, more compelling than any emotive stressing of distinctive traits, emanates from these likenesses. While appropriate in the case of individual portraits, where a human personality speaks for itself, this fine restraint and ordered execution tended to miss the mark when an idea or symbol had to be conveyed. Thus in *The Doubting of St Thomas* (Antwerp) the lateral portraits of the donors, Nicolas Rockox and his wife, where the facial expressions have a wonderful precision and intensity, strongly contrasts with the almost mawkish rendering of the figure of Christ, arisen from the dead. We find the same contrast in the very heart of the picture in Munich showing a curiously wraithlike Christ appearing to Mary Magdalen, a fair-haired young woman of dazzling beauty. Indeed Rubens never felt quite at ease when dealing with immaterial presences; biblical and mythological figures came to life under his brush only in so far as he could convert them into concrete beings of flesh and blood. Thus in his *Christ à la paille* (Antwerp), in the various figures of the Dead Christ represented in foreshortening (as in the Antwerp and Vienna *Pietàs*), and in the *Descent from the Cross* and the Antwerp *Coup de Lance*, the body of the Savior, faintly tinged with the greenish hues of death, acquires a poignant verisimilitude.

Rubens continued to produce, now and again, essentially static works, with dense, solidly constructed volumes. In the *Miraculous Draught of Fishes*, painted in 1618 for the Guild of Fishermen at Malines (Church of Notre-Dame au-delà de la Dyle), we find large planes of uniform, resonant color (notably a garment all in rich vermilion), while certain details, dashed off with an amazing swiftness and sureness of touch (for example, an effect of watery depth conveyed by alternating strokes of brown and green), reveal the change that now was coming over Rubens' art. However, despite its many excellences, this picture, taken all in all, shows a lack of balance. Very different is the *Rape of the Daughters of Leucippus* (Munich), painted at about the same date, where the perfect symmetry of the picture elements, despite the tumultuous movement pervading the whole scene, is a miracle of craftsmanship. Here we have undoubtedly the climactic point of Rubensian classicism, rich in intimations of that "pure painting" visions of which for ever haunted the great artist's thoughts. Light scumbles and rapid brushstrokes bring out the nuances of the horses' manes and hoofs, while sudden high lights on pink flesh and flaxen hair, and faint grey, nacreous shadows picked out with red are rendered with a virtuosity that has rarely, if ever, been surpassed. And all the picture elements coalesce in a swirling circular composition whose fully plastic, mobile masses confront and complement each other.

It was now that Rubens consolidated and made clear his mastery of plastic orchestration, synthesizing the most diverse elements by an overall rhythm, and harmonizing contraries. Thus he moved on from those still somewhat conventional allegories in which sea-gods and exotic animals were presented statically side by side (e.g. the Berlin *Neptune and Amphitrite* and the Vienna *Four Parts of the World*) to the great lion and hippopotamus hunts (Munich) in which the structural problem is solved by a continuous movement of forms caught in a single headlong movement: maddened horses plunging or rearing, bodies flung to the ground, faces convulsed by pain or fury. Movement paths either radiate from a central axis or run along a vast diagonal striking across the picture. Similarly such apparently accessory elements as fruit, game with glossy pelts or feathers, vine-tendrils and grapes, acquire a definite significance when (as often happens) they play an operative part in the compositional scheme. Thus in that fine sketch in the Louvre, *Philopoemen recognized by an Old Woman*, the still life is given a prominent position and forces itself on our attention. Rubens succeeds in making even the most incongruous groupings seem convincing, as in the *Drunken Silenus* (Munich) where we see the burly roisterer staggering forward, escorted by a company of old men, Negroes, children and comely girls. An alternation of dark, monochrome figures with forms in full light, rendered in a thick, unctuous impasto, sets the rhythm of this ignobly triumphal progress, while the well-nigh revolting vulgarity of the foreground motif—a female faun suckling two baby satyrs whose shaggy little heads are splashed with milk—is wholly submerged in the melodious overall harmony of bluish whites and pinks, gossamer-light strokes flicked on with an agile brush.

This was, it seems, a turning-point in his career. Henceforth Rubens gave full scope to the promptings of his genius; refusing to be bound by tradition or to take his lead from any prototype, however illustrious, he accepted no discipline but his own. His most crowded compositions are the least constricted and the very plethora of problems he set himself to solve whetted his creative zest. The shape and size of the canvas mattered little; or, rather, he had a happy knack both of setting forth within a limited compass all the forms that welled up before his inner vision, and also of transposing the subtlest, most delicate nuances of his palette into works of vast dimensions. True, he may have borrowed certain motifs from Leonardo's *Battle of Anghiari* (some of whose central figures he copied in a drawing) or from Titian's *Battle of Cadore* (this had long since perished in a fire and Rubens can only have seen copies), when painting his *Battle of the Amazons*, that maelstrom of galloping horses and human bodies locked in savage conflict or falling from the bridge that spans the composition; nevertheless the method of indicating the forms of the combatants by touches of color, the sudden bursts of light and—last but not least—the amazing "legibility" of this picture as a whole must be credited to Rubens and to Rubens alone.

In the matter of the dimensions of his works we may observe a rather unusual phenomenon. In the case of the *Last Judgment* (a theme to which he reverted several times) it is the first version that is the largest. This "greater" *Last Judgment* (Munich), painted about 1616, still keeps to the conventional tripartite division: a stretch of blue sky upheld by the two human pyramids formed by the Blessed, rendered in pink flesh tints, and by the Damned, rendered in greyish tones. The relations between the various expressive volumes are much better brought out and the masses of moving bodies more fully integrated in the "lesser"

Peter Paul Rubens (1577-1640).

The Fall of the Damned, c. 1620. (9 ft. 5 in.×7 ft. 4 in.) Alte Pinakothek, Munich.

Last Judgment (Munich) in which Rubens imposes more harmonious proportions on the same structural elements. The ascent of the Blessed is relegated to the background and the composition dominated by the tragic struggles of the Damned, thrust down by angels into the bottomless pit. Accented with white, the colors stress the musculature of bodies, while the light has become more otherworldly and fantastic. Finally in the *Fall of the Damned* (Munich), painted about 1620 and engraved by Vorsterman in 1621, Rubens confines himself to a single element of the theme, its most momentous aspect. Between a burst of radiant, celestial light and the dark yawning gulf of the netherworld, long skeins of naked bodies, twisting and turning in tumultuous rhythms, sweep across the composition in a broad diagonal starting

Peter Paul Rubens (1577-1640).

The Martyrdom of St Ursula, c. 1618. Sketch. (19¼×15⅜″)

Musées Royaux des Beaux-Arts, Brussels.

from the top righthand corner of the picture. This *Fall of the Damned* bears comparison with Michelangelo's monumental version of the same theme. It does not present so great a diversity of isolated motifs treated on the heroic scale, but the general conception—of a writhing mass of human forms in headlong movement—has never been excelled, nor has any other artist ever given so awe-inspiring an impression of multitude and vastness.

The way in which Rubens reverted to this theme time and again, as though desiring to exhaust its utmost possibilities, may throw some light on the hotly debated problem of the part played by his studio staff in his enormous output. During those years 1618-1620 this was so large and he turned out masterpieces at such a speed that it seems almost beyond the bounds of possibility that they could have been the work of one man alone, even allowing for the fact that Rubens' energy was nothing short of prodigious. In a letter dated September 13, 1621, he told William Trumbull, English Resident at Brussels, that he felt "better fitted to execute large-scale works," adding: "my endowments are such that I have never lacked courage to undertake any task, however vast." And in 1628, during his second stay in Spain, Pacheco was "positively dumbfounded" by the amount of painting he got through in the rare spells of leisure left over from his diplomatic duties. Indeed what led him to employ an army of assistants was not that he had more work than he could cope with, but that he preferred to leave to them the performance of secondary tasks, such as the execution of purely decorative elements. He was perfectly honest about the matter and specified in his contracts what parts of the picture would be dealt with by his studio. In an early letter (1618) to Sir Dudley Carleton containing a proposal to exchange some works of his for Sir Dudley's collection of antiques, the artist is careful to mention what portions of these works were done by pupils and the cases in which he intends to make retouchings. None of these is a major work; they seem to have formed part of his professional *fonds d'atelier*, samples of the types of picture variants or replicas of which he could supply to order. Nor did Rubens make any secret of the fact that some works were done in collaboration with painters whom he regarded as his peers; when, for example, he was aided by Jan Bruegel, his friend and senior, the pictures on which they co-operated bear the signatures of both. Though, following the common practice of the time, he had recourse to specialists in animal painting, in landscape and the still life, this was not because of any conviction that such motifs would be better handled by "experts" —and in this respect he differed from his contemporaries. For Rubens was a universal artist and he needed no such assistance; his own still lifes and animals are superior to those of Snyders and his own landscape backgrounds more skillfully composed than Van Uden's. When he asked these men to lend a hand, it was probably for works which otherwise would have called for more time and labor than he could expend. This was most certainly the case with the huge decorative projects which he had to carry out in an impossibly short time, such as the vast "Decius Mus" cycle, the *Life of Marie de' Medici*, the elaborate sequences in the church of St Charles at Antwerp and in the Torre de la Parada in Spain. For the last-named work Rubens, then in his sixties, contented himself with making sketches (whose tremendous verve and virtuosity show that there was no flagging of his powers) and left their execution to other painters; their signatures alone appear on the surviving fragments, most of which are in the Prado. Thus each of these artists takes full responsibility for the merits or shortcomings of the execution.

On the other hand, where there are no such qualitative variations, we may assume that Rubens himself saw the work through from beginning to end, and I have little doubt that in such spectacular undertakings as the Marie de' Medici sequence, in which his reputation was at stake, the bulk of the painting, even in the largest compositions (always the most masterfully executed), was by his own hand. This is evidenced by the exceptional brilliance of the handling of minor details, by the use of distinctively Rubensian rhythms, and perhaps also by the equal level of performance in compositions where the execution is, on the face of it, less characteristic. Such are the two large altar pictures which survived the fire that in 1718 destroyed the Jesuit church of St Charles (in Antwerp) and are now on view in the Kunsthistorisches Museum, Vienna, with the artist's preliminary sketches beside them.

Peter Paul Rubens (1577-1640).

The Miracle of St Ignatius of Loyola, 1620-1621. Sketch. (61×29⅛″) Kunsthistorisches Museum, Vienna.

Peter Paul Rubens (1577-1640).

The Miracle of St Francis Xavier, 1619. Sketch. (57⅛×28½″) Kunsthistorisches Museum, Vienna.

These were followed by an extensive decorative sequence, comprising no less than thirty-nine ceiling panels, for the same church; the contract was signed March 29, 1620, and working in collaboration with several of his pupils, Rubens completed the entire sequence within two years. All were destroyed in the fire of 1718.

The two sketches for the St Charles altar pictures (Vienna) are exceptionally large and indeed rank as completed pictures, fully worked out in every detail; notable being the liveliness and variety of the colors and their delicate modulations—yellows kindling into orange, greens melting into brownish hues—even where they are merely scumbled over the ground color. No less remarkable than the bravura of the drawing is its absolute precision.

Peter Paul Rubens (1577-1640).

The Landing of Marie de' Medici at Marseilles, 1622. Sketch. (25¼×19¾″)

Alte Pinakothek, Munich.

Peter Paul Rubens (1577-1640).

The Government of Marie de' Medici, 1622. Sketch. (21¾×36¼")

Alte Pinakothek, Munich.

The modeling of the bodies of the sick and the men possessed by devils has all the plenitude of life. Yet, realistic as are these figures, each scene is bathed in a grey or faintly golden light creating a supernatural ambience. For the subjects are the miracles performed by St Francis Xavier and St Ignatius of Loyola who, each posted like a figurehead on a ship's prow, gaze down with benignant majesty on the sufferers imploring their succor and the groups of awe-struck onlookers. A celestial light issues from the faces of the saints, intercessors between earth and heaven, kindling sudden gleams on twisted limbs and anguished countenances, while the air above them, under the vault and in the precincts of a stately Baroque church, is alive with flying forms, triumphant angels and devils put to rout. We find the same composition reproduced in the large canvases nearby, but shorn of its more dramatic effects. Moreover, the full-size pictures have a smooth enamel finish and, while the ordering of the colors in wide, uniform planes displays the painter's masterly handling of his material, there is, seemingly, no profound emotion behind it. One almost wonders if the sketches were not made by Rubens himself, for his private satisfaction, after completing the full-size pictures. In any case, these powerfully emotive works give the lie to the still too common view that Rubens was incapable of expressing true religious feeling. For despite the opulence of their settings, the faces of the saints breathe a mysticism of the loftiest order and the whole composition is infused with profound religious emotion. His moving picture of the *Last Communion of St Francis of Assisi* (Antwerp), dating from the same period, with its discreetly subdued range of greys and browns, also attests a serene, heartfelt piety.

A study of his preliminary sketches tells us much of the way in which Rubens planned a work and his tentative approaches to it. He began by making rapid, almost monochrome studies indicating the broad lines of the subject as he conceived it; that is to say one or more original, boldly stated interpretations—for, on occasion, he tried out several variants of a theme. Most probably he submitted these alternative versions to prospective buyers so as to make sure of "giving satisfaction." Next—and this he usually did after the contract had been signed—he made a more fully developed study or "modello", setting forth with more precision and in greater detail the composition as a whole. In this final study he gave special care to the organization of space and the placing of the figures, shifting and modifying groups accordingly, and at the same time devising more elaborate color schemes. In the case of some picture sequences, for example the *Life of Marie de' Medici*, both the preliminary drafts and the final studies have survived, and we are thus enabled to trace the development of each picture, stage by stage, and its gradual pervasion by an all-compelling rhythm. For Rubens reserved to himself the right—and this is a proof of his personal and preponderant share in the execution, however large the picture—to modify, improve and if need were remake his compositions up to the very last brushstroke. Finally, there have survived, though these are relatively rare, some works of small dimensions, apparently replicas on a much reduced scale of large compositions—the *Miracle of St Ignatius* and the *Miracle of St Francis Xavier* (both in Vienna) are a case in point—and these, too, throw light on the functioning of the painter's mind from the initial intuition to the final execution of his major works.

It is clear that at each stage of the process, even the most rudimentary, the work is complete in itself. Making a sketch, for Rubens, did not mean jotting down notes or trying to give concrete form to a vague idea; it meant setting forth a full-fledged plastic equivalent of the idea or emotion he proposed to render forth in terms of art. As Leo van Puyvelde has aptly observed, "Rubens thinks, brush in hand." And even in his least significant works we can see this creative process in active operation, since he always composed in the very act of painting, his mind responding to the impulse of his brush. No trace of a preliminary design can be found on any of his canvases, corrections and pentimenti are extremely rare. When he reverted to a theme already dealt with, he always brought to it a new creative élan. Such is his sleight of mind that all the elements of his subjects come simultaneously to life under his hand; a few rapid brushstrokes on the carefully prepared and smoothed foundation suffice to indicate definitively the outlines of forms and the arrangement of the figures in space. Contours are suggested by shadows and high lights on salient edges, while light scumbles indicate varying intensities of color. Rubens seldom resorts to glazes or blended color. Nor does he ever stress the modeling of forms, and the colors, overlapping outlines, spread out in massive waves. He gives a reddish glow to women's flesh, a browner hue to the flesh tints of male figures. Fundamental to his color schemes are red, golden yellow and a greenish blue, sometimes with adjacent passages of grey or black to make them tell out more strongly. He eschews mixtures and expresses a wide range of emotive values simply by varying the intensity of individual colors. The form of the brushstroke plays a large part in his technique; sometimes he indicates high lights by small comma-like accents, sometimes by beadlike spots of paint, and he gives his brush a special twist peculiar to himself, following precisely the curves of bodies and bulging muscles. In a note dated October 21, 1860, Delacroix observes that Rubens' distinctive characteristic is "the prodigious 'bulge' he gives his forms... Even Titian and Veronese look flat beside him."

The Medici cycle illustrates these qualities to perfection. It has now been given a stately, needlessly austere setting in the Louvre and we cannot but regret its removal from its former more congenial and so to say more pliant architectural context in the Luxembourg Palace. Indeed few visitors have the perseverance needed to appraise at their true worth these gigantic panels, replete though they are with admirable passages of "pure painting." Thanks to their preservation in their entirety, undispersed, they constitute our only means of forming a just estimate of Rubens' achievement in the field of decorative cycles. On her return to Paris, after her reconciliation with her son, Marie de' Medici decided to adorn her palace with an allegorized history of her own life and that of her husband Henry IV. It was through the good offices of Archduke Albrecht and his wife Isabella, who had befriended the queen in times of trouble, that Rubens secured this commission, eagerly sought after by all the artists of the day. His program was to celebrate the queen's career, from her birth to her reconciliation with her son, Louis XIII. The preliminary sketches, in grisaille, were submitted to the queen early in 1622 (most of these are now in the Hermitage, Leningrad). On May 19, 1622, Rubens supplied a sequence of much more fully developed sketches, with the basic colors indicated. Some themes were presented in two or three alternative versions. To this phase belongs the large sequence in Munich. Shortly after, at Antwerp, he started work on the final version and the first nine canvases were dispatched to Paris in May 1623. On the occasion of the marriage of Henriette de France, sister of Louis XIII, to Charles I of England, the complete work was exhibited in the Luxembourg Palace. The short time allowed and the novelty of the theme, which relating as it did to contemporary history did not easily lend itself to mythological-allegorical treatment, account for the fact that, despite the high excellence of the sketches, the merits of the final composition can best be seen in the larger, more fully worked-out pictures. None the less, both in the small and in the full-size pictures, we cannot but admire Rubens' imaginative sweep and executive brio, and the skill with which he has glorified —not to say sublimated—a life that, when all is said and done, was rather colorless. The birth of the princess, her travels, her marriage, her tenure of the Regency and the benefits her subjects ostensibly reaped from it, even her quarrels with her son—all alike were used by Rubens as pretexts for metaphors, charming allegories, in which he drew largely on mythology, peopling his scenes with pagan gods and goddesses, water nymphs, Tritons and sprites of the air. And, strangely enough, the fabulous figures do not clash in the least with the historical personages, who are portrayed with remarkable fidelity, the portraits of Henry IV being particularly convincing. Invested as wife and mother with an almost Olympian dignity, the queen seems to figure both on a sublime and on a terrestrial plane. In the *Birth of Louis XIII* there is a profoundly touching beauty in her face, glowing with motherly pride and love; and hardly less impressive is the pearly luster of her feet and bosom. The allegorical figure presents no problem for Rubens; he boldly humanizes it, brings it down to earth. Truth, the Fates and Fortune become real living beings under his brush; and the bodies of the Three Graces and Sirens have the sensuous appeal of healthy young women lavish of their beauty. Even in his most conventional canvases the sudden glory of a nude transfigures all around it. Cases in point are the effigy of Grief in the *Apotheosis of Henry IV* and the young guardian spirit in the *Felicity of the Regency*, one of the few of Rubens' male figures having the absolute perfection of the female nudes. The warm, translucent glow that fills these works, the silken sheen of their colors and their violet-tinted, flickering shadows prefigure the discoveries of Impressionism.

It is to be regretted that Rubens was prevented from carrying out his second commission of this kind, for a *Life of Henry IV*. Here the artist had a subject after his own heart, the celebration of a king whose life had been picturesque, adventurous, rich in heroic deeds and generous gestures. Thus there was no need for allegory and it would seem that Rubens proposed to treat the theme from the angle of reality. The two huge (unfinished) compositions, the *Battle of Ivry* and the *State Entry of Henry IV into Paris* (Uffizi), are perhaps the most spontaneous of all his works. Unfortunately, Richelieu, who sensed in Rubens one of his political opponents and suspected the artist of intriguing against him, saw to it that this second contract was never signed.

The presence of the Medici sequence in Paris had an immense influence on the evolution of the French School in general and in particular on the painters of the 18th century. Watteau made some sketches (British Museum) after the *Coronation of Marie de' Medici* and the *Government of Marie de' Medici* in which he incorporated details from his own pictures. (He also made a charming series of drawings after the *Kermesse*, which very soon after its completion found its way into the collection of Louis XIV.) As the Goncourt brothers wrote: "All of them descend from this father, from this generous initiator, both Watteau and Boucher, Boucher and Chardin. For a hundred years French painting seems to have had no other cradle, no other school, no other homeland than the Luxembourg gallery. *Le dieu est là.*"

The large-scale compositions of this period, when Rubens was at the height of his creative powers, have all the air of splendid improvisations. Even where the execution must have called for the utmost attention and delicacy, colors seem to flow spontaneously from his brush, values blend harmoniously, the patterning of forms shows no trace of effort or constraint.

Peter Paul Rubens (1577-1640).

The Adoration of the Magi, 1624. (14 ft. 8 in.×11 ft.) Musée Royal des Beaux-Arts, Antwerp.

Peter Paul Rubens (1577-1640).

The Crucifixion ("Le Coup de Lance"), 1620. (14 ft.×10 ft. 2 in.) Musée Royal des Beaux-Arts, Antwerp.

Peter Paul Rubens (1577-1640).

The Adoration of the Magi (detail), 1624. Musée Royal des Beaux-Arts, Antwerp.

Thanks to his inspired facility, Rubens was an exceptionally quick worker. The colossal *Adoration of the Magi* (Antwerp), commissioned by Abbot Mathieu Yrsselius for the altar of the Abbey of Saint-Michel in 1624, was painted, we are told, in thirteen days. No work could be more lyrical, more fluent, more immediate in its impact. We must, however, remember that Rubens had dealt with the same theme several times before, beginning with that rather overcrowded composition, charged (in the Venetian manner) with the glamour of the East, which he painted soon after his return to Antwerp. Three other versions, made for the altar of the Capuchins at Tournai (Brussels), for the church of Saint-Jean, Malines, and the church of the Annunciate at Brussels (Louvre), mark successive stages in that progress towards a simplified, more and more coherent composition which culminated in that supreme masterpiece, the Antwerp *Adoration*. In the earlier versions the scene was encumbered with minor figures which tended to confuse the eye. Stage by stage these multifarious groups (carried over in some versions on to the wings of the triptych) were reduced to the essential figures, thrown

Peter Paul Rubens (1577-1640).

The Adoration of the Magi (detail), 1624. Musée Royal des Beaux-Arts, Antwerp.

Peter Paul Rubens (1577-1640).

"Le Coup de Lance" (detail), 1620. Musée Royal des Beaux-Arts, Antwerp.

Peter Paul Rubens (1577-1640). "Le Coup de Lance" (detail), 1620. Musée Royal des Beaux-Arts, Antwerp.

into prominence by their monumental stature. Similarly, violent effects of chiaroscuro and indirect lighting gave place to a clear, calm light bringing out the limpid effulgence of the colors. Thus here, despite its richness and density, the composition achieves a perfect balance between the melodious simplicity of the "duet" of Virgin and Child on the one hand and, on the other, the symphonic splendors of the Magi and their retinues. We are reminded of the measured fall of great waves on a shelving beach when we contemplate those massive and magnificent Eastern potentates, with eyes of flame and broadly curling hair and beards, richly embroidered garments, simultaneously bending forward in humble awe to gaze on the Divine Child. And thus the surging lines of force sweeping across the scene come to a head and are resolved in a rapt, halcyon calm.

The great Crucifixion styled *Le Coup de Lance* (Antwerp), painted a little earlier, in 1620, for the local Church of the Recollects, is remarkable for its highly adroit placing of a great variety of picture elements (Delacroix was much taken by its "organized disorder"). The sky is plunged in darkness but an otherworldly light, streaming from the horizon, plays on the forms of the horses, built to an heroic scale, and on the monumental figures of the Holy Women, relieved against a foreground steeped in shadows, while garments acquire a curious luster in this dramatic colloquy of lights and darks. The composition is based on a system of horizontals, interlocking diagonals, and receding lines, leading the eye successively from group to group, each clearly defined and charged with vivid significance.

The art of Rubens had achieved maturity and such was now his mastery of his means that no enterprise, however great, deterred him. Nevertheless both his life and art were soon to be given a new direction. The year 1626 witnessed the death of Isabella Brant, the artist's charming and devoted helpmate, who, as he wrote, "had none of the failings common to her sex." Heart-broken by his bereavement, Rubens resolved to leave Antwerp, anyhow for a while. Circumstances favored this, since the Archduchess now decided that none was better qualified than he to take charge of the delicate negotiations with the courts of France, Spain and England that the international situation called for. During his stay in Paris, Rubens had become very friendly with the Duke of Buckingham; thus he seemed obviously the right man to be entrusted with a mission to London whose object was to bring about a rapprochement of Spain and England to the detriment of France. However, Richelieu had forestalled him by negotiating an alliance with Spain against England. Rubens had no choice but to leave London and he now proceeded to Madrid, whither he had been summoned by Philip IV. This second visit to Spain (from September 15, 1628, to April 29, 1629), though diplomatically a failure, was a triumph for the painter. He had brought with him some of his pictures, there was keen competition between members of the Court for the honor of sitting to him, and he was deluged with commissions. However, he began by filling an order given him by his patroness: to paint the cartoons for a series of fifteen tapestries for the church of the barefoot Carmelite nuns at Madrid, on the theme of *The Triumph of the Eucharist*. Of the fully developed sketches in the Prado six at least seem to be by the master's hand; the others, of varying dimensions, may be copies. It would seem that Rubens devoted less time to his official mission than to painting, for it was now that he made his admirable "free" copies of the masterpieces of Titian in the royal collections at Madrid. He struck up a friendship with Velazquez, then aged twenty-nine, already famous and a King's Counsellor. The assassination of Buckingham and the taking of La Rochelle opened up new possibilities of negotiations with England and Rubens returned to London, stopping off in Paris and Brussels. Once again he had been forestalled; Charles I had already signed a secret pact with France. But, as an artist, Rubens could not complain of any lack of royal favor; Charles I not only knighted him but commissioned a series of paintings, celebrating the life of James I, for the ceiling of the banquet hall in Whitehall Palace. Finished in 1634 and delivered the following year, these pictures, though much damaged, are still in their original place. Rubens returned to Flanders in 1630 and, disheartened by the failure of a final negotiation with the Prince of Orange, decided to make an end of the political activities which had cost him so much time and pains, and of which his copious correspondence tells us much.

Peter Paul Rubens (1577-1640).

Portrait of Marie de' Medici, 1625? (51¼×42½″) Prado, Madrid.

In 1630 Rubens returned to Antwerp: to his house, his studio and his family. The two surviving children of his first marriage, those handsome boys, Albert and Nicholas, who figure, full-length, sumptuously attired, in the picture in the Liechtenstein Collection, were now sixteen and twelve respectively. On December 6 Rubens, now aged fifty-three, married again; his bride, Helena Fourment, youngest of the many children of a tapestry dealer, a relative by marriage of Isabella Brant, was a girl no older than his elder son. This serenely happy marriage led to a new and splendid flowering of Rubens' art. Four children were born during the ten years of life remaining to him, and domestic happiness went far to compensate for the physical afflictions of his last years.

It now is possible to form an exact idea of the surroundings in which the painter worked, thanks to the careful restoration, under the auspices of the City of Antwerp, of Rubens' house and studio near the Wapper in the center of the city. Work was completed in 1946, only "period" materials being employed. During and after the 18th century a great many alterations were made and new buildings added; but fortunately plans and old prints survived, so it was possible to locate and clear the original foundations, main walls and entrances of the Rubens mansion. While he was still living with his first father-in-law, Johannes Brant, the artist had extensive changes made in the house he had purchased, so as to bring it into line with his professional requirements. The dwelling house proper ran parallel to a very large studio whose two façades were decorated with busts of ancient philosophers and with frescos illustrating "the lives of the gods" executed in grisaille. A handsome Baroque portico with three arches, probably designed by Rubens himself, linked the two buildings. This portico figures in several of his pictures, notably in the Marie de' Medici sequence. Inscribed above the vaults were excerpts from Juvenal's *Satires*. These building operations were not terminated until 1618 at the earliest.

Large as was the studio (thirteen by eight and a half yards), it does not seem to have been intended to accommodate many pupils. At most three big pictures—surprisingly few, considering the number of commissions the artist had to fill—could be proceeded with at the same time. In any case it is known that very often Rubens did merely the preparatory work on his canvases in his studio, and completed them in the edifice where they were to figure. Strangely enough, though the quadrangular courtyard to which the portico gave access was of imposing size, the dwelling house itself was of modest dimensions, containing only a suite of smallish living-rooms and bedrooms, together with a semicircular gallery in which Rubens housed his art collections. These comprised the large collection of antiquities which he had procured, in exchange for pictures, from Sir Dudley Carleton (and subsequently sold with a large profit to the Duke of Buckingham), and also a number of paintings by old Flemish masters and contemporaries. The inventory made after his death includes seventeen pictures by Brouwer and some thirty originals by Italian artists. It would seem, indeed, that, given the smallness of this gallery, only a fraction of his art treasures could be on view at the same time. In short Rubens' house was far from being the palatial mansion described by some biographers; it was no more than the residence of a well-to-do, cultivated Flemish burgher. Equally unpretentious was the delightful little flower garden behind the portico, which is the setting of the picture in Munich where we see the painter doing the honors of her new home to his young wife. What we learn of his personality from the reminiscences of his nephew Roger de Piles goes to show that Rubens led an exemplary, well-regulated life. He rose early, went to Mass, then started his day's work, listening as he plied his brush to his paid reader who entertained him with readings from Latin authors. He took a very light midday meal and continued working until about five in the afternoon; then went for a walk on the ramparts or for a ride on horseback, and often finished the day by supping with friends. Rubens prided himself on counting among the leading humanists of Antwerp; his competence in archeology is vouched for by Nicolas Peiresc, a distinguished contemporary scholar. He also had a gift for languages. Letters written by him in Flemish, French and Italian are extant; he had a thorough knowledge of Latin and had familiarized himself with Spanish and English in the course of his travels.

Peter Paul Rubens (1577-1640).

Landscape with Baucis and Philemon, c. 1620. (58×82⅜″) Kunsthistorisches Museum, Vienna.

Another aspect of Rubens' many-sided personality was his love of nature. Sketches of fallen trees, shrubs and leafage, made in early youth, testify both to his interest in such motifs and to his powers of observation. Notable is the sureness with which he chalks in the high light on a tree-trunk or records the exact color of a bush. On the back of one of his drawings we find this pertinent remark: "Trees reflected in water have a brownish hue and more distinctness than when they are seen in the ordinary way." To begin with he had a country house at Eckeren, north of Antwerp. Later, in 1635, he purchased the manor of Steen, near Malines, consisting of a small château surrounded by a park and orchards. It has been suggested that Rubens developed his interest in landscape only after the acquisition of this estate, that is to say towards the close of his life, when a slowing-down of commissions for large works gave him more leisure and he now could paint for his own satisfaction. The scenery in certain works has been tentatively identified with the environs of Steen and, because Rubens had no studio there, it has been assumed that he painted directly from nature. This is, to my mind, an over-hasty conclusion. True, his early drawings prove that Rubens often sketched from the motif, but there are no good grounds for supposing that he departed from the invariable practice of his contemporaries, which was to do the final painting in the studio, making use of material furnished by the sketches. Admittedly there is difficulty in fixing the chronology of his landscapes. The fact that he used scenes of nature as backgrounds for his early works and that he clearly was familiar with the landscape art of the Carracci and the Venetians, and with Elsheimer's "luminism," no less than with the methods of such contemporary landscapists as Gillis van Coninxloo and Joos de Momper, has led some authorities to date Rubens' first landscapes, in particular the *Landscape with the Shipwreck of Aeneas* (Berlin), as far back as the time of his stay in Italy. The truth lies, doubtless, between these two extremes. Most probably the large landscapes with dramatic light effects—forests swept by gales, and raging torrents—may be safely assigned to the period of his most dynamic works, 1618-1620. This would apply to his numerous "Hunts," such as the Dresden *Wild Boar Hunt* and the *Atalanta* scenes in Brussels and the Prado, in which the entire landscape participates in the action and, bowed by the wind, the very trees seem to be swept along in a wild stampede traversing the canvas. The *Landscape with Baucis and Philemon* (Vienna), with its dark stormy sky and swollen torrents leaping over rocks and fallen trees, has a complexity allied with a nicety of execution equaling that of the *Battle of the Amazons*. On the other hand, in the more restful scenes of nature and country life, where strapping peasant girls, shepherds, milkmaids and cowherds figure prominently, the pigment is given the same rich, smooth texture as in the paintings Rubens made about 1614-1618 with an eye to winning the favor of the Antwerp public. Such is the case with *Summer* and *Winter* (Windsor Castle) and with *Farm at Laeken* (Buckingham Palace) the central motif of which, a peasant woman with a basket, recurs in the *Landscape with Cattle* (Munich).

This interest in rustic life, the prominence given to figures and their perfect cohesion with the surrounding countryside, prove that Rubens was the one artist who carried on successfully the tradition of Pieter Bruegel—whose works, moreover, he collected. Whereas

Peter Paul Rubens (1577-1640).

Landscape with a Tower, c. 1635. (11×14½″) Ashmolean Museum, Oxford.

other landscapists often called in specialists of no great merit to paint in the small figures dotting their compositions, Rubens restores to Man, lord of creation, his due pre-eminence over Nature. For though, to start with, like many of his contemporaries, he was emotionally responsive to the somber, mysterious majesty of the *Urwald* and the mindless powers of wild nature, he soon began to discriminate between the various elements, to set order in the chaos of appearances, and to "humanize" his landscapes by stressing such familiar aspects of the woodlands as clearings and sandy cart-tracks, tokens of man's presence. Moreover, he resolutely excluded the artificial, unnatural rock formations dear to the previous generation. Thus it became easier for him to express the changes brought to the face of nature by the seasons, the changing lights of dawn and sunset, the sudden glamour of a rainbow after storm. Hence the new versimilitude of his landscapes, their greater fidelity to the lights and colors of the seasons.

We are justified in dating to the last years of his life those small, sketch-like works in which he confined himself to recording a few minor yet characteristic aspects of a landscape prospect: a line of small, light-dappled trees on the horizon, a sunken road, a lightly shadowed path, a house or ruined tower, its outlines faintly blurred by distance. Looking at such pictures as the *Landscape with a Tower* (Berlin, Oxford), the *Tourney* (Louvre) or the Vienna *Park of a Château*, we get an impression of scenes that really existed—fragments maybe of the countryside around Steen. The figures, however, are purely fanciful, no longer closely observed peasants, but lords and ladies exchanging compliments, knights jousting in a tournament, characters out of romances or fairy-tales. This remoteness from the contemporary world is stressed by the curiously dream-like quality of the light, though the "actuality" of the picture is ensured by the artist's rapid, fluent calligraphy and the use of very fluid pigment interspersed with bead-like drops of pure color. This new style of pastoral directly pointed the way to Watteau's *Fêtes galantes*.

The dating of one of Rubens' most famous works presents no easy problem, since it combines all the characteristic excellences of his art at its successive peak-points; I refer to the *Kermesse* in the Louvre. Though of small dimensions and treated sketchwise, it is one of the master's most elaborate, fully developed works. So perfect and so vigorous is the execution that we can hardly believe it was painted towards the close of his life, when he was seriously handicapped by illness. Realistic scenes of rustic revelry had always been popular with Flemish painters, but Rubens handles the theme with such gusto that all its grosser sensual elements are purged away. In the *Kermesse* he depicts the climactic moment when the frenzied merrymakers are wildly gyrating, linked in an endless chain weaving across a clearing in the woods. We have here a pictorial synthesis of all the vital urges of simple, happy folk, a cosmic ballet taking place with the benevolent approval of Nature in her friendliest mood, under a smiling sky across which big, swift birds are winging.

During the last decade of his life Rubens followed more and more his personal bent and indulged in an ever wider freedom, while retaining all his consummate power of integrating the picture into an organic whole. He painted now for the sheer joy of creation, of bringing to vivid life forms governed by imperious rhythms and bathed in ever brighter air. Thus in the great St Ildefonso triptych (Vienna), painted in 1630, such is the scintillation of the colors and so fluid the *matière* that it is almost impossible to discern the transitions from one hue to another. Hair, flesh and gorgeous garments dissolve into a dazzling mosaic, a haze of broken lights. Two of his last great religious pictures can be seen in the Royal Museum, Brussels: *The Martyrdom of St Lievin* and *The Bearing of the Cross*, the latter painted in 1636 and placed above the high altar of the Abbey Church of Afflighem in the following year. Though preceded by modellos, both pictures were executed with the utmost boldness and bravura. Notable is the painter's detached attitude towards the tragic content of the scenes depicted, their gruesome or harrowing elements being completely submerged by the dynamic rhythm of the composition. Indeed the Ascent of Calvary has all the air of a triumphal progress, accented by the rearing horses and pink flags flaring out against the sky. Here the prevailing tone is golden, whereas the *St Lievin* has a silvery sheen.

Though in his last years Rubens still accepted commissions for large-scale works, he usually left their execution to others. In 1634 he was put in charge of the street decorations of the City of Antwerp for the welcome of the new Governor of the Low Countries, Archduke Ferdinand of Austria. The City Fathers enacted that the entire route taken by the cortege should be adorned with triumphal arches, trophies and light stages for *tableaux vivants*. Within a few days Rubens had drawn up the general plan and sketched out the architectural elements, paintings and sculpture required. Most of these purely decorative sketches have been preserved in the Royal Museum of Antwerp and they testify both to the artist's fertile imagination and to his encyclopedic knowledge of all forms of art. But he could only take a minor part in the execution of the program he had arranged, as his health was giving way. He had had a first attack of gout when he was in Paris setting the pictures in place in the Medici Gallery, and it had temporarily paralysed his right hand. In 1635 illness prevented his being present at the "Joyous Entry" of the new Governor; however, after the festivities were over, a deputation of the local authorities called at his house to thank and congratulate him for his share in the success of this memorable event. Despite his infirmity he painted with his own hand two pictures commemorating it, one being the *Meeting of Cardinal Infante Ferdinand and Ferdinand of Hungary at Nordlingen* (Vienna). In this evocation of a battle which, it was hoped in Flanders and throughout Europe, heralded an era of long-lasting peace, there is the same skillful intermingling of allegory and reality as in the *Life of Marie de' Medici*. Though the foreground figures (probably intended to harmonize with a big decorative ensemble) may seem disproportionately large, they provide a sort of proscenium, with the two princes bowing to each other, for the distant battle scene viewed in ascending perspective against a smoke-blurred horizon. Though there are signs of haste in the execution, this picture is a not unworthy counterpart of Velazquez' famous *Surrender of Breda*, painted in the same spirit and at almost the same time.

In his sketches for the decorations commissioned by the King of Spain for the twenty-five rooms of his hunting lodge, the Torre de la Parada, Rubens, more and more crippled by gout, had to adopt a more rapid, less exacting technique. Of the mythological themes inspired by Ovid's *Metamorphoses* he retained only the essentials and these sketches combine a fine spareness with much dramatic power. The most effective scenes, the *Fall of Icarus* and the *Fall of Phaethon*, represent single bodies hurtling through the air. So fluid are the brushstrokes that Van Puyvelde believes that Rubens strongly diluted his pigments with essence of turpentine. Ensuring as it did a better admixture of the oil and fatty substances, this volatile essence left a light, transparent coat of color, admirably suited to the "abbreviations" necessitated by the painter's failing health.

It would seem that in this last phase of his life Rubens channeled his remaining energies into creations of an intimate, personal nature, in particular those inspired by his young wife. While the first portraits of Helena show her in the early years of her marriage as an opulent young beauty endowed with a sort of elfin charm, richly attired (Munich) or half clad in dark furs that bring out the pearly luster of her flesh (Vienna), most touching are the last portraits showing her with her children (Munich, Louvre). We see Rubens at his unrivaled best in the unfinished picture in the Louvre, where Helena, a vague pink and golden presence under a huge plumed hat framing the soft curves of her face, is holding on her knee her son Frans who is wearing a black feathered cap and just behind him stands his little sister Clara Johanna. No other picture conveys with such tenderness and tact the fragile joy of a young mother's love; and no other work reveals so tellingly the inmost secret of this great artist's technique: those flowing brushstrokes, light as a caress, with which he conjured up the beauty of human flesh luminous with ardent life. Beside this peerless picture ranks Rubens' last self-portrait made at about the same date, 1637 (Vienna). Following a long sequence of skillfully drawn likenesses in which the painter portrayed himself as a rather dandyfied man-about-town, with a silky, Juanesque moustache, he now shows himself at the end of his long triumphal career, disillusioned by experience, weary of "too much living"—and the change is deeply moving. The fire of life is dying out in the reddened eyes, wrinkles seam the cheeks, and the skin of

Peter Paul Rubens (1577-1640).

Helena Fourment and her Two Children, c. 1637. (44½×32¾″) Louvre, Paris.

the face has lost its suppleness. Here Rubens records with lucid objectivity and stoic resignation the havoc time has wrought upon his handsome features. From 1638 on his hands were all but crippled by gout and the physical effort of painting was becoming more and more difficult for him. After a particularly severe attack in January 1640 he abandoned all hope of working again. Doctors were called in from Brussels, but to no avail, Rubens was forced to realize that the end was near and he now made a new will in Helena's favor. On April 17 he dictated a letter to his friend and pupil, the sculptor Frans Duquesnoy. "Death will soon remove me from the scene for ever." He died of heart failure, due to gout, on May 30, 1640. He lies interred in the Church of Saint-Jacques beneath his own painting of the *Virgin and Child with St George.*

Of much interest not merely on their own account but for their influence on the art of the next century are a group of works produced in the last years of his life: those purely imaginative compositions in which he celebrated feminine beauty under its most sensuous aspects. Gardens of love, lovers' meetings, Graces displaying their ample charms—all these magnificent compositions, after being secluded in the privacy of the artist's studio, were, for the most part, acquired by the King of Spain after Rubens' death and are now in the Prado. More than any of the earlier works, these give an impression of being creations of pure, untrammelled imagination and they had vast repercussions on the future; indeed it is hardly too much to say that all 18th-century painting derives from them. A soft ethereal radiance envelops a company of fair-haired, golden-skinned nudes, amongst whom we can discern, drawn with that superb assurance which never failed the artist even in his darkest hour, the form of his "Helen of Antwerp, lovelier far than Helen of Troy."

Van Dyck and the Society Portrait

Anthony van Dyck (1599-1641).

The Crucifixion. Sketch. (19½×17″) Musées Royaux des Beaux-Arts, Brussels.

Van Dyck and the Society Portrait

ANTHONY VAN DYCK was born in Antwerp on March 22, 1599, in the house quaintly named "The Bear Dance" where his father, far from belonging as used to be thought to an aristocratic family, owned a thriving business in silk (or haberdashery), having started life as a pedlar. Seventh of a family of twelve children, Anthony had to learn a trade at a very early age and when only ten was apprenticed to a historical painter, Hendrick van Balen. He showed exceptional precocity; his first work, the *Old Man* in the Del Monte Collection, dates to 1613 and at the age of fifteen he painted his first *Self-Portrait* (Vienna). When sixteen or seventeen he joined forces with some young fellow artists in setting up a studio that specialized in the production of half-length figures of Apostles, several series of which have survived. In these works Van Dyck displayed both boldness and originality, for instead of producing merely type figures, he strongly individualized each Apostle. Even before obtaining his degree of master in the Painters' Guild (on February 11, 1618), he had laid the foundations of a solid reputation. It was now that he began to work with Rubens, less as a pupil than as a collaborator who could be counted on to give a helping hand when the master was overwhelmed with work, and he filled this post for about two years.

At this time Rubens had achieved Europe-wide renown and the young artist, like his contemporaries, cannot have failed to be deeply impressed by the grandiose scenes with which the Antwerp master was adorning local edifices. Van Dyck took over some of his subjects; he painted a *Silenus Drunk* (Dresden) similar to Rubens' second, milder version, and in his *Calvary* (Louvre) he not only derived the general conception of the composition from the *Coup de Lance*, but exactly reproduced the master's rendering of the Virgin's hands locked in anguish. And though such borrowings were common enough at the time, this led to an (unjustified) belief that Van Dyck had a hand in Rubens' great work. But in his personal creations as in his technique he was highly eclectic and no less responsive to the realism of the rising young artist Jacob Jordaens, and like him much impressed by Caravaggio's *Virgin with the Rosary* which, at Rubens' suggestion, had been acquired for St Paul's Church at Antwerp. In Van Dyck's *St Martin dividing his Cloak*, painted about 1618 for the Church of Saventhem, these various tendencies are fairly well balanced. The figure of the saint reining in his horse provides the axis of the somewhat crowded composition, which is held together in the foreground by the prostrate beggar's naked form and the arrested movement of the horse and rider. The nude body is treated academically, though with considerable emphasis on its muscular structure, whereas the rather vulgar face of the other tramp is frankly realistic. The heads of the horses are convincingly rendered, and the color orchestration is exceptionally rich, containing both some strong contrasts of red and blue and exquisite gradations of greys of varying intensity in garments and the coat of the dapple-grey horse.

One of Van Dyck's chief concerns was to perfect a technique flexible and rapid enough to express fully and instantaneously each fleeting mood. A born dreamer, essentially "temperamental," he troubled himself little over form and structure and, in his eagerness to get the immediate effect that he was aiming at, refused to linger over minor details. Indeed the unevenness of his performance, the ever-increasing tenuity of his *matière* and his occasional lapses into carelessness might give an impression of lack of seriousness, even superficiality. Yet, with all his shortcomings, he had an almost uncanny insight into the human personality and could size up a character at a seeming-casual glance. Quite early in his career it became evident that he had a superlative gift for portrait painting. To this period belong the portrait of Jan Vermeulen dated 1616 (Liechtenstein Collection), that of Cornelius van der Geest (National Gallery, London), those of the painters Paul de Vos (Vienna) and Frans Snyders (Frick Collection, New York), and the double portrait of Snyders and his wife (Cassel). Also belonging to this period is the famous *Self-Portrait* in Munich—that likeness of a young man who will never age, with a slightly girlish face, rippling curls, and a faint, enigmatic smile. Van Dyck was now beginning, if timidly at first, to break with the Flemish tradition, exemplified by Cornelis de Vos, of minutely detailed depictions of physical appearances and character-revealing traits. He sought, rather, to follow in the footsteps of Rubens who, in the portraits made between 1615 and 1618, penetrated so deeply into the minds of his sitters. Subsequently, too, when he had opportunities of seeing the society portraits made by the master during his stay in Italy, he assimilated some of their more superficial aspects.

The two painters' collaboration, though cut short in 1620 by Van Dyck's hasty departure first for England, then to Genoa, had long-lasting effects on the younger man's career. The Countess of Arundel, wife of a rich English patron of the arts, who had come to take a cure at Spa before visiting her children then at school in Padua, had Rubens paint her portrait (Munich). Unable to persuade Rubens to go to England, she sent Van Dyck instead and he made his first stay there in November 1620. He was welcomed at the court of James I but since the aged monarch had no great liking for modern art and preferred the manner of the Elizabethans, and since moreover the young painter had to compete with well-established local artists, he soon returned to Flanders. On October 3, 1621, he set out again for Genoa, arriving there on November 20, and lodging with his Flemish friend, the painter and picture-dealer Cornelis de Wael, who introduced him to the best local society. In February 1622 he left by sea for Civita Vecchia and proceeded to Rome where he stayed about six months. He met the Countess of Arundel again at Venice and returned with her to Genoa. Between November 1622 and March 1623 he put in longish stays at Mantua, Milan and Turin. After the Countess went back to England he lived for some time at Genoa. Meanwhile, however, he made a trip to Palermo (1624) where he was given the order for the *Virgin with the Rosary*. He stopped off at Rome where he was the guest of Cardinal Guido Bentivoglio, former Papal Nuncio to the Low Countries, and made that excellent portrait of the Cardinal which is now in the Pitti Palace, Florence. While in Rome he struck up a friendship with the sculptor Frans Duquesnoy, who hailed from Brussels, and in Florence he met the painter Justus Sustermans. In summer 1625 he journeyed to Marseilles and Aix-en-Provence (where he called on Nicolas Peiresc, Rubens' correspondent), then to Paris. Back in Genoa in 1626, he made several (dated) portraits and next year completed the big picture that had been commissioned in 1624 by the Confraternity of the Rosary at Palermo.

During this long stay in Italy, which lasted till the end of 1627, a gradual change came over Van Dyck's art; he was now beginning to find himself and to strike out on a line more congenial to his temperament. There is no question that he was affected by his contacts with Italian artists. A sketchbook in the Duke of Devonshire's Collection at Chatsworth contains many drawings after Titian, Veronese, Sebastiano del Piombo and Raphael. But despite this token of his respect for these great masters, Van Dyck does not seem to have taken much from them, and he owes more to Bolognese art: to Guercino, Guido Reni and Albani. He now turned more and more to portraiture. For the first time he had occasion to paint, not private individuals—friends or brother artists—but persons representative of a whole social class, the proud and princely Genoese aristocracy. And now that the great Houses of Adorno, Balbi, Spinola, Durazzo, Brignole-Sale, Imperiali, Pallavicini and Grimaldi had adopted him as their "official" portraitist, he produced a series of full-length likenesses in grandiose settings, resplendent with stately pillars and costly fabrics. The model is viewed from below and, to strengthen the perspective effect, is often shown stepping up on to a dais or the first of a flight of steps beginning well in the foreground. Thus bodies are elongated, while faces, viewed from below and at a distance, acquire a delicate distinction. No less original are Van Dyck's color schemes. He has no qualms about using very dark backgrounds for the

Anthony van Dyck (1599-1641).

Self-Portrait, c. 1621. (32×27¼″) Alte Pinakothek, Munich.

Anthony van Dyck (1599-1641).

Portrait of the Marchioness Geronima Spinola, 1623-1627. (87×58") Kaiser Friedrich Museum, Berlin.

voluminous black garments then in fashion, whose folds he indicates with hatchings of greyish light. These somber masses are enlivened here and there with passages of sharply contrasted colors: the bright red of wrist bands, dazzling white of ruffs, pale translucencies of faces and tapering fingers. Not that he was interested in such details for their own sake; his concern was with their color values and he rendered them with little heed to exactitude (this indeed is a distinctive trait of all his portraits). In these works Van Dyck transforms with a fine bravura the traditional techniques of Netherlandish portrait painting, retaining only its spirit, and replaces static presentation by meaningful gesture. All the same he falls far short of Rubens, each of whose figures seems charged with exuberant life, a dynamism that is not arrested at the moment represented, whereas in Van Dyck's portraits movement gives the impression of being momentarily suspended—an ingenious but artificial solution of the artist's problem. Still, there is no question that, handled in this way, the monumental portraits of Van Dyck's Genoese period achieve a certain grandeur and a slightly mannered dignity, doubtless to the liking of his sitters. Many of these works are still in Genoa, chiefly in the Palazzo Bianco and the Palazzo Rosso, but a very fine assortment of them has also been brought together in the Widener Collection (National Gallery, Washington).

We see still more clearly how much the artist owed to his sitters and also how skillfully he could think himself into their minds, when we turn to the portraits he painted some months later on his return to Antwerp in 1627: for example, the likenesses of Pieter Stievens and his wife (The Hague) and that of Gaspard de Crayer (Liechtenstein Collection). Here the mood is one of homely intimacy; Van Dyck has easily and perfectly adapted himself to the spirit of austerity and simplicity animating the exemplary lives of these men of learning and quiet industry. His art has become soberer, perhaps more sincere, and he shows a real comprehension of his sitters, not merely a lively sensitivity to outward appearances. It was now that Van Dyck started on the series of engraved portraits of the most eminent men of his time, known as his "Iconography," on which he continued working up to his death. It contains some hundred portraits and was published at Antwerp in 1645 by Gillis Hendricx; the original plates are preserved in the Louvre. Ten, of an exceptionally high quality, were etched by Van Dyck himself. Many preparatory designs of the others are extant and it is known that the artist carefully supervised their execution, even when away in London.

From the end of 1627 until the beginning of 1632, the period when Rubens was on diplomatic missions to Spain and England, Van Dyck resided in Antwerp. His reputation was steadily rising and, in the master's absence, he received the chief commissions for large-scale pictures for churches, now in great demand as a result of the Catholic revival. These works, which are almost all in Belgium (in St Rombaut's at Malines, St Michael's in Ghent, Notre Dame at Termonde and Notre Dame at Courtrai), differ from Rubens' similar compositions in several ways. They are painted mostly in low-pitched tones with a liberal use of brown, and the would-be heroic gestures of the figures strike a rather affected note. They are at a far remove from those gloriously robust, healthy forms which give a fine distinction to even the most conventional of Rubens' compositions. Sometimes, however, thanks to an expert handling of chiaroscuro and his sure feeling for theatrical effect, Van Dyck more than holds his own beside the master.

At the end of March 1632, summoned to London by Charles I who had come to the throne in 1625 and was a great lover of the arts, Van Dyck left Antwerp once again. In London he received an annual pension, was lodged at the expense of the Crown and provided with a summer residence. Shortly after his arrival he was knighted by the king, who was a frequent visitor to his studio. For the next five years he was the king's chief painter, making a long series of portraits of members of the court and the high society of that troubled age of English history. Many indeed believe that Sir Anthony van Dyck did much to create the "style" of the British aristocracy, a style that has lasted till our time and materially shaped the evolution of English painting. Gifted with an acutely perceptive eye, he could assess a character at a glance and convey with appropriate bravura both the dashing gallantry of the young blades who were the king's boon companions and the time-serving pliability of the courtiers.

Some have thought to see in the steady stream of portraits, hastily executed and sometimes repetitive, that Van Dyck turned out in this phase of his career, signs of a rapid deterioration of his powers, due either to physical weakness or to a dissipated life. But those who take this view lose sight of the heights he could still scale on occasion and the remarkable progress of his technique. True, Van Dyck was always extremely sensitive to the personalities of his sitters, accepted them as they were, uncritically, and he was certainly influenced by the "playboy" atmosphere prevailing in Charles' court, the reckless irresponsibility of the king's

Anthony van Dyck (1599-1641).

St Martin dividing his Cloak, c. 1618. (67½×62¼″) Church of Saventhem (near Brussels).

Anthony van Dyck (1599-1641).

Portrait of Charles I ("Le Roi à la chasse"), c. 1635. (107×87") Louvre, Paris.

associates, blind to the gathering storm. But it is wrong to say that he was losing grip or that his colors were becoming insipid. Though his touch grew ever lighter, he compensated for any textural deficiencies by a brilliant arrangement of small, adroitly placed brushstrokes charged with fluent color, kindling the picture surface into a shimmering haze of silken greys, pale yellows and various shades of pink, and bringing out to perfection the sheen of lace and satin embroideries and glints of gold. If there is no "soul" in his society portraits, it is not the painter's fault. His art regained all its delightful freshness when he portrayed the royal children (Windsor Castle; Galleria Sabauda, Turin) or the young cavaliers whose charming likenesses figure in so many English collections. With their light cloaks elegantly flung back over their shoulders, with their lithe grace and sleekly cambered limbs, they might be treading the mazes of some courtly 17th-century ballet.

In the portraits of Charles, however, we can detect a tragic undertone, suggesting that, however blind the king's entourage, Van Dyck had an intuition of the peril threatening the throne. Though he spared no pains in glorifying and spiritualizing these likenesses, he hid nothing of what his psychological insight had revealed and the superb portraits of that unhappy monarch, Mary Stuart's grandson, temperamentally so unfitted for the throne that Elizabeth had so gloriously occupied, have a revelatory quality that even contemporaries did not fail to notice. The story goes that when Van Dyck sent Bernini that strange portrait of *Charles I in Three Positions* (Windsor Castle), which he had painted to enable the sculptor to make a bust of the king, the Italian exclaimed "What a tragic face!" The portrait of Charles I in the Louvre, known as *Le Roi à la chasse*, in which the texture of the paint has a richness seldom found in Van Dyck's later work, is a masterpiece of its kind, nowise inferior to Velazquez' open-air portraits.

The French bombardment of Brussels in 1695 led to the total destruction in the Town Hall of the large ceremonial picture of *The Magistrates of the City of Brussels*, painted by Van Dyck during a short stay there in 1634-1635. The modello (now in the Ecole des Beaux-Arts, Paris) is remarkable for the finely balanced grouping of the sitters around an allegorical figure of Justice and so admirably conceived is the layout that it is greatly to be regretted Van Dyck was unable to carry out his project for making mural decorations in the banqueting room at Whitehall, where the ceiling had been painted by Rubens.

Sketches by Van Dyck are rare and mostly belong to his second Antwerp period. He lacked that sudden compulsive vision which enabled Rubens to set forth, in a flash of creative inspiration, the full content and rhythmic structure of even the largest compositions. Van Dyck made tentative approaches to his subjects and he found that pen drawings served his purpose best. After singling out the drawing which seemed most promising, he indicated contrasts of light and shade with the brush (or in ink); then proceeded to make numerous studies of details and accessories: draperies, greyhounds, horses, landscape elements and so forth.

Roger de Piles gives an account of what was told him by one of Van Dyck's sitters, a man of whom he made three portraits. From him we learn that as the result of an intensive study of the Italian *fa presto* technique in early youth, Van Dyck was able, towards the close of his life, to work on three paintings at once. He had a sitter pose for an hour at most, then dismissed him and promptly set to work with another sitter; this enabled him to turn out a great many portraits in an incredibly short time. That in the enormous number of works produced by him in England the quality varies so greatly may be partly due to the fact that his health was always precarious and periods of creative energy alternated with moods of profound discouragement when he had little heart for work.

Indeed Van Dyck's life during that last period of feverish activity might be described as a race against time. In 1639 he married Lady Mary Ruthven, who came of a good Scotch family, and thus tightened the link between him and his adoptive country. But the conflict between the monarchy and parliament was coming to a head, England was on the brink of civil war. The King had to cut down expenses and Van Dyck was a victim of this forced economy. On Rubens' death in 1640 he hastily crossed to Antwerp, perhaps in the hope of getting orders, but he was so excessive in his demands that the Archduke declined to have any dealings with him. Next he went to Paris in a vain attempt to obtain the commission for decorating one of the galleries of the Louvre (it ultimately went to Poussin and Vouet). Seriously ill, he returned to London where he summoned up enough energy to paint their wedding portrait for Princess Mary, eldest daughter of Charles I, and William of Orange (Rijksmuseum, Amsterdam). He was about to leave for Holland when his strength failed him. On December 1, 1641, his wife gave birth to a child; on December 9 Van Dyck died, aged forty-two. He was buried in old St Paul's and his remains perished in the fire of 1666.

The deaths of Rubens and Van Dyck within less than two years spelt the decline of Baroque art in Flanders. One has an impression that all Flemish artists, even Jordaens who lived on till 1678, were disheartened by the loss of the two outstanding figures who had been their rallying point and source of inspiration. For two or three decades Gaspard de Crayer (1582-1669) and Erasmus Quellin (1607-1678), who succeeded Rubens as painter to the City of Antwerp, continued decorating churches and public buildings with large historical and religious compositions. But these were less and less vigorous, their colors lusterless, and their only redeeming feature is their occasional provincial flavor, a certain archaic gravity. In any case the period was unpropitious for artists; as a result of the long-drawn struggle with Holland, commerce and industry in Flanders were practically at a standstill, and commissions hard to come by.

None the less, alongside such new art forms as genre painting (dealt with in a later chapter), that typically Flemish branch of art, the portrait continued to have some praiseworthy

Cornelis de Vos (1584-1651).

Family Portrait, 1631. (65×92½″) Musée Royal des Beaux-Arts, Antwerp.

Cornelis de Vos (1584-1651).
Family Portrait (detail), 1631. Musée Royal des Beaux-Arts, Antwerp.

exponents. Justus Sustermans (1597-1681) maintained over a long period the cosmopolitan type of portraiture brought into favor by Van Dyck, whom he had met as a young man in Florence. Trained by Frans Pourbus the Younger at the French court, Sustermans entered the service of the Medici in Florence, before coming to divide his time between the courts of Italy and Austria. He specialized in painting princes, diplomats and military leaders; the chief merit of his work lies in a skillful arrangement of the picture elements and brilliant renderings of damascened cuirasses, ceremonial sashes and plumed helmets (e.g. *Christian of Denmark*, 1638, Pitti Palace, Florence). That great painter Philippe de Champaigne, born at Brussels, might well have revivified the art of the psychological portrait in Flanders; but, since he went to Paris at a very early age, was naturalized French, and played an active part in the religious and intellectual life of his adoptive country, and since his œuvre is one of the glories of the French School, he does not concern us here.

Among Rubens' and Van Dyck's contemporaries it is Cornelis de Vos who ranks nearest to the masters. Born at Hulst in 1584 and trained at Antwerp, where he qualified as master in 1608, he took part in some large-scale Baroque ensembles; for example, in making (in collaboration with Jordaens) the decorations of the City of Antwerp for the state entry of

Cornelis de Vos (1584-1651).

Family Portrait (detail), 1631. Musée Royal des Beaux-Arts, Antwerp.

Archduke Ferdinand and in 1637 in the execution, after sketches made by Rubens, of several mythological scenes for the Torre de la Parada. But his lack of imagination is sadly evident in the arrangement of the narrative elements in his compositions; indeed the only merit of his big historical picture, *The Restitution of the Buried Treasure to the Abbey of Saint-Michel* (1630, Antwerp), lies in the excellence of his portraits of the many persons figuring in the scene. Cornelis de Vos is at his best only when he has real men and women to depict. In such cases he surrenders himself to the persons before him, simply, objectively, wholeheartedly, and is happiest when there is an emotive link between him and his model, as is proved by the fact that his best, most moving portraits are those of members of his family, of people he has known and loved for many years. Noteworthy, too, is the frankness and directness of his approach; we never find any straining after meretricious effects or exhibitionism in his art. His charming pictures in the museums of Brussels and Antwerp give us glimpses of family life, imbued with a tranquil lyricism and bathed in an evenly distributed light.

All these portraits strike a note of absolute sincerity, without any taint of vulgarity or exaggeration. And while he gives close attention to details—always handled with a fine discretion—his chief concern is to reveal the personality of the sitter, the sort of man he really is, and this he does with tactful understanding and a fine objectivity. Given his temperament, it was natural that Cornelis should excel in portraits of children, and he has a delightful gift for capturing their candid gaze, their shyness in the presence of a grown-up, their naive grace. His portraits of his own children are minutely observed, devoid of any sentimental idealization, yet convey to perfection the winsomeness of childhood. Some of these, masterpieces of their kind, are in the Mayer van den Bergh Museum at Antwerp and in Berlin. We find traces of fatigue in the output of his declining years and, though he made some good, if rather stiff, individual likenesses of adults, he seems to have given up painting groups, perhaps because he felt their composition was beyond his strength.

We find a notable revival of the group portrait in the work of Gonzales Coques (1614-1684), who often posed his models in the open air. Distinctive of his figures are the elegance of their bearing and the refinement of the faces. They are usually shown walking in a park or on a terrace; but sometimes in an interior in the Terborch manner. His preference for works of very small dimensions led Coques to employ a technique of tiny, sharply defined brushstrokes, high lights being shown by touches of bright color. He brings off some original and agreeable effects by associating brilliant hues of garments—vivid blue, carmine and gamboge yellow— with a neutral landscape ground, brownish in tone. The artist's delicate sensibility makes itself felt in the reserved, faintly melancholy expressions of faces both in his isolated figures (depicted in medallions on copper) and in his family groups.

Some minor painters in provincial centers, working in the same tradition, call for mention. At Malines Peeter Franchoys (1606-1654) and his younger brother Lucas (1616-1681) enjoyed considerable success. Some of the extant portraits (of men) by Peeter Franchoys are treated in a manner deriving from Van Dyck's *Iconography*. The model is shown in an easy, natural attitude, with a strong light on his face; the flesh tint is a uniform, full-bodied pink with brown shadows to indicate modeling. From Pieter Meert of Brussels (1619-1669) we have some excellent portrait groups, notably *The Governors of the Brussels Corporation of Fishmongers* (Brussels) which, with its fine spareness of means, recalls the art of Philippe de Champaigne. The same austerity is found in individual portraits, for example the *Old Man* and *Old Woman* (Brussels) where a light brown ground of varying intensity sets off a neutral color scheme of greys and blacks. At Bruges Jacob van Oost the Elder (1601-1671), otherwise known only by some rather inferior portraits, produced one outstanding work in which the figure gives a fine effect of solidity: the *Boy with a Muff* (1650) in the National Gallery, London. Jacob van Oost the Younger (1639-1713), who succeeded him as favorite painter of the local upper class, successfully revived the tradition of exact, painstaking craftsmanship in the manner of the Pourbus "dynasty." Meanwhile, not far away, in the peaceful town of Furnes, Victor Boucquet (1619-1677) was working for the Spanish garrison. In his *Standard Bearer* (1664, Louvre) this artist's gifts as a colorist are seen to admirable effect.

Jordaens and Flemish Opulence

Jacob Jordaens (1593-1678).

Fecundity (detail), c. 1622. Musées Royaux des Beaux-Arts, Brussels.

Jordaens and Flemish Opulence

THE contrast between Jordaens and Rubens provides an illustration of two different and enduring aspects of the Flemish temperament. Rubens was one of those supreme artists who see the world instinctively in terms of painting, the resources of his palette were unlimited and he almost effortlessly created plastic equivalents, as eloquent as apposite, of scenes of history, of allegories and indeed of the whole range of human sentiments and passions. Jordaens, on the other hand, deliberately narrowed his field of vision and never lost sight of the "message" he felt called on to voice. Thus he has no scruples about repeating himself with tedious insistence and, whatever the subject of the picture, he usually manages to include some of his favorite type figures, the result being that in many cases they are little more than incongruous accessories. The strange thing is that though his outlook was so prosaic and dogmatic, Jordaens was gifted with undeniable creative power and often attains a certain grandeur; even when a work as a whole seems incoherent or disappointing, there are always fragments so beautifully executed as to atone for these shortcomings.

There has been much, perhaps over-much, talk of Jordaens' realism and he has been regarded as a pioneer of naturalism, born out of his due time, an unimaginative exponent of Flemish truculence and triviality. Indeed his art has always provoked greatly varying responses. Some insist on describing him as a "low-life" painter because he employs rustic types in his *Satyr and Peasant* and *Tribute Money*; others, in view of his many scenes entitled *The King Drinks*, illustrating the Twelfth Night rejoicings in Flemish homes, regard him as a chronicler of the bourgeoisie. Moreover attempts have been made to identify the faces that persistently recur in his pictures as those of his father-in-law, his wife and his children. Actually, however, this so-called realist pays little heed to visual reality; he never lets himself be guided by appearances or seeks to convey "impressions." On the contrary he composes with patient application (for he has little imagination and still less gusto) certain conventional figures, since such to his thinking are best suited for the program he has constantly in mind: to fill the entire picture space with significant volumes and produce a work that will "hold the wall" on which it hangs.

For Jordaens, all form is primarily volume. He seldom tries to create the illusion of depth and uses light only as a means of emphasizing the thickness and rotundity of objects at once frontally illuminated and shown up against indirect light coming from another source. The effect is to bring them forward, rendered by purely painterly means, just as they would appear to a spectator present at the scene. It was said of Monet that he was "only an eye—but what an eye!" It might be said of Jordaens that he is only a hand, but a hand gifted with extraordinary skill in defining forms, making us sense their palpability. Moreover, as a painter he goes much further than the moralistic commentator, the man with a message —which is the first impression he produces. For the narrative elements of his pictures are quickly forgotten; not so his treatment of them. Though his work has little interest as to its subject matter, it ranks as the most advanced of the entire century, so far as execution is concerned. Thus when we single out particular fragments, we discover that Jordaens is the finest painter of nudes, still lifes and animals of his time and in fact the true initiator of the various genres of 17th-century painting found in the works of specialists. But he excels them all, since he has not only a broader outlook but a deeper interest in the human situation; beneath the surface virtuosity of his paintings there is always a profound significance.

There was nothing of the "Bohemian" in Jordaens; unlike many of his fellow artists, he led an exemplary, domesticated, almost puritanically sober life. Born at Antwerp in May 1593, he began by painting in tempera and it was as a bodycolor painter that he qualified as master in the Painters' Guild in 1615. He always kept to this medium for his sketches and tapestry cartoons. He studied, like Rubens, under Adam van Noort, in whose studio he worked from 1607 onward, and after marrying his teacher's daughter Katharina in 1616, continued living with him until 1633. He had three children (1617, 1625, 1629), was devoted to his family and home, and never traveled except for occasional visits to Holland late in life, due to his Protestant leanings. He had no wish for social distinction and pressure had to be brought to make him accept the post of Dean of the Guild of Painters in 1621. In 1639 he bought a house in the Rue Haute, then had it torn down and rebuilt to his own design. This handsome building still exists but has unfortunately been stripped of the very fine decorations, on religious and mythological themes, painted by Jordaens himself. One sequence, *The Signs of the Zodiac*, now figures on the ceiling of a gallery in the East wing of the Palais du Luxembourg in Paris.

Jordaens seldom collaborated on large decorative ensembles and, when he did so, always showed traces of timidity and none of the confidence and bravura that characterize the works he executed single-handed. His share in the decorations made for the state entry of Archduke Ferdinand into Antwerp in 1635, his contributions to some of the paintings which Rubens made to the order of the King of Spain and which he left it to his colleague to complete, and some mythological scenes made for the Torre de la Parada hardly call for mention; nor does the contract Jordaens entered into in 1648 for painting (along with collaborators) thirty-five ceiling panels for Christina of Sweden, or the order given in 1661, when he was nearly seventy, for some decorations in the Town Hall of Amsterdam.

One of his decorations, however, painted in 1651-1652, is a brilliant exception: that on the main wall of the octagonal "Orange Hall" in the famous villa near The Hague built for Princess Amelia of Solms in memory of her husband Frederick Henry of Orange, and known as the Huis ten Bosch (House in the Woods). An allegorical picture celebrating the triumph of the deceased Stadholder, it is a work of huge dimensions, measuring twenty-eight feet by twenty-seven. Jordaens executed it in bold, sweeping brushstrokes applied with fine precision and unfailing verve. The composition is extremely dense, crowded with allegories due to the fertile imagination of Constantin Huygens, secretary to the Princess. A letter dated April 23, 1651, shows that Jordaens was given a complete plan of the work and expected to conform to this. The number of preliminary sketches (three are preserved in Warsaw, Brussels and Antwerp) shows both the difficulties he had to cope with and the conscientiousness with which he carried out his instructions to the letter. But here again what counts is not the scene itself but the superb execution, the dynamic modeling of figures, the splendor of the white horses drawing the triumphal car, the powerful relief of the simulated statues, the wealth of floral ornamentation and the masterly renderings of animal forms. Like all his sketches, these show remarkable powers of simplification; employing a technique both forthright and flexible, Jordaens indulges in a host of bold, clean-cut, almost geometrical abbreviations, which have no parallel in his finished pictures.

Having embraced Protestantism late in life, Jordaens suffered a certain amount of persecution; on one occasion he was fined for publishing "heretical" pamphlets. All the same he never broke completely with the faith of his forefathers and still received occasional commissions from the Catholic authorities. In any case his change of faith does not seem to have had much effect on his work, which was already declining in quality and, from 1660 on, his output fell off sharply. He long outlived the failure of his powers. When he died, October 16, 1678, he was in his dotage and a chronic invalid. As was customary in the case of Protestants living in Antwerp his remains were interred in Dutch soil.

The outstanding quality of his early work is its forcefulness, a juvenile vigor that could but diminish as the years went by. He brings his figures forward to the picture surface as if seen in close-up—usually half-length—and employs a richly worked impasto whose texture

Jacob Jordaens (1593-1678).

The Satyr and the Peasant (detail). Musées Royaux des Beaux-Arts, Brussels (no. 1044).

brings out wrinkles and folds of flesh. He has a habit of representing figures side-face, so as to accentuate profiles and features. We see this in that well-known picture in the Louvre usually known as the *Four Evangelists* (c. 1616-1618), but more probably illustrating "Christ among the Doctors." It contains some of the type figures, rugged-faced old men with gnarled hands and limbs, which he employs indifferently as satyrs, saints and peasants. True, in the period 1614-1618, when he was in his twenties, Jordaens was strongly influenced by Rubens' technique, but he carried the master's smoothly finished manipulation of the pigment to the point of giving it a porcelain-like gloss. This we see in the magnificent nudes of the *Daughters of Cecrops discovering Erechtheus* (1617, Antwerp) and *Meleager and Atalanta* (Antwerp); there is an enlarged version of the latter in the Prado. The light flesh tints stand out brightly against a pool of shadows that sometimes creep up to faces, the effect being that of blazing sunlight, high noon in some southern land far from the mists of Flanders.

We find the same arbitrary but dynamic handling of light, quite other than the faintly glimmering daybreaks of the Primitives, in the *Adoration of the Shepherds* (1618, Stockholm). Stripped of its wonted accessories, the scene is handled in a curiously modern spirit. The Mother and Child are hardly distinguishable from the robust peasants grouped around them, who seem oddly ill at ease in the constricted space. Their responses vary greatly; some are stolidly indifferent, some lost in thought, others carried away by emotion. With a fine economy of means Jordaens represents the diverse gestures of massive, elongated hands, the

Jacob Jordaens (1593-1678).

Fecundity, c. 1622. (71×95″) Musées Royaux des Beaux-Arts, Brussels.

cubic forms of faces partly sheltered from the light by rustic headdresses or their drooping posture. The juxtaposition of strong, saturated colors—vermilion, yellow, blue and green— gives rise to violent contrasts and the painter does not need to make use of black, since tones are harmonized by shadows touched with glints of light.

Jordaens made several interpretations of Aesop's fable, *The Satyr and the Peasant*, in which the Satyr is so much puzzled by seeing the Peasant alternately blowing on his soup to cool it and on his hands to warm them. This subject gave him good opportunities of grouping together those massive figures in which he excelled. In the Brussels version (acquired by the Royal Museum in 1940; other versions are in Cassel and Munich) the color scheme is remarkably successful. Here for once the figures are full-length. On the left we see the strapping peasant woman wearing a straw hat who is one of Jordaens' stock figures. The rustic setting is stressed by the presence of animals: a rooster with gaudy plumage, a dog under the table. In the case of the dog color alone suffices to bring out the plastic values of the body, and its coat has a rich velvety luster glowing across the shadows. All the *Satyr and Peasant* pictures contain old women with furrowed faces slumped in wicker chairs, and bearded oldsters, figures of ancient wisdom, chuckling to themselves. These type figures, symbolic of the ages of human life, reappear in the artist's religious scenes as well.

Fecundity (c. 1622, Brussels) is the best and final version of a theme which Jordaens had already handled several times (1617, Munich; variants at Ghent and in the Wallace Collection, London). A group of female figures—two of them nudes, one presented standing in back view and the other squatting—is surrounded by a company of fauns and satyrs, one of them holding a cornucopia filled with the fruits of the earth. This detail has often been attributed to Snyders but the texture of the painting seems more uniform than in any picture by that virtuoso of the banquet piece, and I am inclined to think it is by Jordaens' hand. The figure of the satyr, whose sharply incised features stand out against a Negro's upturned face, is a superb creation, and equally unforgettable is the plump little girl with parted lips, whose curly golden tresses are bedecked with flowers. The wealth of colors is nothing short of prodigious: exquisitely varied shades of pink for flesh tints, dark green of leafage, the softly glowing, iridescent bloom of fruit, finely balanced alternations of warm and cool tones. Noteworthy in such works as this is the unqualified success with which Jordaens fuses these multifarious elements (some, perhaps, not by his hand) into an organic whole.

During the 17th century Frans Snyders' huge displays of fruit and game and the hunting scenes of Paul de Vos were in great demand. Born at Antwerp in 1579 and a contemporary of Rubens, with whom he regularly collaborated from 1613 on, Snyders had specialized since his return from Italy (1609) in large still lifes of the "larder" or "market" type, containing meat, fish, fruit and vegetables, usually displaying each kind of foodstuff separately. The effect is eminently restful and pleasing to the eye, though the artist shows no concern with rhythm. The real value of these works, executed with painstaking precision, is their rich color orchestration, and it more than justifies the artist's arbitrary recourse to the most spectacular specimens of the animal and vegetable kingdoms. He also made some fine studies of animals at rest (Berlin, Brussels, Leningrad) remarkable for the incisive precision of the drawing. In this connection there is an interesting passage in the letter from Tobias Matthew to Sir Dudley Carleton (1617) in which he informed Sir Dudley that Rubens had been struck by Snyders' reluctance to draw animals in movement; what fascinated him was the still-life aspect of feathers and fur, preferably those of dead animals.

The art of Frans Snyders was carried a stage further by his brother-in-law Paul de Vos, born at Hulst about 1596 and thus an almost exact contemporary of Jordaens. Some of his works used to be attributed to Snyders, though actually there are many differences. De Vos spent his entire career at Antwerp and was chiefly influenced by Rubens' big hunting scenes. In his *Stag Hunt* (Brussels) and scenes of animals fighting he employs violently baroque rhythms, showing animals wildly leaping, with their forms elongated out of all proportion. But his color schemes (with brown as the dominant tone) are less rich and his execution is more banal than Snyders'. His work is essentially decorative and often sadly uninspired. For all the virtuosity and brio of these two artists and some of their contemporaries, we would gladly discard their works today (if a choice had to be made) in favor of the brief expositions of similar themes figuring as mere decorative accessories in the pictures of Rubens and Jordaens.

A fine example of Jordaens' gift for combining still-life elements with portraiture is his *Portrait of the Artist and his Family* (Prado), which he seems to have painted at about the same time as *Fecundity*, in the early 1620s. He portrays himself standing beside his wife, his little daughter and a servant girl in a setting in which discreetly figure all the stock accessories he employs in his carefully contrived compositions: domestic animals (a parrot and a dog), various kinds of flowers and fruit, a statuette. All merge delightfully into the simple décor which, if somewhat shallow, is animated by their presence and acts as a foil to the figures, posed with monumental simplicity well in the foreground, as if viewed from a slightly lower level. The painter's mastery of pictorial effect is seen in the varied treatment of the women's faces, one in full light, the other faintly shadowed, and no less masterly is the detailed rendering of costumes, particularly that of the laughing little girl with the blue kerchief. We have also here a fine example of full-bodied colors toned down to create an atmosphere of intimacy; rich and unctuous as is the pigment, it has undertones of shadow. But in portraying contemporaries Jordaens often indulges his propensity for a rather brutal forthrightness and far from flattering them as Van Dyck was apt to do, stresses facial peculiarities and volumes. Thus in the *Portrait of Van Zurpelen and his Wife* (Chatsworth) the figures are bulky, almost uncouth, and the austerity of the setting is redeemed only by the presence of some animals, which, given the theme, seem quite uncalled-for.

Jordaens is at his best when handling subjects with which he has familiarized himself by frequent repetition and containing a limited number of stock figures; he often seems ill at ease when tackling bigger compositions and seeking to enlarge his range of vision. None the less in that ambitious work, *The Tribute Money* (Copenhagen), he scores a notable success. The subject proper is relegated to the extreme right, where we see St Peter drawing up a large fish from the water and taking the coin from its mouth. The entire picture surface is filled by a boat laden to the gunwales with peasants and animals. We have here presumably a more or less exact representation of the Antwerp ferry boat that plied between the two banks of the Scheldt, though one may wonder how, with a human and animal cargo so disproportionate to its capacity, it managed to keep afloat. For all the surface realism there is no mistaking the symbolic meaning of the theme, a ship freighted with "all sorts and conditions of men." The air seems charged with the invigorating breath of a sea breeze and, despite the overcrowded boat, the composition as a whole produces an effect of spaciousness. Details are skillfully arranged in an alternating rhythm between strongly lit faces gazing skywards—for example that of a woman suckling her child—and faces overshadowed by huge straw hats, such as that of the burly peasant leaning on his ox.

Too often, however, his large-scale works—with their echoes (usually remote and indirect) of Caravaggio and Bassano—fail to hold together; there is a disturbing incongruity between the baroque gesturings of minor figures, merely decorative adjuncts devoid of personality, and the essentially static quality of the leading figures, treated in isolation and with that delicate precision characteristic of Jordaens in his best moments. This applies in particular to the religious works painted after 1625 and pervaded with a violent agitation vaguely reminiscent of Van Dyck's treatment of such themes. A case in point is the big *Calvary* in Bordeaux Cathedral (Chapel of the Treasure). This was the time when he was receiving orders for large-scale compositions intended to figure in churches and thus was obliged to forgo the kind of painting in which he felt at ease and to tackle an unfamiliar problem, that of rendering movement. In the *Martyrdom of St Apollonia* (St Augustine's, Antwerp) Jordaens applies his usual method of violent color contrasts to a thickly crowded composition, the result being an incoherent rhythm that distracts the eye, allowing it no point of rest. The *Miracle of St Martin* (1630, Brussels), which was made for the high altar of St Martin's Church at Tournai, contains a number of gigantic figures whose limbs are oddly

Jacob Jordaens (1593-1678).

Portrait of the Artist and his Family, 1622-1623. (71¼×73¾″) Prado, Madrid.

imbricated without giving any suggestion of depth. The composition of his most famous religious work, the *Adoration of the Magi* in Dixmude Church (destroyed in the 1914-1918 war), was equally chaotic and fell far short of the work by Rubens which inspired it.

For once, however, Jordaens made an effort to convey an idea of space between his figures in *St Yves, Patron Saint of Lawyers* (1645, Brussels) where we see a crowd of suppliants flocking into a nobly proportioned edifice to seek counsel from the saint. And in *Showing Off the Paces of a Horse* (c. 1644, Cassel) the composition is quite clear and comprehensible; the arrangement of the servant and the restive horse relieved against a landscape background could not be bettered. Jordaens' conception of the nude also underwent a notable change in this phase of his career, as can be seen in his *King Candaules* (1648, Stockholm). The naked body, shown in back view, is given proportions that bring out its rotundities to the full; placed in the center of the picture, a glowing mass of vivid pink, it looks like a colossal statue flooded with light. Something of this eye-filling opulence is also found in *Susanna and the Elders* (1653, Copenhagen; replica in Brussels), though here the execution is somewhat careless and the modeling lacks vigor.

Over a period of ten years (1638-1648) Jordaens put the best of himself into depictions of Twelfth Night festivities, generally entitled *The King Drinks*. A great many versions are extant (Louvre, Brussels, Antwerp, Leningrad, Munich, Vienna) and they were the prototypes of numerous works by the master's pupils and followers. In Flanders the Feast of the Epiphany was celebrated with a jollity that delighted the painter's eye. At Twelfth Night gatherings a "king," chosen by lot, and attended by a train of comic courtiers, presided over the revels. It is not, however, the rather forced joviality of these Twelfth Night pictures that interests the modern observer. He is more inclined to wonder whether behind the plethora of expressive, willfully vulgar attitudes and the general effect of uncontrolled exuberance, these scenes may not contain a deeper significance. Hints of this are discernible in the Brussels version, where thanks to the cleaning of 1930 some ill-advised repaintings have been eliminated. First to catch the eye is the architectural arrangement of the group on the extreme left, given the exact form of a pyramid, its apex formed by the pointed cap of a smoker waving his pipe above his head; he has a strongly foreshortened face and is making a grimace as

Jacob Jordaens (1593-1678).

The King Drinks, c. 1638. (59⅛×82¾″) Musées Royaux des Beaux-Arts, Brussels.

Jacob Jordaens (1593-1678).

The King Drinks (detail), c. 1638. Musées Royaux des Beaux-Arts, Brussels.

he purses his lips to expel a puff of smoke. Just in front of him a drinker is bawling out a song and behind the dark mass of his body we see two cheerful but relatively sedate young girls: an oasis of calm filled with flickering shadows that impart a curious vibrancy to flesh tints and a translucent wine glass. It is as if in the midst of all the crazy antics of the revellers we had a sudden glimpse of Vermeer's fine serenity.

Somewhat similar is another set of paintings on the theme of the Flemish proverb *As Old Folk Sing, Young Folk Pipe* (Antwerp, Dresden, Louvre) showing a cheerful company gathered round a table, the young people playing musical instruments, the grandfather and grandmother singing. Here again the figures, shown half length, represent the various ages of man. In these less crowded compositions the distribution of light is well balanced and atmosphere suggested with much skill. But by this time Jordaens' art was deteriorating, his color losing its distinctive resonance and richness. None the less, up to the very end of his life, this great artist's sincerity was never in question; always he gave of his best.

Jacob Jordaens (1593-1678).
The King Drinks (detail), c. 1638. Musées Royaux des Beaux-Arts, Brussels.

Brouwer and Life in the Raw

David Teniers the Younger (1610-1690).

The Five Senses (fragment). Musées Royaux des Beaux-Arts, Brussels.

Brouwer and Life in the Raw

WHEN a painter of Rubens' stature takes a lead from foreign art, he can do so without detriment to his native vision and he transforms his "borrowings" out of recognition. In early 17th-century Flanders, however, foreign influences were clearly visible in the work of several artists. For example, there were Flemish Caravaggeschi, painting in the manner of Manfredi, Honthorst or Valentin, who specialized in night pieces with people playing cards or backgammon, soldiers and prostitutes, tipplers, guitar players and so forth. The figures are presented half length, grouped around a table, and much use is made of artificial, violently contrasting light effects. Such were the works of Gerard Seghers (1591-1651) and Theodore Rombouts (1597-1637), both of them pupils of Abraham Janssens (1575-1632), who combined gesticulation and the cool, iridescent hues of the Antwerp mannerists with reminiscences of antique statuary. Seghers, who had spent some years in Italy and probably in Spain as well between 1611 and 1620, fell completely under the spell of Rubens soon after his return to Antwerp. Before that, however, he had produced some more original works and (as A. von Schneider has pointed out) followed a line of evolution running parallel to that of the Spanish painter Ribalta. Two other artists somewhat resembled Rombouts: Adam de Coster of Malines (1586-1643), whose *Judith* (Prado) has analogies with Saraceni's picture on the same subject, and Jan Cossiers (1600-1671), who painted smokers and beggars in a somber, opaque tonality (Antwerp and Cassel). But alongside these art forms deriving from abroad, the influence of Bruegel's sons persisted. Pieter II specialized in scenes of peasant life and exploited their burlesque possibilities, while in his landscapes Jan Bruegel the Younger stressed the poetic aspects of nature, sometimes making them the leading theme of his pictures.

In the works of the artists named above we have all the ingredients of the "genre" painting which achieved its flowering in Flanders in the art of Adriaen Brouwer and David Teniers the Younger, as in Holland with Adriaen van Ostade. That very great artist Adriaen Brouwer had a personality so rich and independent that it is hard to say whether he properly belongs to the Flemish or to the Dutch School. We do best, perhaps, to regard him as a connecting link between the two, and in fact he spent much of his short life in Holland. However, since the Flemish vein predominates in the best of his work, we are justified in regarding him as one of the brilliant generation of artists shaped in Antwerp.

Brouwer was born in Flanders in 1605 or 1606, at Audenarde, his father being a designer of tapestry cartoons for the local factories. Adriaen, who ran away from home at sixteen, is thought to have received his early training in Antwerp and his first works, treated anecdotally and composed of more or less disjointed fragments with a wealth of vivid colors, are obviously Bruegelian in inspiration. In 1625 we find him in Amsterdam, then in Haarlem where he worked in the studio of Frans Hals, whose alert, spontaneous touch he skillfully assimilated. After qualifying as a free master in 1631-1632 he led an erratic life in Antwerp, often in conditions of extreme poverty, but meanwhile turned out a quite amazing quantity of work. Brouwer's career was one long struggle against adversity, he was always in debt and in 1633 was incarcerated for some months in the citadel. Nevertheless he went on working while in confinement and even found time to give painting lessons to the prison baker Joos van Craesbeeck, who subsequently made a name for himself as the best of Brouwer's disciples. On several occasions he was befriended by Rubens, who not only showed him much kindness but thought highly of him as an artist and bought a number of his works.

Brouwer's pictures are always of small dimensions: scenes in village taverns, brawls of peasants and gamblers tippling and smoking in sordid hovels. But the subjects were merely pretexts, he did not pick on them for their intrinsic interest or linger over anecdotal elements; his aim was always to depict humanity in the raw and the elemental facts of life. During his Antwerp period, when he developed a personal style, without any trace of caricature or over-insistence on the picturesque detail, he created an œuvre whose significance and scope form a remarkable contrast with the small size of his pictures and the apparent triviality of their subjects. He concentrates on a few figures, sometimes treated separately, and his rendering of faces in well-marked planes gives them a remarkable monumentality. Everyday reality is charged with magical overtones, tragedy mingled with hilarity. The bare, grimy wall of a hovel becomes a finely shaded monochrome backdrop bringing out the delicious blue of a rough peasant smock, the red of a draggled cap, the brownish grey of a pitcher, the green or brown of an earthenware pot. Though the figures are ignoble and the domestic utensils of the humblest description, roughly made and devoid of any elegance of form, the colors enveloping them have a softly glowing sheen, without emphasis or sparkle, and are of such exquisite delicacy that squalor is transmuted into beauty. Brouwer's forthright, fluid execution has affinities with that of Rubens' sketches. And we find no less vitality, combined with fine precision, in his pen-and-ink drawings.

Adriaen Brouwer (1605/06-1638).

Card Players. (13×17″) Alte Pinakothek, Munich.

Adriaen Brouwer (1605/06-1638).

Peasants drinking in a Courtyard, c. 1631-1632. (10×8¼″)

Musées Royaux des Beaux-Arts, Brussels.

His psychological approach to his characters is equally original. He depicts the most unprepossessing creatures with a humor that is far from ruling out fellow-feeling and kindly comprehension. For the artist had much in common with his models; he shared their plight, for he too was one of life's misfits and capable of acts of brutal violence; yet we feel that he was always haunted by dreams of better things. He never judges, never sermonizes, never moralizes; all he does is to record, with a rare perfection, what no previous artist had thought worthy of his brush. Towards the close of his life he took to painting landscapes and in these he reveals, perhaps, his deepest feelings. Thus in the wonderful *Landscape in Moonlight* (Berlin) there is a curiously haunting beauty in the human figures engaged in some mysterious colloquy, the moonlit dunes, and that dazzling white of the sky which rivals Gossart at his most dramatic. Of all time and no time, this strange work is at a far remove from the artificial lighting of the Caravaggeschi, and in some respects prefigures Daumier.

As was only to be expected, Brouwer's disciples and imitators found it hard to grasp the deeper implications of his art. They merely took over the more picturesque aspects of his subjects, adding piquant details, novel turns of expression or moralistic innuendos. In their execution, too, they were far less successful in achieving that unity of atmosphere in which the master excelled. Craesbeeck's small touches of vivid color are discordant and the efforts of David Ryckaert (1612-1661), third of the name, to enlarge the compositional field and bring more air into it, were clumsily conceived and in the main abortive.

The only artist to make a truly personal approach to genre painting was David Teniers the Younger and in at least two branches of art—landscape and still life—he displayed true originality. Born in 1610, he came of a family of artists and married one of Jan Bruegel's daughters, Rubens' ward. He began his career in Antwerp but in 1651 was summoned to Brussels by Archduke Leopold William, Governor of the Spanish Netherlands, who made him his official painter. The art-loving Archduke commissioned Teniers to get together a collection of pictures for the Ducal Gallery; many of these subsequently found their way to the Kunsthistorisches Museum, Vienna. Teniers made a sort of pictorial catalogue of the Duke's art treasures in his pictures of Leopold William visiting his gallery (Vienna and Brussels). In 1662 Teniers bought the "Château of the Three Towers" at Perck, near Brussels (of which there is a picture in the National Gallery, London), and he died there in 1690.

He began by keeping to Bruegel's themes and by following the Flemish tradition perfected by that master, but he also showed no hesitation about going still further back, to Bosch and his *diableries*. But his depictions of alchemists and his "Temptations of St Anthony" are singularly innocuous, not to say bowdlerized, versions of the weird imaginings of his great forerunner. Louis Gillet has said of him that he "purged the genre scene of its grossness." That, however, is hardly to his credit since, handled in this way, his low life scenes lose much of the astringent flavor we find in Brouwer's work. There are far too many needless accessories in Teniers' pictures of taverns, soldiers' guardrooms and kitchens, and they are usually overcrowded. But when he turns to more congenial subjects, his habit of viewing things and people from the outside, with amiable indifference, saves him from any obsession with the anecdotal element, and he can concentrate his efforts on the actual execution. Slighter and daintier than Brouwer's, his forms have a charm of their own, in keeping with the social milieu he depicts, that of the prosperous middle class. Teniers' scenes of home life foreshadow those of the next century. Lively little figures disport themselves in well-appointed interiors where silvery gleams enliven the plain monochrome walls. Here Teniers aims at more than mere entertainment; these works are a visual commentary on the manners of the day. He has a flair for the significant placing of accessories and the best parts of his compositions are often mere "impressionist" suggestions—as when a picture relieves the monotony of a wall with some blurred but well-placed patches of color. (Even Vermeer, though handling it with more precision, did not employ this motif to better effect.) In his *Studies of Accessories* (Brussels), where he groups in a delightfully natural way a disorderly pile of books and a terrestrial globe, Teniers brings out the poetic quality of inanimate objects in a delicate color scheme of greys and browns. His landscapes (of which some hundred are extant) are handled

Adriaen Brouwer (1605/06-1638).

Landscape in Moonlight, c. 1635-1637. (9⅞×13½″) Kaiser Friedrich Museum, Berlin.

in much the same way as Brouwer's, merely picturesque details being ruled out, colors limited in number, planes much simplified. Again like Brouwer, Teniers often chooses for his subject a lonely cottage in a bare countryside veiled in evening dusk. Usually there are two or three finely rendered figures of peasants in the foreground and chromatic unity is ensured by the use of two dominant colors, brown and grey.

The uncompromisingly modern trends apparent in these two artists' handling of landscape and still life were bound to make the works of those who still clung to the old tradition seem hopelessly outmoded. Hence the archaistic effect of those exquisitely painted flower and banquet pieces, with butterflies and insects, in which so many Flemish still-life artists continued to exploit formulas dating to the beginning of the century. Only one man, Jan Fyt (1611-1661), ranks as a master in this field; a pupil of Frans Snyders, he lightened the texture of his teacher's cumbrous compositions by grouping the picture elements in a much freer way and stressing only such as lent themselves to interesting effects.

Nor need we linger on the huge mythologies of Frans Wouters (1612-1659) or on the landscapes of Jacques d'Artois (1613-1686?), excellent as are his renderings of the Brabant countryside. The works of both artists are at once conventional and basically decorative.

Mention must, however, be made of the work of an Antwerp painter, Jan Siberechts (1627-1703?), which, while quite unpretentious, bears the stamp of fine sincerity. He stood outside the main current of the time and painted as if Rubens had never lived. Rejecting the Baroque conception of landscape, he built up static compositions, in which both scenery and figures seem to be taking part in a tranquil celebration of the beauties of nature—hence Paul Fierens' description of him as "a sort of Flemish Le Nain." In a carefully planned décor of fields and rivers fringed with willows he places healthy, convincingly natural countryfolk, herds of cattle, carts, buxom peasant women lifting their skirts to wade across a ford. Disdaining the artifice of oblique illumination, he places forms under a light falling directly from above; with the result that volumes are accentuated and figures acquire a sculpturesque solidity. Still, it cannot be denied that the inner life we sense in Le Nain's stately peasant women is sadly absent; these have more in common with Courbet's heavily built matrons. Siberechts had little imagination and persistently reverted to the same themes. He also painted farmyards, and here the composition is more crowded and darker in tone. He moved to England in 1672 and while in that country specialized in the topographical landscape and somewhat pompous views of castles.

Implicit in these 17th-century works, whatever their nature and however limited their scope, we find constructive elements and effects of atmosphere destined to play a vital part in the great flowering of painting that took place a century and a half later. In them we have the sunset glow of Flemish art before it lapsed into a long quiescence, but not before confiding to the soil of Western Europe the seeds of a magnificent renewal.

David Teniers the Younger (1610-1690).

Study of Accessories, c. 1645-1650. (20½×27″) Musées Royaux des Beaux-Arts, Brussels.

BIBLIOGRAPHY
INDEX OF NAMES
LIST OF COLORPLATES

BIBLIOGRAPHY

GENERAL

L. GUICCIARDINI, *Descrittione di tutti i Paesi Bassi*, Antwerp 1567 (French translation, *Description de touts les Pays-Bas*, Amsterdam 1625). — LAMPSONIUS, *Pictorum aliquot celebrium Germaniae inferioris Effigies*, Antwerp 1572. — G. P. LOMAZZO, *Trattato della Pittura, Scultura et Architettura*, 1585. — C. VAN MANDER, *Het Schilderboeck*, Haarlem 1604 (French translation by H. HYMANS, *Le Livre des Peintres*, 1884; English translation in C. VAN DE WALL, *Dutch and Flemish Painters*, New York 1936). — G. GEVARTIUS and T. VAN THULDEN, *Pompa triomphalis introitus H. S. Principis Ferdinandi Austriaci*, Antwerp 1642. — G. P. BELLORI, *Le Vite dei Pittori, Scultori, Architetti moderni*, Rome 1672. — Joachim VON SANDRART, *Teutsche Academie*, Nuremberg 1675. — Roger DE PILES, *Dissertations sur les ouvrages des plus fameux peintres avec la vie de Rubens*, Paris 1681. — A. FÉLIBIEN, *Entretiens sur les vies et sur les ouvrages des plus excellents peintres anciens et modernes*, Paris 1685. — Roger DE PILES, *Abrégé de la vie des peintres avec des réflexions sur leurs ouvrages*, Paris 1699. — J. B. DESCAMPS, *La vie des peintres flamands, allemands et hollandais*, Paris 1753. — P. GUARIENTI, *Abecedario pittorico d'Orlandi*, Venice 1753. — *Description des principaux ouvrages de peinture et de sculpture actuelles existant dans les églises, couvents et lieux publics d'Anvers*, Antwerp 1774. — J. B. DESCAMPS, *Voyage pittoresque de la Flandre et du Brabant*, Paris 1792. — J. SMITH, *A Catalogue Raisonné of the Works of the most eminent Dutch, Flemish and French Painters*, London 1833. — C. KRAMM, *De Levens en Werken der Hollandsche en Vlaamsche Kunstschilders*, Amsterdam 1856-1863. — C. BLANC, *Histoire des Peintres, école flamande*, Paris 1864. — P. ROMBOUTS and T. VAN LERIUS, *Les Liggeren et autres archives historiques de la Guilde anversoise de Saint-Luc*, Antwerp 1864-1876. — E. FÉTIS, *Les artistes belges à l'étranger*, Brussels 1865. — A. MICHIELS, *Histoire de la Peinture flamande*, Paris 1865-1878, 11 vols. — C. NARREY, *Voyage d'Albert Dürer dans les Pays-Bas, écrit par lui-même pendant les années 1520 et 1521*, Gazette des Beaux-Arts, Paris, October 1865, February 1866. — J. A. CROWE and G. B. CAVALCASELLE, *The Early Flemish Painters*, London 1872. — E. FROMENTIN, *Les maîtres d'autrefois*, Paris 1876 (English edition, *The Masters of Past Time*, Phaidon, London 1948). — E. NEEFFS, *Histoire de la Peinture et de la Sculpture à Malines*, Ghent 1876. — T. VAN LERIUS, *Biographies d'artistes anversois*, Antwerp 1880. — F. J. VAN DEN BRANDEN, *Geschiedenis der Antwerpsche Schilderschool*, Antwerp 1883. — A. WAUTERS, *La peinture flamande*, Paris 1883. — A. MICHEL, *Histoire de l'Art*, Paris 1905-1929: vol. V, Ist part, chapter V, *La Peinture dans les Pays-Bas, depuis les successeurs des Van Eyck et de Roger van der Weyden jusque dans la seconde moitié du XVIe siècle* (by L. DE FOURCAUD); idem, vol. VI, Ist part, chapter VII, *La Peinture dans les Pays-Bas au XVIIIe siècle* (by Louis GILLET), — H. PIRENNE, *Histoire de Belgique*, vols. II, III, Brussels 1907. — THIEME-BECKER, *Allgemeines Lexikon der bildenden Künstler*, Leipzig 1907-1950. — H. WÖLFFLIN, *Kunstgeschichtliche Grundbegriffe*, Munich 1915 (English edition, *Principles of Art History*, London 1929; French edition, *Principes fondamentaux de l'Histoire de l'Art*, Paris 1952). — M. J. FRIEDLÄNDER, *Von van Eyck bis Brueghel*, Berlin 1921 (English edition, *From Van Eyck to Bruegel*, Phaidon, London 1956). — R. OLDENBURG, *Die flämische Malerei des 17. Jahrhunderts*, Berlin-Leipzig 1922. — FIERENS-GEVAERT, *La Peinture à Bruges*, Brussels 1922. — FIERENS-GEVAERT, *La peinture au Musée ancien de Bruxelles*, Brussels 1923. — F. WINKLER, *Die altniederländische Malerei*, Berlin 1924. — J. HUIZINGA, *The Waning of the Middle Ages*, London 1924. — M. J. FRIEDLÄNDER, in *Repertorium für Kunstwissenschaft*, XLVI, 1915. — A. WEBER, *Histoire de la philosophie européenne*. Paris 1925. — M. J. FRIEDLÄNDER, *Die altniederländische Malerei*, vols. V, VII, VIII, IX, XI, XII, XIII, XIV, Berlin-Leyden 1924-1937. — H. HYMANS, *L'art dans les Pays-Bas*, Brussels 1926. — *Trésors de l'art flamand du Moyen Age au XVIIIe siècle par un groupe de spécialistes* (Antwerp Memorial Exhibition, 1930), 2 vols., Brussels 1932. — A. VON SCHNEIDER, *Caravaggio und die Niederländer*, Munich 1933. — A. J. J. DELEN, *Histoire de la gravure dans les Anciens Pays-Bas*, Brussels 1935. — WERF, *Vlaamsche Kunst en Italiaansche Renaissance*, Malines 1935. — R. SCHNEIDER and G. COHEN, *La formation du génie moderne dans l'art d'Occident*, Paris 1936. — H. PIRENNE, *Histoire de l'Europe, des invasions au XVIe siècle*, Paris 1936. — W. KRÖNIG, *Der italienische Einfluss in der flämischen Malerei im ersten Drittel des 16. Jahrhunderts*, Würzburg 1936. — J. LAVALLEYE and A. VERMEYEN, in *Geschiedenis van de Vlaamsche Kunst*, Antwerp 1936-1937. — J. A. GORIS and G. MARLIER, *A. Dürer, Journal de voyage dans les Pays-Bas*, Brussels 1937. — H. FOCILLON, *Art d'Occident*, Paris 1938. — L. VENTURI, *Histoire de la critique d'art*, Brussels 1938. — G. MARLIER, *La Peinture au XVIe siècle* and A. J. J. DELEN, *La Peinture au XVIIe siècle*, in *L'Art en Belgique du moyen âge à nos jours*, published under the direction of P. FIERENS, Brussels 1939. — A. LHOTE, *Traité du paysage*, Paris 1939. — E. MICHEL, *La Peinture flamande au XVIIe siècle*, Paris 1939. — A. BLUNT, *Artistic Theory in Italy 1400-1600*, London 1940. — L. FEBVRE, *Le Problème de l'Incroyance au XVIe siècle*, Paris 1942. — G. J. HOOGEWERFF, *De Noord-Nederlandsche Schilderkunst*, The Hague 1939 (1942). — P. FIERENS, *L'Art flamand*, Paris 1945. — P. FIERENS, *Le fantastique dans l'art flamand*, Brussels 1947. — C. BRANDI, *Carmine o della Pittura*, Florence 1947. — H. B. WEHLE and M. SALINGER, *Catalogue of Early Flemish, Dutch and German Paintings*, Metropolitan Museum, New York 1947. — E. BAIE, *Le Siècle des Gueux*, Brussels 1947-1948. — H. VAN DER TUIN, *Les vieux peintres des Pays-Bas et la critique artistique en France dans la première moitié du XIXe siècle*, Paris 1948. — J. HUIZINGA, *Renaissance en Realisme, Verzamelde Werken*, Haarlem 1949. — *Dictionnaire des peintres*, preface by P. FIERENS, notices on the Flemish painters of the 16th and 17th centuries by R. L. DELEVOY, P. FIERENS and Edith GREINDL, Brussels 1950. — H. SÉE and A. RÉBILLON, *Le XVIe siècle*, Paris 1950. — A. GERLO, *Erasme et ses portraitistes*, Brussels 1950. — L. VAN PUYVELDE, *La Peinture flamande à Rome*, Brussels 1950. — A. JANSSENS DE BISTHOVEN and E. A. PARMENTIER, *Le Musée communal de Bruges*, Antwerp 1951. — P. FRANCASTEL, *Peinture et société*, Lyons 1951. — S. BERGMANS, *La Peinture ancienne*, Brussels 1952. — C. STERLING, *La nature morte de l'Antiquité à nos jours*, Paris 1952. — L. VAN PUYVELDE, *Le Siècle des Van Eyck*, Brussels 1953. — M. DUFRENNE, *Phénoménologie de l'expérience esthétique*, Paris 1953. — J. LAVALLEYE, *Répertoire des peintures flamandes des XVe et XVIe siècles: collections d'Espagne*, Antwerp 1953. — E. PANOFSKY, *Early Netherlandish Painting*, Cambridge, Mass. 1953. — E. MICHEL, *Catalogue raisonné des peintures flamandes des XVe et XVIe siècles*, Musées nationaux, Paris 1954. — R. GENAILLE, *La peinture dans les anciens Pays-Bas, De Van Eyck à*

Bruegel, Paris 1954. — Martin DAVIES, *Les Primitifs flamands: The National Gallery of London*, Antwerp 1954, 2 vols. — G. MARLIER, *Erasme et la peinture flamande de son temps*, Damme 1954. — J. BALTRU-ŠAITIS, *Le moyen âge fantastique*, Paris 1955. — M. L. HAIRS, *Les peintres flamands de fleurs au XVIIe siècle*, Brussels 1955. — A. CHASTEL, *La « Manière » italienne*, L'Œil N° 6, Lausanne 1955. — S. SULZBERGER, *L'influence de Léonard de Vinci et ses répercussions à Anvers*, Arte Lombarda I, 1955. — L. VENTURI, *The Sixteenth Century, From Leonardo to El Greco*, Geneva 1956. — E. GREINDL, *Les peintres flamands de nature morte au XVIIe siècle*, Brussels 1956. — J. LEYMARIE, *Dutch Painting*, Geneva 1956. — M. J. FRIEDLÄNDER, *From Van Eyck to Bruegel*, London 1956. — S. SPETH-HOLTERHOFF, *Les peintres flamands de cabinets d'amateurs*, Brussels 1957. — J. LASSAIGNE, *Flemish Painting, The Century of Van Eyck*, Geneva 1957.

CHAPTER I

BOSCH: MASTER OF THE FANTASTIC

M. G. GOSSART, *Jérôme Bosch, « Le Faiseur de Diables » de Bois-le-Duc*, Lille 1907. — P. LAFOND, *Hieronymus Bosch*, Brussels 1914. — M. J. FRIEDLÄNDER, *Die altniederländische Malerei, Geertgen und Bosch*, vol. V, Berlin 1927. — C. DE TOLNAY, *Hieronymus Bosch*, Basel 1937. — J. DUPONT, *Le retable de saint Antoine du Musée national de Lisbonne*, Paris 1938. — M. BRION, *Jérôme Bosch*, Paris 1938. — L. BALDASS, *Zur künstlerischen Entwicklung des Hieronymus Bosch*, Annuaire des Musées royaux des Beaux-Arts, Brussels 1938. — *A Great Jerome Bosch for San Diego: Christ taken in Captivity*, Art News, December 1938. — L. LEBEER, *Het Hooi en de Hooiwagen in de Beeldende Kunsten*, Gentsche Bijdragen tot de Kunstgeschiedenis, Ghent 1938. — J. GRAULS, *Taalkundige toelichting bij het Hooi en de Hooiwagen*, Gentsche Bijdragen tot de Kunstgeschiedenis, Ghent 1938. — A. VERMEYLEN, *Hieronymus Bosch*, Amsterdam 1939. — J. G. VAN GELDER, *Teekeningen van Jeroen Bosch*, Beeldende Kunst, N° 8, 1941. — L. BALDASS, *Hieronymus Bosch*, Vienna 1943. — L. VAN DEN BOSSCHE, *Jérôme Bosch*, Diest 1944. — A.T.W. BELLEMANS, *Tondalus' Visioen*, Antwerp 1945. — J. COMBE, *Jérôme Bosch*, Paris 1946 (revised edition Paris 1957; in English, Paris 1946 and 1957). — J. DE BOSSCHÈRE, *Jérôme Bosch*, Brussels 1947. — W. FRAENGER, *Hieronymus Bosch, Das Tausendjährige Reich*, Coburg 1947 (English translation, *The Millennium of Hieronymus Bosch*, Chicago 1951 and London 1952). — D. HOWARD, *Hieronymus Bosch*, New York 1947. — J. MOSMANS, *Jheronimus Anthoniszoon van Aken, alias Hieronymus Bosch, Zijn leven en zijn werk,*'s Hertogenbosch 1947. — J. V. L. BRANS, *El Bosco en el Prado y en el Escorial*, Barcelona 1948. — W. FRAENGER, *Hieronymus Bosch: Johannes der Täufer*, Zeitschrift für Kunst 1948, pp. 163-175. — H. J. M. EBELING, *J. van Aken*, Miscellanea J. Gessler, 1948. — G. VAN CAMP, *Considérations sur le paysage de Jérôme Bosch*, Miscellanea Leo van Puyvelde, Brussels 1949. — J. LEYMARIE, *Jérôme Bosch*, Paris 1949. — D. BAX, *Ontcijfering van Jeroen Bosch*, The Hague 1949. — A. PIGLER, *Astrology and Jerome Bosch*, Burlington Magazine, May 1950. — W. VOGELSANG, *Hieronymus Bosch*, Amsterdam 1951. — C. JANSON, *Le « Christ en Croix » de Jérôme Bosch*, Bulletin des Musées royaux des Beaux-Arts, 1, Brussels 1952. — W. FRAENGER, *Hieronymus Bosch, der verlorene Sohn*, Cristianesimo e Ragione di Stato, Rome 1952. — L. BRAND PHILIP, *The Prado Epiphany by Jerome Bosch*, The Art Bulletin XXXV, 4, 1953. — R. H. WILENSKI, *Hieronymus Bosch*, London 1953. — G. DORFLES, *Bosch*, Milan

1954. — L. VAN PUYVELDE, *De Geest van Hieronymus Bosch*, Revue belge d'Archéologie et d'Histoire de l'art, 1954, p. 238. — G. VAN CAMP, *Autonomie de Jérôme Bosch et récentes interprétations de ses œuvres*, Bulletin des Musées royaux des Beaux-Arts, 3, Brussels 1954. — L. BRAND PHILIP, *Hieronymus Bosch*, 1955. — J. V. L. BRANS, *Los Ermitanos de Jeronimo Bosco, San Juan Bautista en el desierto*, Goya, 4, Madrid 1955. — C. D. CUTTLER, *The Lisbon Temptation of St Anthony by Jerome Bosch*, The Art Bulletin XXXIX, 2, 1957. — Id., *Witchcraft in a Work by Bosch*, The Art Quarterly XX, 2, 1957. — O. BENESCH, Konsthistorisk tidskrift, Stockholm 1957. — K. G. BOON, *De eerste bloei van de Noord-nederlandse Kunst*, preface to the catalogue of the exhibition *Middeleeuwse Kunst der Noordelijke Nederlanden*, Amsterdam 1958. — L. BRAND PHILIP, *Hieronymus Bosch*, Nederlandsche Kunst Jaarboek 1958.

For the evolution of Flemish landscape painting, see also the general works listed in the bibliography for Chapter V (p. 190).

Patinir: G. J. HOOGEWERFF, *Joachim Patinir in Italie*, Onze Kunst I, 1926. — H. B. WEHLE, *A Triptych by Patinir*, Bulletin of the Metropolitan Museum, New York 1936.

Herri Met de Bles: E. LARSEN, *Quelques notes à propos de Herry de Patenier et Henri Blès*, Oud Holland I, 1940. — F. COURTOY, *Henri Blès de Bouvignes*, Namurcum, 1947. — M. J. FRIEDLÄNDER, *Noch einmal: Herry Met de Bles-Herry de Patenier?*, Oud Holland, 1949. — A. DASNOY, *Henri Blès, peintre de la réalité et de la fantaisie*, Etudes d'histoire et d'archéologie namuroises, 2, 1952. — A. DUPONT, *Note sur le Saint Jérôme de H. Blès*, Etudes d'histoire et d'archéologie namuroises, 1952. — R. A. KOCH, *The Road to Calvary by Herry met de Bles*, Princeton University, Museum of Historic Art 2, 1955.

Matthys, Hieronymus and Lucas Cock: G. J. HOOGEWERFF, *Matthys Wellens de Cock en Hans Dooven Keynoogh*, Mededelingen van het nederlandsch historisch Institut te Rome, V, 1935. — M. J. FRIEDLÄNDER, *Jan de Cock oder Lucas Koch*, Miscellanea Leo van Puyvelde, Brussels 1949. — K. G. BOON, *De Tekenaar van het Errera-Schetsboek*, Miscellanea E. Panofsky, Brussels 1955.

Peeter Huys: E. MICHEL, *Peeter Huys au Musée du Louvre*, Gazette des Beaux-Arts, II, 1935. — E. MICHEL, *Une Tentation de saint Antoine par Peeter Huys*, Bulletin des Musées de France, November 1935. — E. P. RICHARDSON, *Peeter Huys*, Bulletin of the Detroit Institute of Art, March 1938. — R. L. DELEVOY, *Peeter Huys*, Actes du Congrès d'Histoire de l'Art, London 1939. — R. L. DELEVOY, *Une étude de Peeter Huys au Musée de Bruxelles*, Apollo, 14, Brussels 1942.

Jan Mandyn: Grete RING, *Der Meister des Verlorenen Sohnes, Jan Mandijn und Lenaert Kroes*, Jahrbuch für Kunstwissenschaft, Leipzig 1923.

CHAPTER II

BRUEGEL: MAN'S PLACE IN THE UNIVERSE

R. VAN BASTELAER and G. HULIN DE LOO, *Pierre Bruegel l'Ancien*, Brussels 1907. — R. VAN BASTELAER, *Les Estampes de Pierre Bruegel l'Ancien*, Brussels 1908. — C. BERNARD, *Pierre Brueghel l'Ancien*, Brussels 1908. — M. J. FRIEDLÄNDER, *Pieter Bruegel*, Berlin 1921. — K. TOLNAI, *Die Zeichnungen Pieter Bruegels*, Munich 1924 (revised and enlarged edition in English: *The Drawings of Pieter Bruegel the Elder*, New York and London 1952). — F. TIMMERMANS, *Pierre Bruegel*, Brussels 1927. — F. CRUCY, *Les Bruegel*, Paris 1928. — E. MICHEL, *Bruegel*, Paris 1931. — C. DE TOLNAY, *Pierre Bruegel l'Ancien*, Brussels 1935. — G. GLÜCK,

Bruegels Gemälde, Vienna 1935 (English edition, *The Large Bruegel Book*, Vienna 1952). — M. BRION, *Bruegel*, Paris 1936. — P. COLIN, *Bruegel le Vieux*, Paris 1936. — M. J. FRIEDLÄNDER, *Pieter Bruegel*, Leyden 1937. — L. VAN PUYVELDE, *Un nouveau Massacre des Innocents de Pierre Bruegel l'Ancien*, Annuaire des Musées royaux des Beaux-Arts, Brussels 1938. — C. DE TOLNAY, *La seconde Tour de Babel de Pierre l'Ancien*, Annuaire des Musées royaux des Beaux-Arts, Brussels 1938. — E. MICHEL, *Bruegel et la critique moderne*, Gazette des Beaux-Arts I, 1938. — G. JEDLICKA, *Pieter Bruegel, Der Maler in seiner Zeit*, Zurich 1938 (new edition, 1947). — J. GRAULS, *Uit Bruegels Spreekwoorden*, Annuaire des Musées royaux des Beaux-Arts, Brussels 1939. — L. LEBEER, *De Blauwe Huyck*, Gentsche Bijdragen tot de Kunstgeschiedenis, VI, Ghent 1939-1940. — L. LEBEER, *Nog enkele wetenswaardigheden in verband met Pieter Bruegel den Oude*, Gentsche Bijdragen tot de Kunstgeschiedenis, IX, Ghent 1943. — G. GLÜCK, *Pieter Bruegel the Elder and Classical Antiquity*, Art Quarterly VI, 1943. — P. MINNAERT, *Essai d'interprétation de la Dulle Griet de P. Bruegel*, Apollo, 22, Brussels 1943. — W. VAN BESELAERE, *Pieter Bruegel en het Nederlandsche manierisme*, Tielt 1944. — L. VAN PUYVELDE, *Pieter Bruegel, The Dulle Griet*, London 1945. — A. J. BARNOUW, *The Fantasy of Pieter Bruegel*, New York 1947. — F. NOVOTNY, *Die Monatsbilder Pieter Bruegels*, Vienna 1948. — Special number of Les Arts Plastiques, 11-12, Brussels 1948: articles by G. GLÜCK, *Le paysage avec la Fuite en Egypte de Pierre Bruegel le Vieux*; J. COMBE, *Jérôme Bosch dans l'art de Pierre Bruegel*; C. DE TOLNAY, *"Le peintre et l'amateur" de P. Bruegel le Vieux*; E. MICHEL, *Bruegel ou non Bruegel*; L. VON BALDASS, *Les paysanneries de Pierre Bruegel*. — P. FIERENS, *Sur la "Tempête" de Bruegel*, Miscellanea J. Gessler, 1948. — R. VERDEYEN, *Bruegel en de dialektgeografie*, Miscellanea J. Gessler, 1948. — L. LEBEER, *La kermesse d'Hoboken*, Miscellanea Leo van Puyvelde, Brussels 1949. — A. J. BARNOUW, *Bruegels Verzoeking van den heiligen Antonius*, Miscellanea Leo van Puyvelde, Brussels 1949. — A. L. ROMDAHL, *Le style figuré de P. Brueghel*, Miscellanea Leo van Puyvelde, Brussels 1949. — L. LEBEER, *Propos sur les dessins de Bruegel le Vieux*, Les Beaux-Arts, 445, Brussels 1949. — P. FIERENS, *Pierre Bruegel, sa vie, son temps*, Paris 1949. — G. GLÜCK, *Peter Bruegel the Elder and the Legend of St Christopher in Early Flemish Painting*, Art Quarterly, XIII, Detroit 1950. — W. FISCHER, *Peter Bruegel's "Winterlandschaft", ein Blick auf die Amraser Gefilde im Jahre 1553*, Veröffentlichungen Museum Ferdinandeum, 31, Berlin 1951. — C. DE TOLNAY, *The Drawings of Pieter Bruegel the Elder*, New York and London 1952. — F. GROSSMANN, *Bruegel's "Woman taken in Adultery" and other Grisailles*, Burlington Magazine, 94, 1952. — R. GENAILLE, *Bruegel l'Ancien*, Paris 1953. — G. FAGGIN, *Brueghel*, Verona 1953. — C. BOSSUS, *Sur la date de naissance de Brueghel le Vieux*, Gazette des Beaux-Arts 41, Paris 1953. — L. VON BALDASS, *La tendenza moralizzante in Bosch e Bruegel*, Cristianesimo e ragione di Stato, L'Umanesimo e il demoniaco nell'arte, Milan-Rome 1953. — C. G. STRIDBECK, *Bruegel und der niederländische Romanismus*, Stockholm 1953. — G. VAN CAMP, *Pierre Bruegel a-t-il peint une série des Sept Péchés Capitaux?*, Revue belge d'Archéologie et d'Histoire de l'Art, 23, Brussels 1954. — H. SHIPP, *The original "Winter Landscape with a Birdtrap" by Bruegel in the collection of M. A. Hassid*, Apollo, 59, London 1954. — R. KLIMOW, *P. Brueghel*, Moscow 1954. — O. BUYSSENS, *De schepen bij Pieter Brueghel de Oude*, Mededelingen der Academie van Marine van België 8, 1954. — C. G. STRIDBECK, *Bruegels Fidesdarstellung. Ein Dokument seiner religiösen Gesinnung*,

Konsthistorisk Tidskrift, 23, Stockholm 1954. — L. LEBEER, *Le Pays de Cocagne (Het Luilekkerland)*, Miscellanea E. Panofsky, Brussels 1955. — C. DE TOLNAY, *Unknown Early Panel by Pieter Bruegel the Elder*, Burlington Magazine, 1955. — G. C. ARGAN, *Cultura e Realismo di Pietro Bruegel*, Letteratura 15-16, Rome 1955. — F. GROSSMANN, *Bruegel, The Paintings*, London 1955. — J. BIALOSTOCKI, *Bruegel*, Poznan 1956. — F. GROSSMANN, *Tutta la pittura di Bruegel*, Florence 1956. — C. DE TOLNAY, *Une vue d'Anvers de Pierre Bruegel l'Ancien?*, Gazette des Beaux-Arts 2, 1957.

CHAPTER III

FROM MASSYS TO MANNERISM

W. COHEN, *Studien zu Quentin Matsys*, Bonn 1904. — J. DE BOSSCHÈRE, *Quentin Metsys*, Brussels 1907. — H. BRISING, *Quinten Matsys und der Ursprung des Italianismus in der Kunst der Niederlande*, Leipzig 1908. — H. BRISING, *Quentin Metsys*, Upsala 1909. — A. J. J. DELEN, *Metsys*, Brussels 1929. — M. J. FRIEDLÄNDER, *Metsys, Die altniederländische Malerei*, vol. VII, Leyden 1939. — F. PRIMS, *Antwerpiensa, Quinten Massijs in de Kempen*, IV, Antwerp 1931. — J. DE FIGUEIREDO, *Metsys e Portugal*, Mélanges Hulin de Loo, Brussels 1931. — F. PRIMS, *Drie ascetische schrijvers der Throonpriorij: Storm, Roecx, Bellens*, Koninklijke Vlaamsche Academie voor Taal- en Letterkunde, Verslagen en Mededelingen, Brussels 1932. — M. J. FRIEDLÄNDER, *Quentin Massys, Reflexions on his Development*, Burlington Magazine, 72, 1932. — L. VON BALDASS, *Gotik und Renaissance im Werke des Quinten Massys*, Jahrbuch der Kunsthistorischen Sammlungen, Vienna 1933. — J. DE FIGUEIREDO, *Metsys et le Portugal*, Revue belge d'Archéologie et d'Histoire de l'Art, III, Brussels 1933. — L. REIS SANTOS, *A lost work of Massys and a hitherto unknown Van der Goes*, Burlington Magazine 75, 1939. — H. ROOSEN-RUNGE, *Die Gestaltung der Farbe bei Quentin Metsys*, Munich 1940. — L. REIS SANTOS, *Quentin Metsys, seus discipulos e continuadores em Portugal*, Panorama II, Lisbon 1942. — K. G. BOON, *Quinten Massys*, Amsterdam 1942. — Grete RING, *Additions to the Works of Jan Provost and Quentin Massys*, Burlington Magazine, 80, 1942. — C. DE MAEYER, *L'iconographie de Cranach, la Parenté de la Vierge*, Apollo, 8, Brussels 1942. — W. VAN BESELAERE, *Quinten Metsys*, Gentsche Bijdragen tot de Kunstgeschiedenis, Ghent 1943. — A. GERLO, *Erasmus en Quinten Metsijs*, Revue belge d'Archéologie et d'Histoire de l'Art, XIV, Brussels, 1944. — L. VAN PUYVELDE, *Le retable de Sainte-Anne de Quentin Metsys*, Les Arts Plastiques, 5-6, Brussels 1947. — E. K. WATERHOUSE, *An unnoticed Quentin Massys*, Burlington Magazine, October 1947. — M. J. FRIEDLÄNDER, *Quentin Metsys as a Painter of Genre*, Burlington Magazine, May 1947. — A. C. SEWETR, *A Portrait by Quentin Massys at the Barber Institute, Birmingham*, Gazette des Beaux-Arts, 1948. — L. REIS SANTOS, *Le Portrait de saint Bernardin de Sienne par Quentin Metsys*, Lisbon 1949. — L. REIS SANTOS, *Obras Primas da Pintura Flamenga dos seculos XV e XVI em Portugal*, Lisbon 1953. — L. REIS SANTOS, *Catalogo de Arte flamenga da secolo XVI*, Coimbra 1954. — A. DE LAET, *Quinten Massys, Voorgeslacht, leven en kunst*, De Schakel, 9, 1954.

Jan Gossart: M. GOSSART, *Jean Gossart de Maubeuge*, Lille 1902. — E. WEISZ, *Jan Gossart genannt Mabuse*, 1913. — A. SEGARD, *Jean Gossart*, Brussels 1924. — M. J. FRIEDLÄNDER, *Gossart, Die altniederländische Malerei*, vol. VIII, Leyden 1930. — W. KRÖNIG, *Zur Frühzeit Jan Gossarts*, Zeitschrift für Kunstgeschichte III, 1934. — J. G. VAN GELDER, *Jan Gossart in Rome, 1508-1509*, Oud Holland 1942. —

G. GLÜCK, *Mabuse and the Development of the Flemish Renaissance*, Art Quarterly, VIII, Detroit 1945. — P. FIERENS, *"Vénus et l'Amour" de Gossart*, Bulletin des Musées royaux des Beaux-Arts, Brussels 1952. — P. FIERENS, *Une nouvelle Madone de Gossart*, Bulletin des Musées royaux des Beaux-Arts, 3, Brussels 1954.

Joos van Cleve: L. VON BALDASS, *Joos van Cleve, der Meister des Todes Mariae*, Vienna 1925. — L. VON BALDASS, *Porträts von J. van Cleve*, Zeitschrift für bildende Kunst, 1928-1929. — M. J. FRIEDLÄNDER, *Van Cleve, Die altniederländische Malerei*, vol. IX, Leyden 1931.

Jan Massys: C. MARCENARO, *Ancora Jan Massys al Palazzo Bianco*, Emporium, Bergamo, September 1950.

Bernard van Orley: C. DE MAEYER. *A propos d'un portrait de Marguerite d'Autriche*, Apollo, Brussels, May 1941. — J. LAVALLEYE, J. MAQUET-TOMBU, etc. *Bernard van Orley*, Société royale d'Archéologie, Brussels 1943. — L. VON BALDASS, *Die Entwicklung des Bernard van Orley*, Jahrbuch der Kunsthistorischen Sammlungen, Vienna 1944.

Jan Sanders van Hemessen: F. GRAEFE, *Jan Sanders van Hemessen und seine Identifikation mit dem Braunschweiger Monogrammisten*, Leipzig 1909. — M. J. SCHRELTEN, *Twee werken van Jan Sanders van Hemessen*, Oud Holland, 1937. — L. NINANE, *Van Hemessen*, Actes du Congrès d'Histoire de l'Art, London 1939. — C. DE MAEYER, *Les Peintres de la Réalité*, Apollo, 3, Brussels 1941. — L. VAN PUYVELDE, *Nouvelles œuvres de Jan van Hemessen*, Revue belge d'Archéologie et d'Histoire de l'Art, XX, Brussels 1951.

Pieter Aertsen: J. SIEVERS, *Pieter Aertsen*, Leipzig 1906. — S. BERGMANS, *Deux portraits de Pieter Pieters par son père Pieter Aertsen*, Oud Holland III, 1936. — E. GREINDL, *Einige Stileigentümlichkeiten an den Werken des Pieter Aertsen und des Joachim Beuckelaers*, Pantheon, 1942. — R. GENAILLE, *L'œuvre de Pieter Aertsen*, Gazette des Beaux-Arts, 44, 1954.

Master of the Antwerp Epiphany: P. PHILIPPOT, *Le monogrammiste G, Maître de l'Epiphanie d'Anvers*, Bulletin des Musées royaux des Beaux-Arts, Brussels 1956. — P. VANAISE: *Nadere identiteitsbepaling van de Meester der Antwerpse aanbidding*, Bulletin de l'Institut royal du Patrimoine artistique, I, Brussels, 1958.

CHAPTER IV

THE HUMANIST PORTRAIT

Anthonis Mor: G. MARLIER, *Anthonis Mor van Dashorst*, Brussels 1934. — G. MARLIER, *Nieuwe gegevens omtrent Anthonis Mor*, Gentsche Bijdragen, VIII, Ghent 1942. — L. FRERICHS, *Antonio Moro*, Amsterdam 1947. — H. E. VAN GELDER, *Moro's "Goudsmid"*, Nederlandsch Kunsthistorisch Jaarboek, 1947. — H. B. DE VRIES, *Antonio Moro*, Les Arts Plastiques, 6, Brussels 1953. — H. L. C. JAFFÉ, *Antonio Moro, sa personnalité par rapport au Nord*, Cahiers de Bordeaux, 1954.

Pieter Pourbus: G. MARLIER, *Le maniérisme dans l'art de Pierre Pourbus*, Annuaire des Musées royaux des Beaux-Arts, Brussels 1939. — R. A. D'HULST, *Pieter Pourbus, Portretschilder van de Brugse Burgerij uit de tweede helft der XVIde eeuw*, Gentsche Bijdragen tot de Kunstgeschiedenis, XIII, Ghent 1951.

Other painters: L. VAN PUYVELDE, *"L'enfant à l'oiseau mort", de Juan de Flandes*, Les Arts Plastiques, 7-8, Brussels 1948. — P. PHILIPPOT, *Le Maître du Portrait de Famille d'Anvers*, Bulletin des Musées royaux des Beaux-Arts, 3-4, Brussels 1957.

CHAPTER V

IMAGINATIVE LANDSCAPE

General Works:

E. PLIETZSCH, *Die Frankenthaler Maler, ein Beitrag zur Entwicklungsgeschichte der niederländischen Landschaftsmalerei*, Leipzig 1910. — L. VON BALDASS, *Die niederländische Landschaftsmalerei von Patinir bis Brueghel*, Jahrbuch der Kunsthistorischen Sammlungen XXXIV, 4, 1918. — FIERENS-GEVAERT, *Préface au catalogue de l'Exposition rétrospective du Paysage flamand*, Brussels 1926. — C. STERLING, *Le paysage fantastique néerlandais*, Art Vivant 1930. — J. A. RACZYNSKI, *Die flämische Landschaft vor Rubens*, Frankfort 1937. — A. LAES, *Shorter Notices on Flemish Landscape Art in the Seventeenth Century*, Burlington Magazine XXXV, December 1944. — A. LAES, *Le paysage flamand. Notes, remarques et réflexions*, Miscellanea Leo van Puyvelde, Brussels 1949. — M. J. FRIEDLÄNDER, *Préface au catalogue de l'Exposition Gérard David*, Bruges 1949. — C. LAURIOL, *Les influences réciproques du paysage flamand et du paysage italien pendant la Renaissance*, Les Arts Plastiques, 2, Brussels 1951. — Y. THIÉRY, *Le paysage flamand au XVIIᵉ siècle*, Brussels 1953.

Jan Bruegel: G. CRIVELLI, *Giovanni Bruegel pittore fiammingo, e sue lettere e quadretti esistenti presso l'Ambrosiana*, Milan 1868. — Mgr. VAES, *Le journal de Jean Bruegel II*, Bulletin de l'Institut historique belge de Rome, 1926. — F. CRUCY, *Les Brueghel*, Paris 1928. — J. DENUCÉ, *Brieven en Documenten betreffende Jan Breughel I en II*, Antwerp 1934. — L. VAN PUYVELDE, *Unknown Works by Jan Bruegel*, Burlington Magazine CCCLXVI, July 1934. — J. COMBE, *Breughel de Velours*, Paris 1942.

Gillis van Coninxloo: J. L. SPONSEL, *Gillis van Coninxloo und seine Schule*, Jahrbuch der königl. Preuss. Kunstsammlungen, Berlin 1889. — G. J. HOOGEWERFF, *Een onbekend Landschap van Gillis van Coninxloo*, Onze Kunst XXXV, Antwerp 1919. — A. LAES, *Gilles van Coninxloo, rénovateur du paysage flamand au XVIIᵉ siècle*, Annuaire des Musées royaux des Beaux-Arts, Brussels 1939. — H. WELLENSIEK, *Das Brüsseler "Elias-Bild", ein Werk des Gillis van Coninxloo*, Bulletin des Musées royaux des Beaux-Arts, 3, Brussels 1954.

Roelandt Savery: E. FÉTIS, *Roelandt Savery*, Bulletin de l'Académie royale des Sciences, des Lettres et des Beaux-Arts de Belgique, 1858, 2ᵉ série, IV. — T. VON FRIMMEL, *Roland Savery*, Bamberg 1892. — K. ERASMUS, *Roelandt Savery, sein Leben und seine Werke*, Halle 1908. — A. LAES, *Le peintre courtraisien R. Savery*, Revue belge d'Archéologie et d'Histoire de l'art, IV, 1931.

The Valckenborghs: E. MICHEL, *Lucas van Valckenborgh*, Bulletin des Musées de France 1931. — W. ZÜLCH, *Die Künstlerfamilie van Valckenborgh*, Oud Holland XLIX, 1932. — W. ZÜLCH, *Frankfurter Künstler 1223-1700*, Frankfort 1933. — A. LAES, *Marten van Valckenborgh*, Annuaire des Musées royaux des Beaux-Arts, I, Brussels 1938. — *Les sites mosans de Lucas I et Martin I van Valckenborgh*, Société royale des Beaux-Arts, Liège 1954.

Other landscapists: G. CAULLET, *Le peintre Chrétien de Coninck et sa famille*, Bulletin du Cercle historique et archéologique de Courtrai, 1903. — A. LAES, *Un paysagiste flamand de la fin du XVIᵉ siècle, K. de Keuninck*, Mélanges Hulin de Loo, Brussels 1931. — A. LAES, *Abel Grimmer*, Annuaire des Amis des Musées royaux de l'Etat, Brussels 1932. — G. J. HOOGEWERFF, *Lucas Gassel, Schilder van Helmond*, Oud Holland, I, 1936. — R. L. DELEVOY, *L'œuvre gravé de Lucas van Uden*, Revue belge d'Archéologie et d'Histoire de l'Art, I, 1940. — P. F. J. J. REELICK, *Identificatie van de Meester der Winterlandscappen (Gysbrecht Leytens?)*, Oud Holland 1942. — E. GREINDL, *La conception du paysage chez Alexandre Keirinckx*, Annuaire du Musée royal des Beaux-Arts, Antwerp 1942-1947. — P. M. AUZAS, *Les douze Mois de Grimmer*, Pro Arte, Geneva, January 1948. — A. LAES, *Paysages de Josse et Frans de Momper*, Bulletin des Musées royaux des Beaux-Arts, 2, Brussels 1952. — J. C. AZNAR, *Un lienzo de Lucas Gassel en el Museo Lazaro*, Goya, 16, Madrid, 1957.

CHAPTER VI

RUBENS AND LIVING FORMS

A. MICHIELS, *Rubens et l'école d'Anvers*, Paris 1854. — F. GOELER VAN RAVENSBURG, *Rubens und die Antike*, Jena 1882. — M. ROOSES, *L'œuvre de P. P. Rubens*, Antwerp 1886-1892. — C. RUELENS and M. ROOSES, *Correspondance de Rubens*, Antwerp 1887-1907. — G. GEFFROY, *Rubens*, Paris 1902. — M. ROOSES, *P. P. Rubens*, Paris 1903. — L. HOURTICQ, *Rubens*, Paris 1905. — A. ROSENBERG, *Rubens*, Klassiker der Kunst, 1905. — W. BODE, *Kritik und Chronologie der Gemälde von Peter Paul Rubens*, Zeitschrift für Bildende Kunst, 1905. — H. REA, *Rubens*, Leipzig 1905. — H. KNACKFUSS, *Rubens*, Leipzig 1905. — K. GROSSMANN, *Der Gemäldezyklus der Galerie der Maria von Medici von Peter Paulus Rubens*, Strasbourg 1906. — E. VERHAEREN, *Rubens*, Leipzig 1913. — R. OLDENBURG, *Rubens*, Munich 1922. — F. LUGT *Notes sur Rubens*, Gazette des Beaux-Arts, 1925. — G. VAN ZYPE, *Rubens*, Paris 1926. — P. COLIN, *Correspondance de Rubens*, Paris 1927. — G. GLÜCK and F. M. HABERDITZL, *Handzeichnungen von P. P. Rubens*, Berlin 1928. — C. STERLING, *Les Paysages de Rubens*, Travaux des étudiants du groupe d'Histoire de l'Art de la Faculté des Lettres de Paris, Paris 1928. — A. BERTRAM, *The Life of Sir Peter Paul Rubens*, London 1928. — A. STUBBE, *P. P. Rubens*, Brussels 1929. — H. BERGNER, *Rubens, eine Skizze seines Lebens und Wirkens*, Leipzig 1930. — P. FIERENS, *Rubens*, Paris 1931. — E. CAMMAERTS, *Rubens, Painter and Diplomat*, London 1932. — R. OLDENBURG, *P. P. Rubens*, Klassiker der Kunst, Berlin 1932. — R. AVERMAETE, *Rubens*, Brussels 1933. — G. GLÜCK, *Rubens, Van Dyck und ihr Kreis*, Vienna 1933. — A. J. J. DELEN, *Het Huis van Pieter Pauwel Rubens*, Brussels 1933. — W. BAUNVIG, *Rubens*, Copenhagen 1936. — P. JAMOT, *Rubens*, Paris 1936. — Special number of L'Amour de l'Art, *Rubens et son temps*, November 1936 (G. BAZIN, P. COLIN). — Claire JANSON, *L'influence de Véronèse sur Rubens*, Gazette des Beaux-Arts, January 1937. — C. STERLING and L. BURCHARD, *Découverte et histoire d'une œuvre inconnue de Rubens*, L'Amour de l'Art, November 1937. — J. BURCKHARDT, *Rubens*, Vienna 1937 and 1938. — G. GLÜCK, *De landschappen van Peter Paul Rubens*, Amsterdam 1940. — L. VAN PUYVELDE, *Les esquisses de Rubens*, Basel 1940. — A. CORNETTE, *Rubens*, Antwerp 1940. — P. DAYE, *Rubens*, Paris 1941. — J. BURCKHARDT, *Rubens*, Berlin 1942. — H. G. EVERS, *Peter Paul Rubens*, Munich 1942. — L. VAN PUYVELDE, *Rubens' Aanbilding door de herders te Antwerpen*, Annuaire du Musée royal des Beaux-Arts, Antwerp 1942-1947. — H. G. EVERS, *Rubens und sein Werk*, Brussels 1943. — L. VAN PUYVELDE, *Le génie de Rubens*, Brussels 1943. — Ghislaine VAN PUYVELDE-LASSALLE, *Watteau et Rubens*, Brussels 1943. — E. GREINDL, *Deux esquisses du Martyre de saint Liévin*, Phoebus I, Basel 1946. — M. DE LANNOY, *Peter Pauwel Rubens*, Tielt 1946. — H. G. EVERS, *Peter Paul Rubens* (Flemish translation by K. Ruyssinck), Antwerp

1946. — Z. HARSANYI, *Dit was leven Peter Paul Rubens* (translated from the Hungarian by P. van Deurningen), Antwerp 1946. — L. VAN HOEK, *P. P. Rubens*, Brussels 1946. — J. CRICK, *Petrus Paulus Rubens. De roman van zijn leven*, Antwerp 1947. — J. CRICK, *Les vies multiples de Rubens*, Brussels 1947. — I. WALLACH, *The Horn and the Roses. A novel based on the life of P. P. Rubens*, New York 1947. — Baron STALINS, *La maison de P. P. Rubens à Anvers*, L'Amour de l'Art II, 1947. — G. SOYER, *Rubens inconnu*, Antwerp 1947. — J. A. GORIS and J. S. HELD, *Rubens in America*, Pantheon, New York 1947. — A. MORASSI, *Alcune opere del Rubens a Genova*, Emporium, Bergamo 1947. — J. BOUCHOT-SAUPICQUE, *Rubens et Hélène Fourment*, Paris 1947. — Bock VON WÜLFINGEN, *Zwei Bilder aus Rubens' italienischer Zeit*, Kunst 1948. — G. GLÜCK, *Die Landschaften von P. P. Rubens*, Vienna 1948. — A. BLUM, *Rubens*, Paris 1949. — W. G. CONSTABLE, *Rubens in the Museum of Fine Arts*, Boston, Miscellanea Leo van Puyvelde, Brussels 1949. — J. THIÉRY, *La Chasse d'Atalante de Rubens aux Musées royaux des Beaux-Arts de Bruxelles*, Miscellanea Leo van Puyvelde, Brussels 1949. — L. NINANE, *Rubens et Snyders*, Miscellanea Leo van Puyvelde, Brussels 1949. — L. VAN PUYVELDE, *L'atelier et les collaborateurs de Rubens*, Gazette des Beaux-Arts, October-December 1949. — J. BURCKHARDT, *Recollections of Rubens*, Phaidon, London 1950. — L. VAN PUYVELDE, *Rubens*, Brussels 1952. — E. LARSEN, *P. P. Rubens, with a complete catalogue of his works in America* (in English), Antwerp 1952. — F. LEHMANN, *Rubens und seine Welt*, Stuttgart 1954. — A. BLUM, *Rubens*, Copenhagen 1955. — R. EIGENBERGER, *Peter Paul Rubens*, Vienna 1955. — J. MULS, *P. P. Rubens als levenskunstenaar*, Antwerp 1956. — W. COHN, *Rubens*, Paris 1956. — E. HAVERKAMP BEGEMANN, *De Kroning van Maria door Rubens*, Bulletin Museum Boymans VIII, 3, Rotterdam 1957. — F. BRESSELEERS and H. KANORA, *P. P. Rubens te Ekeren*, Ekeren 1957. — F. BAUDOIN, *Guide sommaire de la maison de Rubens*, Antwerp 1957. — M. JAFFÉ, *Un chef-d'œuvre mieux connu, la récente découverte d'une esquisse pour la "Descente de Croix" de Rubens*, L'Œil 43-44, Lausanne 1958.

CHAPTER VII

VAN DYCK AND THE SOCIETY PORTRAIT

DUPLESSIS, *Eaux-fortes d'Antoine van Dyck*, Paris 1874. — A. MICHIELS, *Van Dyck et ses élèves*, Paris 1882. — J. GUIFFREY, *Antoine van Dyck*, Paris 1882. — A. SALINAS, *Antonio van Dyck e il suo quadro per la compagnia del Rosario in S. Domenico in Palermo*, L'Arte II, 1899. — M. ROOSES, *Vijftig Meesterwerken van Anthony van Dyck*, Amsterdam 1900. — Sir Lionel CUST, *Anthony van Dyck*, London 1900. — Sir Lionel CUST, *A Description of the Sketch Book by Sir Anthony van Dyck*, London 1902. — H. KNACKFUSS, *Van Dyck*, Leipzig 1902. — Sir Lionel CUST, *Van Dyck*, London 1903. — FIERENS-GEVAERT, *Van Dyck*, Paris 1903. — Pol DE MONT, *A. van Dyck*, Haarlem 1906. — E. SCHAEFFER, *Van Dyck*, Klassiker der Kunst, 1909. — Sir Lionel CUST, *A. van Dyck, a further Study*, London 1911. — R. OLDENBURG, *Studien zu van Dyck*, Münchener Jahrbuch der bildenden Kunst, 1914-1915. — Mgr. VAES, *Le séjour d'Antoine van Dyck en Italie*, Bulletin de l'Institut historique belge de Rome, 1924. — C. BERNARD, *Van Dyck*, Brussels 1924. — G. GLÜCK, *Van Dyck*, Klassiker der Kunst, 1931. — M. DELACRE, *Recherches sur le rôle du dessin dans l'Iconographie de Van Dyck*, Brussels 1932. — G. GLÜCK, *Rubens, van Dyck und ihr Kreis*, Vienna 1933. — L. VAN PUYVELDE, *Les débuts de Van Dyck*, Revue belge d'Archéologie et d'Histoire de l'Art, 1933. — L. VAN

Saventhem, Burlington Magazine, LXXVII, 1940. — L. VAN PUYVELDE, *Van Dyck's Replicas of the Virgin and Child*, The Journal of the Walters Art Gallery, Baltimore 1940. — G. ADRIANI, *Anton van Dyck, Italienisches Skizzenbuch*, Vienna 1940. — A. MUÑOZ, *Van Dyck*, Rome 1941. — J. REDER, *Research on Sir Anthony van Dyck and Samuel Hofmann*, New York 1941. — L. VAN PUYVELDE, *The young Van Dyck*, Burlington Magazine, LXXIX, 1941. — A. MUÑOZ, *Van Dyck*, Leipzig 1942. — F. VAN DEN WYNGAERT, *Van Dyck*, Antwerp 1943. — L. VAN PUYVELDE, *Van Dyck and the Amsterdam Double-Portrait*, Burlington Magazine 32, 1943. — L. VAN PUYVELDE, *Van Dyck and Bernini*, The Connoisseur, 1944. — F. R. BOSCHVOGEL, *A. van Dyck*, Tielt 1945. — H. COMSTOCK, *Van Dyck's Portrait of the Duc de Guise*, The Connoisseur, 1948. — P. CLARIJS, *A. van Dyck*, Amsterdam 1949. — G. J. HOOGEWERFF, *Een "Noods Gods" door Van Dyck geschilderd*, Miscellanea Leo van Puyvelde, Brussels 1949. — L. VAN PUYVELDE, *Van Dyck*, Brussels 1950. — M. MAUQUOY-HENDRICKZ, *L'Iconographie d'Antoine van Dyck*, Académie royale de Belgique, 1956. — H. VEY, *De tekeningen van Anthonie van Dyck in het Museum Boymans*, Bulletin Museum Boymans, VII, 2-3, Rotterdam 1956. — W. VAN BESELAERE, *In memoriam A. van Dyck*, Antwerp 1957. — E. DU GUÉ TRAPIER, *The School of Madrid and Van Dyck*, Burlington Magazine, August 1957. — L. VON BALDASS, *Quelques notes sur le développement de Van Dyck*, Gazette des Beaux-Arts, November 1957. — H. VEY, *Einige unveröffentlichte Zeichnungen Van Dycks*, Bulletin des Musées royaux de Belgique, 3-4, Brussels 1957.

Cornelis de Vos: J. MULS, *Cornelis de Vos, Schilder van Hulst*, Antwerp 1933. — E. GREINDL, *Les portraits de Corneille de Vos*, Annuaire des Musées royaux des Beaux-Arts, II, Brussels 1939. — E. GREINDL, *Corneille de Vos*, Brussels 1944.

Justus Sustermans: P. BAUTIER, *Juste Suttermans*, Brussels 1912.

CHAPTER VIII

JORDAENS AND FLEMISH OPULENCE

P. GÉNARD, *Notices sur Jordaens*, Messager des sciences historiques, 1852. — P. BUSCHMANN, *J. Jordaens*, Brussels 1905. — FIERENS-GEVAERT, *Jordaens*, Paris 1905. — Max ROOSES, *J. Jordaens*, Antwerp 1906. — H. COOPMAN, *Jordaens*, Brussels 1922. — L. VAN PUYVELDE, *L'œuvre authentique d'Adam van Noort*, Bulletin des Musées royaux de Belgique II, 1929. — O. BENESCH, *Eine Zeichnung aus Jakob Jordaens' Frühzeit*, Actes du Congrès d'Histoire de l'Art, I, Brussels 1930. — L. VAN PUYVELDE, *Nouvelles œuvres d'Adam van Noort*, Annuaire des Musées royaux de Belgique, I, 1938. — E. MICHEL and Mlle DE VALLÉE, *Jordaens et les quatre évangélistes*, Paris 1938. — M. CRICK-KUNTZIGER, *Les cartons de Jordaens du Musée du Louvre et leur traduction en tapisserie*, Bulletin de la Société royale d'Archéologie de Bruxelles, 1938. — J. S. HELD, *Jordaens' Portraits of his Family*, The Art Bulletin XXII, 1940. — G. MARLIER, *Jordaens*, Antwerp 1941. — J. S. HELD, *Jordaens and the Equestrian Astrology*, Miscellanea Leo van Puyvelde, Brussels 1949. — L. VAN PUYVELDE, *Jordaens*, Brussels 1953. — Idem, *Jordaens zoals hij was*, Verslagen en Mededelingen van de Kon. Vlaamse Academie voor Taal- en Letterkunde, Brussels 1953. — B. BUSHART, *Une tête d'étude inédite de Jordaens*, Revue belge d'Archéologie et d'Histoire de l'Art, XXV, 1946. — *Les signes du Zodiaque de Jordaens au Palais du Luxembourg*, Paris 1957.

Frans Snyders and Paul de Vos: P. BUSCHMANN, *F. Snyders*, Biographie nationale XXIII, Brussels 1921-1924. — M. MANNEBACK, *Paul de Vos*, Actes du Congrès d'Histoire de l'art, London 1939. — M. MANNEBACK, *Paul de Vos et Snyders*, Miscellanea Leo van Puyvelde, Brussels 1949.

CHAPTER IX

BROUWER AND LIFE IN THE RAW

Adriaen Brouwer: F. SCHMIDT, *Das Leben des Malers A. Brouwer*, Leipzig 1873. — F. SCHMIDT-DEGENER, *A. Brouwer*, Brussels 1908. — W. VON BODE, *A. Brouwer*, Berlin 1923.

David Teniers the Younger: DE PAUW, *Les trois peintres David Teniers et leurs homonymes*, Annuaire de l'Académie royale de Belgique, 4e série, X, 1897. — A. ROSENBERG, *Teniers der Jüngere*, Künstler Monographien 8, Bielefeld 1895. — R. PEYRE, *D. Teniers*, 1914. — VON TERCY, *David Teniers und der Samt Bruegel*, Kunstkronik 1922. — L. BOCQUET, *David Teniers*, 1924. — P. BAUTIER, *Les tableaux de singeries attribués à David Teniers*, 1926. — G. EECKHOUD, *Teniers*, 1926.

Jan Siberechts: H. MARCEL, *Un peintre de la vie rustique du XVIIe siècle, Jan Sieberechts*, Gazette des Beaux-Arts, 1912. — T. H. FOKKER, *Jan Siberechts, peintre de la paysannerie flamande*, Brussels-Paris 1931. — A. LAES, *Jan Siberechts, peintre anversois du XVIIe siècle*, Gedenkboek A. Vermeylen, Brussels 1933.

EXHIBITIONS

1902 Bruges, Musée Communal, *The Flemish Primitives*.

1923 Paris, Musée du Jeu de Paume, *Belgian Art*.

1926 Brussels, Musées Royaux des Beaux-Arts, *Retrospective Exhibition of Flemish Landscape Painting*.

1926 Bern, Kunstmuseum, *Belgian Art, Ancient and Modern*.

1927 London, Burlington House, *Flemish and Belgian Art*.

1930 Antwerp, International Exhibition, *Early Flemish Art*.

1935 Brussels, World's Fair, *Five Centuries of Art*.

1935 Paris, Musée de l'Orangerie, *From Van Eyck to Bruegel*.

1936 Paris, Musée de l'Orangerie, *Rubens and his Times*.

1936 Rotterdam, Boymans Museum, *Hieronymus Bosch and the Primitives of the Northern Netherlands*.

1936 Antwerp, *Exhibition of Drawings and Prints by Antwerp Artists*.

1937 Brussels, Palais des Beaux-Arts, *Drawings from Bosch to Rembrandt*.

1937 Brussels, Musées Royaux des Beaux-Arts, *The Sketches of Rubens*.

1938 Brussels, Palais des Beaux-Arts, *Drawings by Peter Paul Rubens*.

1939 Philadelphia Museum of Art, *Flemish Painting*.

1939 Worcester Art Museum, *Flemish Painting*.

1946 Brussels, Palais des Beaux-Arts, *From Bosch to Rembrandt*.

1947 Paris, Musée de l'Orangerie, *The Flemish Primitives*.

1948 Eindhoven, Van Abbe Museum, *Netherlandish Landscape Art*.

1949 Brussels, Palais des Beaux-Arts, *Drawings by Flemish Masters from Van Eyck to Rubens*.

1949 Paris, Bibliothèque Nationale, *Drawings by Flemish Masters from Van Eyck to Rubens*.

1949 Bruges, Musée Communal, *Gerard David and his Entourage*.

1949 Rotterdam, Boymans Museum, *Masterpieces from the D. G. van Beuningen Collection*.

1950 Dijon, Musée des Beaux-Arts, *From Hieronymus Bosch to Rembrandt*.

1950 Brussels, Palais des Beaux-Arts, *"Le Patrimoine artistique de l'Assistance Publique de Bruxelles"*.

1951 Bruges, Musée Communal, *Flemings and Italy*.

1951 Brussels, Palais des Beaux-Arts, *The Examination of the Ghent Altarpiece*.

1952 Paris, Petit-Palais, *Masterpieces from the D.G. van Beuningen Collection*.

1952 Luxemburg, State Museum, *Prints by Pieter Bruegel the Elder*.

1952 Paris, Musée de l'Orangerie, *The Still Life from Antiquity to the Present Day*.

1953 Paris, Musée de l'Orangerie, *The Portrait in Flemish Art from Memling to Van Dyck*.

1953-1954 London, Royal Academy of Arts, *Flemish Art 1300-1700*.

1954 Bordeaux, Musée des Beaux-Arts, *Flanders, Spain and Portugal from the 15th to the 17th Century*.

1954 Brussels, Palais des Beaux-Arts, *Humanist Europe*.

1955 Amsterdam, Rijksmuseum, *The Triumph of European Mannerism*.

1956 Bruges, Musée Communal, *Flemish Art in British Collections*.

1957 Ghent, Musée des Beaux-Arts, *Joos van Ghent, Pedro Berruguete and the Court of Urbino*.

1957 Brussels, Palais des Beaux-Arts, *Dirk Bouts and his Times*.

1958 Amsterdam, Rijksmuseum, *Medieval Art in the Northern Netherlands*.

1958 Bruges, Musée Communal, *Flemish Art in Spanish Collections*.

1958 Brussels, *Trésors de la Bibliothèque Royale de Belgique*.

THE COLORPLATES

CONTENTS

THIS VOLUME OF THE COLLECTION "PAINTING ○ COLOR ○ HISTORY" WAS PRODUCED BY THE TECHNICAL STAFF OF EDITIONS D'ART ALBERT SKIRA, FINISHED THE FIFTEENTH DAY OF NOVEMBER, NINETEEN HUNDRED AND FIFTY-EIGHT.

TEXT AND COLORPLATES BY

COLOR STUDIO AT IMPRIMERIES RÉUNIES S.A., LAUSANNE.

PLATES ENGRAVED BY GUEZELLE ET RENOUARD, PARIS.

PHOTOGRAPHS BY

Editions Skira, Geneva (pages 13, 14, 15, 25, 26, 27, 28, 31, 35, 45, 46, 47, 62, 67, 69, 70, 74, 82, 85, 86, 87, 89, 92, 94, 95, 99, 102, 104, 105, 107, 108, 111, 112, 113, 114, 115, 121, 128, 136, 137, 138, 139, 140, 141, 152, 158, 161, 162, 163, 166, 169, 170, 174, 175, 176, 178, 181, 184), Hans Hinz, Basel (pages 11, 17, 19, 20, 21, 22, 23, 29, 30, 73, 81, 97, 118, 123, 124, 127, 132, 133, 143, 155, 173, 180), Claudio Emmer, Milan (pages 33, 109), Louis Laniepce, Paris (pages 149, 159), Paul I. Bessem, Amsterdam (page 34), Karl Meyer, Vienna (pages 38, 40, 41, 42, 43, 48, 49, 51, 53, 54, 55, 56, 57, 58, 59, 130, 131, 145), Laurence Reverdin, London (page 77), Walter Steinkopf, Berlin (pages 79, 156, 183) and Zoltan Wegner, London (page 146).